Studies of Love in Religion 2

14/ 1/ 2023

Loving the Planet

Loving the Planet
Interfaith Essays on Ecology, Love, and Theology

Edited by
Paul S. Fiddes

~ **F P** ~
Firedint Publishing
Oxford

ISBN 978-1-9999407-4-4

December 2022

Contents

Preface

This book has its genesis in an online conference called 'Loving the Planet', which was held in November 2021 and co-sponsored by the Oxford Centre for Religion and Culture at Regent's Park College in the University of Oxford, and the Caritas Center at Brescia University, Kentucky, USA. Three of essays, by Jewish, Islamic and Christian scholars, have their origin in papers given on the day. The remaining essays have been added by scholars from these three faiths who are interested in the theme. Finally, as editor I have written a piece which draws on all the essays and which suggests the elements for a way of thinking which might be seen as a new shoot from the stem of 'ecotheology'—namely, an 'eco-love-theology'.

The conference was part of a series of events promoted by an interfaith project for 'The Study of Love in Religion', based at Regent's Park College, Oxford. The project was founded in 2012 with the support of HRH Prince Ghazi bin Muhammad bin Talal of Jordan, who was the main author of the widely-acclaimed Open Letter to world Christian leaders called 'A Common Word' (2007). This document, signed by many Muslim scholars, took its title from a verse in the Qur'an which urged Muslims to issue the following call to Christians and Jews: *O People of the Scripture! Come to a common word between us and you* (*Aal 'Imran* 3:64). This 'common word', the letter proposed at its beginning, was a 'common ground' between Islam and Christianity (and, by implication, also Judaism), and consisted of three principles— the unity of God, love of God, and love of neighbour.[1] With great

---

[1] *A Common Word Between Us and You.* 5–Year Anniversary Edition (Amman: MABDA, 2012), 53–4. See Miroslav Volf, Ghazi bin Muhammad, and Melissa

courtesy, it took its point of departure from the words of Jesus in the New Testament, themselves drawn from the Jewish Torah, that 'The Lord is One, and you shall love the Lord your God with all your heart, and you shall love your neighbour as yourself' (Mark 12:29–31). At a conference celebrating five years of 'A Common Word' at Regent's Park College, Oxford, the project for 'The Study of Love in Religion' was created as a development from 'A Common Word', and in its early years enjoyed the generous support of the John Templeton Foundation.

Participants in the project collaborated to produce a first volume of essays, drawing upon work done during the first decade of the project, and this was published under the title *Love as Common Ground. Essays on Love in Religion* (Lexington Books, 2021) with contributions by Muslim, Jewish and Christian scholars. The essays made clear that this 'common ground' was not some kind of 'lowest common denominator', but that the study of love was a 'ground' or 'place' where people of different faiths could meet and explore convergences as well as differences. The conviction that 'love, in religious consciousness and in practice today, is the ultimate reality of the universe'[2] is now being worked out in a second volume which we place in the hands of our readers at a time of ecological crisis.

Paul S. Fiddes
Advent 2022

Yarrington (eds.), *A Common Word: Muslims and Christians on Loving God and Neighbor*, (Grand Rapids: Eerdmans, 2010).
[2] Statement of aims from the website of the project, loveinreligion.org.

Editor's Note

In order to be respectful to the religions represented in this volume, contributors have been permitted their own choice about capitalization of personal pronouns relating to God. Contributors have also used their own, differing transliterations of ancient languages.

About the Contributors

Celia Deane-Drummond is Director of the Laudato Si' Research Institute and Senior Research Fellow in theology at Campion Hall, University of Oxford.

Emily A. DeMoor is Director of the Caritas Center, and Associate Professor of Theology, at Brescia University, Kentucky, USA.

Paul S. Fiddes is Professor of Systematic Theology in the University of Oxford, Principal Emeritus of Regent's Park College, Oxford, Senior Research Fellow of the College, and Fellow of the British Academy.

Greg Marcar is Harold Turner Research Fellow at the Centre for Theology and Public Issues, University of Otago, New Zealand.

Tareq Moqbel is H.M. King Abdullah II ibn Al Hussein of Jordan Fellow for the Study of Love in Religion, Regent's Park College in the University of Oxford.

Melissa Raphael is Professor Emerita in Jewish Theology at the University of Gloucestershire and lecturer in Modern Jewish Thought at Leo Baeck College, London.

Naftali Rothenberg is a Senior Research Fellow at the Van Leer Jerusalem Institute, and a co-investigator in the Project for the Study of Love in Religion at Regent's Park College, Oxford

Leyla Tajer is a freelance scholar and writer in Islamic Studies, Vienna, formerly Lecturer in Islamic Studies, HELP University, Malaysia, and a co-investigator in the Project for the Study of Love in Religion at Regent's Park College, Oxford

Amir Hossein Zekrgoo is formerly Professor of Islamic and Oriental Arts, the International Institute of Islamic Thought and Civilization, and is an Associate Member of the Iranian Academy of Arts and Sciences.

1

Love, Intersubjectivity and the Natural World

Emily A. DeMoor

The natural world as subject and intersubjective

Cultural historian and ecotheologian Thomas Berry often spoke of the universe as a communion of subjects rather than a collection of objects. This vision has profound theological and ecological implications. The concept of the natural world[3] as subject is premised on the belief that it has intrinsic value in and of itself apart from any value humans ascribe to it. In a piece entitled 'Mapping the Sacred Landscape', theologian Douglas Burton-Christie suggests that poetry and literature play a crucial role in re-imagining our relationship with the natural world.[4] This essay will draw on the work of theologians, nature writers, and philosophers, as well as scientific texts to explore the notion of the natural world as a subject exercising its own intersubjectivity, and as being related to the intersubjectivity of human life. This, I suggest, is the context for knowledge, meaning-making, spiritual encounter, and ultimately, love. It is this love that compels us to participate with God in the life of the planet for its well-being.

---

[3] Although humans are part of rather than separate from the natural world, the terms 'natural world' and 'nature' will be used throughout this essay to indicate non-human nature, in keeping with the literature reviewed in this essay.

[4] Douglas Burton-Christie, 'Mapping the Sacred Landscape: Spirituality and the Contemporary Literature of Nature'. *Horizons* 21/1 (1994): 22–47.

The Judaeo-Christian scriptures are grounded in a participatory worldview in which nature has subjectivity. In Psalm 19 the psalmist writes:

> The heavens are telling the glory of God;
>   And the firmament proclaims his handiwork.
> Day to day pours forth speech,
>   And night to night declares knowledge.
> There is no speech, nor are there words;
>   Their voice is not heard;
> Yet their voice goes out through all the earth,
>   And their words to the end of the world.[5]

In Psalm 148 all of creation praises the Lord:

> Praise him, sun and moon;
>   Praise him, all you shining stars!
> Praise him, you highest heavens,
>   And you waters above the heavens!
> …Praise the LORD from the earth,
>   You sea monsters and all deeps,
> Fire and hail, snow and frost,
>   Stormy wind fulfilling his command!
> Mountains and all hills,
>   Fruit trees and all cedars!
> Wild animals and all cattle,
>   Creeping things and flying birds![6]

In this worldview, the land and its creatures alike have voice and agency.

In his book, *The Spell of the Sensuous,* ecologist and philosopher David Abram describes the land as 'the sensible site or matrix wherein

---

[5] Ps 19:1–6, *NRSV*
[6] Ps 148:3–4, 7–10, *NRSV*

meaning occurs and proliferates.'[7] Abram explores the narratives of indigenous peoples in which moral teachings are tied to the land and its inhabitants and explains that the places where these stories occur might even be considered the source or primary power that is expressing itself through the events that occur there. He proposes that through reawakening one's senses, along with a renewed trust in the intelligence of one's sensing body, she or he may once again begin to notice and respond to 'the subtle logos of the land.'[8]

Burton-Christie emphasizes the quality of one's emotional response to nature when he writes 'To the extent that we can still be moved by the natural world ... we are acknowledging the possibility of responding to the earth as a living subject.'[9] When we lose the sense of the natural world as subject, we diminish 'the sense of the world as a place where the shimmering force of the transcendent, the elusive traces of mystery can shine through.'[10] Thomas Berry similarly reflects that 'the way to the world of the sacred is through the place of our dwelling';[11] 'If the outer world is diminished in its grandeur, then the emotional, imaginative, intellectual, and spiritual life of the human is diminished or extinguished.'[12]

Burton-Christie finds in the genre of nature-writing, 'endless possibilities for genuine encounter with the natural world, for entering

---

[7] David Abram, *The Spell of the Sensuous: Perception and Language in a More-Than-Human World* (New York: Vintage Books, 1996), 162.

[8] Abram, *Spell of the Sensuous*, 268.

[9] Douglas Burton-Christie, 'A Feeling for The Natural World: Spirituality and Contemporary Nature Writing', *Continuum* 2/2–3 (1993): 162.

[10] Ibid.

[11] Thomas Berry, 'Caring for Creation.' Paper presented at *Caring for Creation*, hosted by the Episcopal Diocese of Kansas and the Stewardship Office of the Episcopal Church, Kansas City. 1994 , n.p.

[12] Thomas Berry, *The Great Work, Our Way into the Future* (New York: Bell Tower, 1999), 200.

into relationships of mystery.'[13] He refers to 'narratives of conversion' as those which convey the place and way in which an author is 'beckoned, even seized' by a sense of mystery in nature.[14] These narratives suggest 'both the revelatory power of natural epiphanies and their capacity to transform those who experience them.'[15]

In a piece entitled 'Words Beneath the Water', Burton-Christie dwells upon the concept of 'logos' as one that possesses a wealth of meaning and gives expression to 'a constellation of Christian mysteries, all grounded in the sense that God comes to us as a kind of utterance.'[16] He elaborates:

> like the cottonwood tree deep in the desert canyon that draws into its branches wrens, juncos, hawks, and ravens and pulses with their movement and color, so the Word has attracted to itself diverse symbols and metaphors, many drawn from the natural world, that have deepened and enriched the Word's expressive power.[17]

Nature writer Loren Eiseley likewise portrays the natural world as revelatory as he describes the work of the nature-writer who puts down his reflections:

> in the hope that they will come to the eye of those who have retained a true taste for the marvelous, and who are capable of discerning in the flow of ordinary events the point at which the

---

[13] Douglas Burton-Christie, 'The Literature of Nature and the Quest for the Sacred', *The Way Supplement* 81 (1994): 12 (5–14).

[14] Ibid.

[15] Ibid.

[16] Douglas Burton-Christie, 'Words Beneath the Water: Logos, Cosmos, and the Spirit of Place', in Dieter T. Hessel, and Rosemary Radford Ruether (eds.), *Christianity and Ecology: Seeking the Well-Being of Earth and Humans* (Boston: Harvard University, Center for the Study of World Religions, 2000) 318.

[17] Burton-Christie, 'Words Beneath the Water,' 318–19.

mundane world gives way to quite another dimension.[18]

He advises that the time must be right: 'one has to be, by chance or intention, upon the border of two worlds. And sometimes these two borders may shift or interpenetrate and one sees the miraculous.'[19]

In 'Hymn to Matter' by Pierre Teilhard de Chardin, the natural world itself is a divine utterance. Teilhard blesses matter, which, in both its violence and benevolence, reveals the sacred. He immerses the reader in a sacramental theology in which the divine is not only manifested in the human, but in all of creation. The Word takes on flesh in nature:

> Blessed be you, universal matter, immeasurable time, boundless ether, triple abyss of stars and atoms and generations: you who by overflowing and dissolving our narrow standards of measurement reveal to us the dimensions of God ... You who batter us and then dress our wounds, you who resist us and yield to us, you who wreck and build, you who shackle and liberate, the sap of our souls, the hand of God, the flesh of Christ: it is you, matter, that I bless ... I acclaim you as the divine milieu, charged with creative power, as the ocean stirred by the Spirit, as the clay molded and infused with life by the incarnate Word ... Your realm comprises those serene heights where saints think to avoid you—but where your flesh is so transparent and so agile as to be no longer distinguishable from spirit.[20]

The philosophical movement of phenomenology provides a useful lens for exploring Teilhard's worldview. In the early 1900s, Edmund Husserl sought to rejuvenate the world of sensorial experience and to

---

[18] Loren Eiseley, 'The Judgment of the Birds', in R. Finch and J. Elder (eds.), *The Norton Book of Nature Writing*, College Edition (New York: W. W. Norton & Company, 2002), 486.

[19] Eisley, 'Judgment', 527.

[20] Pierre Teilhard de Chardin, 'Hymn to Matter', in *Hymn of the Universe* (London: Collins, 1965), 68–70.

ignite the recognition of Earth as the forgotten foundation of human awareness.[21] Phenomenology, he proposed, is a knowledge that grows out of lived experience.

Husserl and Maurice Merleau-Ponty wished to return to experience as it is immediately lived, experience that precedes thought about it. Through this quality of experience, they believe that a person returns to Earth as the primal source of awareness. For Husserl, human consciousness is always consciousness *of something* in the world that is presenting itself to perception, such as a blossoming apple tree.[22] So the world is indispensable to consciousness and the subject is immersed into the world. In his later work he alludes to an 'intersubjectivity' to describe the relational quality of experience that forms the basis of knowledge about the same world as others perceive.[23]

David Abram builds on this Husserlian approach, proposing that there are 'at least two regions of the experiential or phenomenal field: one of phenomena that unfold entirely for me—images that arise, as it were, on this side of my body—and another region of phenomena that are, evidently, responded to and experienced by other embodied subjects as well as by myself.' [24] This intersubjective experience, he explains, is an embodied one:

> It is as visible, animate bodies that other selves or subjects make themselves evident in my subjective experience, and it is only as a body that I am visible and sensible to others. The body is precisely my insertion in the common, or intersubjective, field of

---

[21] Abram, *Spell of the Sensuous*, 44.

[22] Edmund Husserl, *Ideas Pertaining to a Pure Phenomenology and to a Phenomenological Philosophy*, trans. F. Kersten (Dordrecht: Kluwer Academic Publishers, 1983), 214.

[23] Edmund Husserl, *Cartesian Meditations. An Introduction to Phenomenology*, trans. Dorion Cairns (Dordrecht: Springer, 1950), 120–28.

[24] Abram, *Spell of the Sensuous*, 38.

experience.[25]

The living, sensing body has open and indeterminate, membranelike boundaries that define a surface of metamorphosis and exchange. An active and open form, the body is 'continually improvising its relations to things and to the world.'[26] Thus Abram goes on to draw out what he sees as the implication of Husserl's approach, that there must be an intersubjective relation with the natural world itself: 'my body is a sort of open circuit that completes itself only in things, in others, in the encompassing earth … the world is perceiving itself *through* us.'[27] Abram describes this as 'a ceaseless dance between the carnal subject and its world.'[28]

In his book *The Reenchantment of the World*, cultural historian Morris Berman refers to the notion of 'participatory consciousness' in which one merges and identifies with one's surroundings. Participatory knowledge is sensual. Berman maintains that 'reality that is not "tasted" does not remain real to us. In order to make a thing real, we must go out to it with our bodies and absorb it with our bodies.'[29]

Abram explains that the phenomenologists propose that language is an ongoing exchange 'between our own flesh and the flesh of the world', belonging to the animate landscape as well as the human community.[30] He reflects that by making language a code to be understood on a secondary level rather than immediately experienced in relation to the world, humans created an abstraction, setting themselves apart from the animal world. He writes:

---

[25] Abram, *Spell of the Sensuous*, 45.

[26] Abram, *Spell of the Sensuous*, 49.

[27] Abram, *Spell of the Sensuous*, 62, 68.

[28] Abram, *Spell of the Sensuous*, 54.

[29] Morris Berman, *The Reenchantment of the World* (Ithaca: Cornell University Press, 1981), 181.

[30] Abram, *Spell of the Sensuous*, 89, 82.

> As technological civilization diminishes the biotic diversity of the earth, language itself is diminished ... As the splashing speech of the rivers is silenced by more and more dams, as we drive more and more of the land's wild voices into the oblivion of extinction, our own languages become increasingly impoverished and weightless, progressively emptied of their earthly resonance.[31]

When a culture shifts its participation from the outer world to the printed text, 'the stones fall silent'.[32] It follows, then, that literature which grows directly from a participatory experience of the natural world might enable the stones to speak once again.

Empathetic love in intersubjective relations

The notion of 'participatory consciousness' finds resonance in the writings of José Vasconcelos who moves the discussion into the realm of beauty and, ultimately, love. Vasconcelos proposed an aesthetic philosophy in which what he calls 'empathetic fusion' between subject and object occurs. In this experience, the person or subject loses him or herself in the experience of connection.[33] For Vasconcelos the compenetration through love contradicts reason, which analyses and creates barriers. Love, in this framework, is intersubjective in that it involves an intimate exchange between subjects that mutually give of themselves and receive of the other.

We might turn to the works of the nature-writers for further insight.

---

[31] Abram, *Spell of the Sensuous*, 86.

[32] Abram, *Spell of the Sensuous*, 131.

[33] Roberto S. Goizuetta, *Caminemos Con Jesús: Toward A Hispanic/Latino Theology of Accompaniment*. Maryknoll (New York: Orbis Books, 1995), 91. See José Vasconcelos, *Obras Completas*, 4 vols (México, DF: Libreros Mexicanos Unidos, 1958–61), 4:16.

Burton-Christie explains that nature writing 'inhabits and searches out those charged borderlands, those places of encounter where longing gives way to relationship, communion, intimacy.'[34] This 'simple, radical relationality' lies at the heart of nature writing. He continues:

> Here, in this liminal space, it becomes possible to imagine the apparently impermeable boundaries that separate one place from another, spirit from matter, ourselves from other living species, ourselves from God, as permeable. It becomes possible to imagine ourselves as no longer standing aloof and distant from the world, but as caught up into, transformed by the intimate presence of the living world within and around us.[35]

Burton-Christie underscores the importance of emotional engagement with the subject matter as an integral part of this transformative process. In the words of scientist Edward Wilson, 'You start by loving a subject.'[36] Reminiscent of Vasconcelos, Edward Abby explains that the nature writer needs 'a sympathy for the object under study, and more than sympathy, love. A love based on prolonged contact and interaction.'[37]

In a piece entitled 'Fire and Silence', Burton-Christie tells the story of Anthony, a fourth-century monk, who emerges from the wild with special healing powers after twenty years of solitary prayer, fasting, meditating on sacred texts, and wrestling with demons. Spiritual transformation, in this tradition, does not occur apart from the natural

---

[34] Douglas Burton-Christie, 'A Sense of Place', *The Way* 39/1 (1999): 64.

[35] Ibid.

[36] Edward O. Wilson, *Biophelia: The Human Bond with Other Species* (Cambridge MA: Harvard University Press, 1984), 65; cit. Burton-Christie, 'Literature of Nature', 10.

[37] Edward Abbey, 'Down the River with Henry Thoreau', in Stephen Trimble (ed.), *Words from the Land: Encounters with Natural History Writing* (Kaysville: Gibbs Smith, 1988), 62; cit. Burton-Christie, 'Literature of Nature', 11.

world, but in intersubjectivity with it:

> deepening one's capacity to respond to the world ... learning to
> see and celebrate ... the traces of spirit arising from the palpable
> world ... It means learning that the pores of the soul can be
> opened, that we can drink deeply from the verdure of the world,
> and pour ourselves back with unstinting generosity. It means
> entering the great dance of the spirit in the world.[38]

Experiencing this transformation, one of the early desert monks, Abba
Joseph of Panephysis, declared, 'If you will, you can become all
flame.'[39]

In *The Star Thrower*, by nature-writer Loren Eiseley, the inner fires
of the main character are rekindled through an intersubjective encounter
with the natural world. In this piece a nameless narrator describes
himself bleakly as 'the skull ... the inhumanely stripped skeleton
without voice, without shape, wandering alone upon the shores of the
world.'[40] The narrator comes upon another man wandering the coasts
and throwing the many starfish on the beach back into the sea. He
converses with him and learns that the star thrower wishes to save the
starfish from death on the dry beaches. After a conversation with the
star thrower, he vacillates between his inner darkness and a newfound
sense of hope born of a fleeting glimpse of the holy:

> I turned as I neared a bend in the coast and saw him toss another
> star, skimming it skillfully far out over the ravening and
> tumultuous water. For a moment, in the changing light, the sower
> appeared magnified, as though casting larger stars upon some
> greater sea.[41]

---

[38] Douglas Burton-Christie, 'Fire and Silence', *Orion* 15/4 (1996): 67.

[39] Cit. Burton-Christie, 'Fire and Silence', 67.

[40] Loren Eiseley, *The Star Thrower* (New York: Harcourt Brace & Company, 1978), 169.

[41] Eiseley, *Star Thrower*, 172–173.

The narrator remembers the Biblical injunction, 'Love not the world,' and responds in a whisper:

> But I *do* love the world … I love its small ones, the things beaten in the strangling surf, the bird, singing, which flies and falls and is not seen again. I choked and said, with the torn eye still upon me, "I love the lost ones, the failures of the world." It was like the renunciation of my scientific heritage. The torn eye surveyed me sadly and was gone. I had come full upon one of the last great rifts in nature, and the merciless beam no longer was in traverse around my skull. But no, it was not a rift but a joining: the expression of love projected beyond the species boundary by a creature born of Darwinian struggle, in the silent war under the tangled bank … I had seen the star thrower cross that rift and, in so doing, he had reasserted the human right to define his own frontier. He had moved to the utmost edge of natural being, if not across its boundaries. It was as though at some point the supernatural had touched hesitantly, for an instant, upon the natural.[42]

In this interpenetration of the natural and supernatural, the main character is transformed. He too becomes a star thrower and experiences himself as part of something larger, 'We were part of the rainbow—an unexplained projection into the natural.'[43] He recalls:

> I picked up a star whose tube feet ventured timidly among my fingers while, like a true star, it cried soundlessly for life. I saw it with an unaccustomed clarity and cast far out. With it, I flung myself as forfeit for the first time, into some unknown dimension of existence.[44]

---

[42] Eiseley, *Star Thrower*, 182.
[43] Eiseley, *Star Thrower*, 184.
[44] Eiseley, *Star Thrower*, 185.

In Eiseley's story there is a sense of allurement that compels the main character to overcome his demons and seek something higher. In my own poem, 'Divine Encounter' (1995) I seek to capture this sense of allurement:

> You called me.
> I tried to resist. ...
>
> I resisted because
> you are so beautiful
> that it is painful.
>
> But you shot
> your soft evening rays
> through my window.
> And the dancing leaves
> outside the glass
> took on the colors
> of your twilight gown.
>
> You teased me
> and coaxed me
> till I could no longer
> resist you.

After several descriptive verses depicting divine courtship through the natural world, I conclude:

> You called me here
> and my soul drank
> with deep refreshment.
> You invited me
> and my heart exploded
> with gladness.
> You beckoned me
> and the sky
> made love to me.

And now, like Mary,
I carry you within me.
I birth you again and again,
overflowing with you,
spilling you out
like uncontrollable laughter
or tears,
I don't know which;
I cannot contain you.
I am dangerously in love.
I want to spill you
crazily into another heart.
I cannot bear
the burden of this joy alone.

You called me
and we commingled
here tonight.
Now I am sky,
I am ice-blue water,
I am purple,
I am orange,
I am on fire.

In this poem, heaven and earth alike participate in a cosmic courtship that results in spiritual transformation.

Entanglement, love, and Trinity

In his book, *Entangled Life*, Merlin Sheldrake explains that 'we are ecosystems, composed of— and decomposed by—an ecology of microbes, the significance of which is only now coming to light.'[45]

---

[45] Merlin Sheldrake, *Entangled Life: How Fungi Make Our Worlds, Change Our Minds and Shape Our Futures* (New York: Random House, 2020), 17.

Symbiosis is ubiquitous in this entangled world. Sheldrake reflects that it no longer makes sense to speak of individuals. Rather, biology, which studies living organisms, is transformed into ecology, which studies the relationship between living organisms.[46]

Sheldrake devotes a chapter of his book to the topic of 'lure', in which he discusses truffles, or *tuber magnatum*, which are the underground fruiting bodies of mycorrhizal fungi. These fungi communicate chemically their readiness to be eaten by animals or humans. In describing various fungal relationships, including those *within* truffles and *between* truffle fungi and their partner trees, Sheldrake speaks in terms of attraction and allure, or 'chemical call-and-response.'[47] He quotes Paride, a truffle hunter, as saying, 'the truffle and its tree are like lovers, or husband and wife.'[48]

The features of attraction, entanglement and love thus belong together in inter-subjective spaces, within symbiotic relationships. In her book, *Symbiotic Planet*, scientist Lynn Margulis proposes a new model of evolution based primarily on symbiosis—the living together of very different kinds of organisms in order to survive. This theory is a departure from the Darwinian model of competition and survival of the fittest that has dominated evolutionary science for over a century. In symbiosis, the author explains, long-term cohabitation may result in symbiogenesis, the appearance of new bodies, new organs, and new species, such as the emergence of the green algal cell from four once entirely separate ancestors. She asserts that most evolutionary novelty arose and still arises directly from symbiosis. The concept of symbiosis presents us with a relational model that generates new social metaphors of mutuality, cooperation, community, and innovation.[49]

---

[46] Ibid.

[47] Sheldrake, *Entangled Life*, 37.

[48] Sheldrake, *Entangled Life*, 41.

[49] Lynn Margulis, *Symbiotic Planet: A New Look at Evolution* (New York: Basic

Now, I suggest that this relational model can be aligned with Christian theology. In his book, *Participating in God*, theologian Paul Fiddes maintains that 'the divine Word will not be spoken without physical mediation. God takes on bodies in order to draw us into the triune relationships in God.'[50] Fiddes suggests that if one is to embrace an incarnational theology, then personal encounters with God are possible in many and varied ways and places. He proposes a trinitarian doctrine of God in which we shift from static substance language to 'dynamic ideas of movement and relationship' based on love. For, he writes, 'God happens in an interweaving flow of relationships like those between a father and a son, opened up and deepened by the currents of the Spirit.'[51] Fiddes points out that, since the 'persons' of the Trinity are movements of love, such as active movements of 'originating, responding, and opening' as well as passive movements of 'being glorified, being sent, being breathed', they can be gendered in a variety of ways, including the images of mother and daughter.[52] We become part of these divine movements through participation, while sharing in relations between the many bodies of the universe.

Fiddes' notion of participating in God, based in a pastoral praxis, can be seen as a kind of entanglement with the divine, like the entanglement that science finds at every level of creation, human and other-than-human. Scientist and theologian Ilia Delio, in her book *The Unbearable Wholeness of Being*, provides a succinct definition of Erwin Schrödinger's theory of quantum entanglement as 'nonlocal interaction or unmediated action at a distance, without crossing space, without decay, and without delay.'[53] She draws here on the work of Teilhard,

---

Books, 1998).

[50] Paul S. Fiddes, *Participating in God: A Pastoral Doctrine of the Trinity* (Louisville: Westminster John Knox Press, 2000), 227.

[51] Fiddes, *Participating in God*, 281.

[52] Fiddes, *Participating in God*, 38.

[53] Ilia Delio, I., *The Unbearable Wholeness of Being: God, Evolution and the Power*

who proposed that love is the physical unitive structure of the universe.[54] Delio writes, 'Love energy is intrinsically relational and as core energy undergirds relationality in the universe.'[55] While we may not think of attraction and lure in the natural world as love, Delio points out, 'If there was no internal propensity to unite, even at a rudimentary level—indeed in the molecule itself—it would be physically impossible for love to appear higher up, in a hominized form.'[56] This view correlates with Arthur Koestler's work on the 'holon'—an entity that is whole in itself while also part of some other whole.[57] Love, then, must exist in the parts in order to exist in the whole.

Delio describes love as 'an irresistible ocean of attraction whose infinite goodness leads into the heart of God.'[58] She maintains that there is a divine depth-dimension within all of life; that God is 'the whole of every whole ... God is one with created/cosmic being and created/cosmic being is one with God.'[59]   Making a case for panentheism, she continues, 'God is in the cosmos and the cosmos is in God, but God is more than the cosmos by the nature of being God.'[60] With this view in mind, one might argue that to enter into an intersubjective relationship with any aspect of creation creates a sacred space for participating in the life of the divine.

---

of Love (Maryknoll, New York: Orbis Books, 2013) 27.

[54] Pierre Teilhard de Chardin, *The Phenomenon of Man* (London: Collins, 1963), 264–8; de Chardin, *Le Milieu Divin* (London: Collins, 1961), 135–8.

[55] Delio, *Unbearable Wholeness of Being*, 45.

[56] Ibid.

[57] Arthur Koestler, *The Ghost in the Machine* (London: Hutchinson, 1967), 48. The word is cited by Delio, *Unbearable Wholeness of Being*, 34.

[58] Ilia Delio, *The Primacy of Love* (Minneapolis: Fortress Press, 2022), 11.

[59] Delio, *Unbearable Wholeness of Being*, 58.

[60] Ibid. In developing her argument, she draws upon the work of Raimon Panikkar in his *The Rhythm of Being: The Gifford Lectures* (Maryknoll: Orbis Books, 2010), 187–88.

Intersubjective spaces and the question of identity

So far I have been exploring intersubjective relationships with and within the natural world as transformative spaces of encounter. They also provide us with a clue to the identity of every living thing. Drawing upon the work of Pierre Teilhard de Chardin, Ilia Delio uses his word 'interbeing' to speak of reality as being interwoven and relational. Humans as cosmic beings are thus intrinsically relational. But this raises questions about what identity might look like in marginal or edge spaces with permeable boundaries. Thomas Berry provides insight into this issue when he proposes that we are the universe made conscious of itself in multiple distinct forms: the universe celebrating itself. In *The Dream of the Earth*, he writes, 'the human is that being in whom the universe comes to itself in a special mode of conscious reflection.'[61] Berry speaks of a spiritual capacity in matter: 'Mind and matter are two dimensions of the single reality that comes into being in an immense diversity of expression throughout the universe by some self-organizing process.'[62] He provides a rich language for articulating how humans participate in a wholeness that also allows for individuality, as individuality is what makes relationship possible. In addition to being wholes and parts of wholes,[63] one may create intersubjective spaces between wholes; spaces that have identity in themselves and the capacity for 'holiness'.

Sheldrake's findings from the field of mycology further raise the question about locating identity within inter-subjective spaces. He explains that organisms cannot be understood in isolation. Lichens, for example, 'confuse our concept of identity and force us to question where one organism stops and another begins.'[64] Whereas branches of the tree

---

[61] Thomas Berry, *The Dream of the Earth* (Berkeley: Sierra Club Books, 1990), 16.
[62] Berry, *Dream of the Earth*, 26.
[63] Delio, *Unbearable Wholeness*, 34.
[64] Sheldrake, *Entangled Life*, 71.

of life have been diverging for hundreds of millions of years, lichens, he discovered, are also converging:

> Lichens are places where an organism unravels into an ecosystem and where an ecosystem congeals into an organism. They flicker between "wholes" and "collections of parts." Shuttling between the two perspectives is a confusing experience .... Lichens are a product less of their parts than of the exchanges between these parts.[65]

Sheldrake uses Gregory Bateson's question about a blind man with a stick as an illustration of this idea. Bateson raises the question: 'where does the blind man's self begin? At the tip of the stick? At the handle of the stick? Or at some point halfway up the stick?'[66]

Mycorrhizae are examples of mutual interdependence and boundary functions that are   performed at the interfaces of different organisms. One organism is a fungus while the other is a plant. That same fungus may also connect with other plants of the same species. The total number and types of connections in a mycorrhizal network function across boundaries of difference to create new, intersubjective relationships. Thus, mycorrhizae raise similar issues regarding identity. Sheldrake asks:

> Can we think about a plant without also thinking about the mycorrhizal networks that lace outward—extravagantly—from its roots into the soil? If we follow the tangled sprawl of mycelium that emanates from its roots, then where do we stop?[67]

Since human beings are living systems, and thus open systems, we might ask the same regarding humans and the networks in which we

---

[65] Sheldrake, *Entangled Life*, 88.
[66] Sheldrake, *Entangled Life*, 148.
[67] Ibid.

participate.

In *The Universe Story from the Primordial Flaring Forth to the Ecozoic Era,* Brian Swimme and Thomas Berry effectively identify differentiation as an answer to this question. They name differentiation, autopoiesis and communion as three basic principles of the cosmological order and warn that our present trajectory on the planet violates each of them. The universe unfolds and is ordered by differentiation, as matter becomes more complex and diverse.[68] Differentiation also relates to the quality of relationships in the universe. Autopoiesis, which the authors also refer to as 'subjectivity', is the power of each thing to participate in the ongoing creation of the universe. It is an interior dimension of things and capacity for self-manifestation.[69] Communion, a third organizing principle, is the capacity for the components of the universe to bond together and unify, as 'nothing is itself without everything else.'[70] Each of these has implications for the phenomenon of intersubjective identity as the universe evolves into 'a differentiated web of relationships around sentient centers of creativity.'[71]

Differentiation results in 'inscape', a term coined by the poet Gerard Manley Hopkins to indicate the distinctive design and particular identity of every creature.[72] In *The Groaning of Creation: God, Evolution and the Problem of Evil* Christopher Southgate, a biochemist and theologian, explains that 'every creature has both its pattern of life

---

[68] Brian Swimme and Thomas, *The Universe Story from the Primordial Flaring Forth to the Ecozoic Era* (San Francisco: HarperCollins Publishers, 1992), 73.

[69] Swimme and Berry, *Universe Story*, 74.

[70] Swimme and Berry, *Universe Story*, 77.

[71] Ibid.

[72] For 'inscape' and 'instress' see *The Journals and Papers of Gerard Manley Hopkins,* Second Edition, Revised and Enlarged, Edited by Humphry House, Completed by Graham Storey (Oxford University Press, London, 1967), 127.

and membership of its species, and also its particularity, its 'thisness.'[73] Each creature, then, may be considered to be a unique manifestation of God's presence and love. Delio's metaphor for humanity speaks to this idea: 'Each person is like a pane of glass in the great cathedral of life; the divine light shining through every person in a unique way.'[74] 'Each person is a new way of being love.'[75]

Intersubjective spaces and the presence of a God of love: 'lovescapes'

The term 'instress', also coined by Hopkins, allows us to empathize with and see the distinctiveness and essence of another person or thing.[76] Southgate explains that Hopkins uses 'instress' to describe 'the cohesive energy that binds individual entities into the Whole, the impact the inscape of entities makes on the observer, and the observer's will to receive that impact,' with the Holy Spirit being the 'go-between God.'[77] This idea locates God in intersubjective spaces and, since God is love, supports Teilhard's view of love-energy as the foundational and connective energy of the universe. Southgate's discussion of inscape and instress lead him to a theology of the Trinity. He writes:

> What God fathers forth, for which he is always to be praised, is in its truest inscape the Word, which plays in return in all selving and all self-giving love to the Father. The Christ imminent in the inscapes of the world is always the suffering Christ, the Christ

---

[73] Christopher Southgate, *The Groaning of Creation: God, Evolution and the Problem of Evil* (Louisville: Westminster John Knox Press, 2008), 97.

[74] Ilia Delio, 'Word Made Matter.' Inaugural Fireside Zoom Webinar, 28 February 2022. https://vimeo.com/689715984, accessed 28 April 2022.

[75] Delio, 'Word Made Matter'.

[76] Hopkins, *Journals and Papers*, 127.

[77] Southgate, *Groaning of Creation*, 97.

that bears the "no" along with creation's "yes," the Christ that bears the "no" of the human will, the Christ that-would-be-crucified.[78]

Through the kenosis or 'self-emptying sacrifice of Christ' humans are free to respond to God and the world.

This image of Christ lies at the heart of Hopkins' use of the word 'lovescape' in his poem 'The Wreck of the Deutschland' (1875–76), which commemorates the death of five exiled Franciscan sisters in a shipwreck near Kent, England. Hopkins uses the expression 'lovescape crucified'[79] to connect the nuns' drowning to the stigmata of St. Francis of Assisi, the founder of their religious order, suggesting that they also participated in Christ's suffering. The phenomenon of stigmata might be seen as a kind of intersubjectivity with Christ. Delio also writes of crucified love as reciprocal: 'The cross reveals to us the heart of God because it reveals the vulnerability of God's love.'[80] Because God is the 'fountain fullness of Love,' God shares in the sufferings of the world, and thereby 'draws life into new life.'[81]

Like Southgate and Delio, Fiddes proposes the idea of love as a space for divine encounter; he writes that encountering each other in the spatiality given by love is only possible because 'at the same time it is knowledge of the God who holds us all in the fellowship (*koinonia*) of God's own life.' It is 'human participation in the relational currents of love in God'.[82] In a comparative study of love in mystical religion,

---

[78] Southgate, *Groaning of Creation*, 101.

[79] Gerard Manley Hopkins, 'The Wreck of the Deutschland', in *Poems of Gerard Manley Hopkins*, 4th. Ed., edited by W. H. Gardner and N. H. Mackenzie (London: Oxford University Press, 1967), 59.

[80] Delio, *Unbearable Wholeness of Being*, 85.

[81] Delio, *Unbearable Wholeness of Being*, 87.

[82] Paul S. Fiddes (ed.), *Love as Common Ground: Essays on Love in Religion* (Lanham: Lexington Books, 2021), ix; cf. Fiddes, 'God Is Love, But Is Love God? Towards a Theology of Love as Knowledge', in Fiddes (ed.), *Love as Common*

Minlib Dallh explores bridal mysticism and erotic imagery in the writings of some Islamic and Christian women mystics as sites of encounters of a transcendent kind. The writings of these women attempted to 'bridge the incommensurable gap between God and humanity and to highlight the neglected and yet positive role that marital love plays in understanding the ineffable encounter with the divine.' In both traditions, women mystics show us that erotic encounters with the divine create 'new possibilities for a deeper life in God.'[83] These encounters take place in the core of our being even as the world is fragmented. Might they, then, also be considered 'lovescapes?' And might lovescapes—the patterns of God's love—be found in non-human life as well? Might these spaces be both human and divine spaces, each with their own distinctive inscape and instress? If so, the energy at work in spaces would be love.

One may also consider the networks of the universe in terms of edge spaces. Rachel Carson writes of borderline, marginal spaces as places of meeting, interpenetration, and mystery: 'Looking out over the cove I felt a strong sense of the interchangeability of land and sea in this marginal world of the shore, and of the links between the life of the two.'[84] Boundaries between land and sea become blurred. Bill Mollison and Reney-Mia Slay, farmers who practice and teach about permaculture, write of edge spaces as places of varied ecology within which productivity increases because the resources from both systems can be utilized. Reef ecologies—on the edge between coral and ocean—for example, are highly productive systems.[85] Edge spaces are akin to

---

Ground, 18–19.

[83] Minlib Dallh, 'Bridal Symbolism, Eroticization of Divine Love, and Friendship', in Fiddes (ed.), *Love as Common Ground,* 91.

[84] Rachel Carson, 'The Edge of the Sea', in Finch and Elder, *Norton Book of Nature Writing,* 464.

[85] Bill Mollison and Reney-Mia Slay, *Introduction to Permaculture* (Sisters Creek, Tasmania: Tagari Publications, 1991), 26.

what spiritual director William Barry refers to as 'thin places' wherein one can more readily encounter God: they are meeting places between the immanent and transcendent.[86] The relationships that emerge from these encounters may be considered a third thing, each with its particular inscape. Intersubjective relationships within 'edge' or 'thin' places, then, provide a way for humans to participate intersubjectively in the Trinity. As Fiddes proposes, God is not only in the spaces, but the spaces are in God. That is, the spaces of the universe are held within the spaces between the interweaving relations of the triune God.[87]

Attraction, love and Trinity

Earlier, I explored the notions of attraction and allure at the quantum, microbial, human, and interspecies levels and I maintained that this attraction is best understood in inter-subjective terms, and that is in fact a form of love. Now I want to work towards the point where this inter-subjective attraction at the collective or systemic level might be understood within a theology of the Trinity.

In *The Primacy of Love*, Ilia Delio explains Pierre Teilhard de Chardin's claim that 'the characteristics of human love such as attraction, irresistibility and union, can be found on the most fundamental levels of physical life.'[88] Delio explains Teilhard's belief that love is a force of attraction that is present at the atomic level: 'If matter is a form of energy, and the core energy of the universe is love,

---

[86] William A. Barry, SJ, *A Friendship Like No Other* (Chicago: Loyola Press, 2008), 163.

[87] Paul S. Fiddes, *Seeing the World and Knowing God. Hebrew Wisdom and Christian Doctrine in a Late-Modern Context* (Oxford: Oxford University Press, 2015), 249–265

[88] Delio, *Primacy of Love* (Minneapolis: Fortress Press, 2022), 16; cf. de Chardin, *Phenomenon of Man*, 264.

then all matter is a form of love.'[89] Given that energy is matter, it follows that love energy is the physical structure and fabric of the universe, with attraction and union as its organizing principles: 'Love is a cosmic force before it is a human one.'[90] She maintains that union precedes being, which is why we seek to reunited into a higher unity. Attraction and love draw us into this union.

Delio proposes the idea of spontaneously appearing 'Christ fields' as drawing us into new patterns of community, oneness and relationship with our planet. Christ fields are 'basins of attraction, transcending institutional religion, signaling a new religious consciousness, a new God-centeredness that inspires and empowers co-creativity for a new humanity and a new Earth.'[91] They are 'holons', whole parts and a larger consciousness that participates in the universe. Christ fields, then, are the power of attraction in mycorrhizal and other networks in nature as well as in human communities.

Sheldrake presents a compelling case for the ability of fungi to solve problems, communicate, make decisions, learn and remember.[92] He explains that intelligent behaviours can arise without brains, so long as there is a dynamic and responsive network.[93] My question, though not his, is whether these behaviours also show love, and in doing so, participate in Christ. Sheldrake cites a study by forest ecologist Suzanne Simard in which she found that phosphorus was passed from the roots of dying plants to nearby healthy plants through a shared fungal network. She also discovered carbon transfers between Paper Birch and Douglas Fir that flowed in both directions, depending upon the seasons and needs of the plants.

---

[89] Delio, *Primacy of Love*, 19.

[90] Delio, *Primacy of Love*, 18.

[91] Ilia Delio, *The Emergent Christ* (Maryknoll: Orbis Books, 2011), 145.

[92] Sheldrake, *Entangled Life*, 16.

[93] Sheldrake, *Entangled Life*, 66.

Simard found that the birch and fir were transmitting carbon back and forth through a mycorrhizal network, working together like a system, with Paper Birch receiving more than it gave. The birch's vitality, however, was not diminished. Over time, Simard observed that over the growing season the exchange of resources between trees changed; during the summer the birch sent more carbon to the fir, but in the Spring and Fall the fir sent more carbon to the birch. She explains, 'This trading system between the two species, shifting with the seasons, suggested that the trees were in a sophisticated exchange pattern, possibly reaching a balance over the course of a year.'[94]

Puzzled by the behaviours found in Simard's study, Sheldrake asks, 'why would plants give resources to a fungus that goes on to give them to a neighbouring plant—a potential competitor?'[95] This appears to be altruism, which is problematic to him, as it does not appear to support evolutionary theory. Sheldrake resolves:

> There are a number of ways around this impasse. One relies on the idea that the costs to donor plants aren't actually costs. Many plants have plenty of access to light. For such plants, carbon is not a limited resource. If a plant's surplus carbon passes into a mycorrhizal network where it is enjoyed by many as a "public good," the charge of altruism can be avoided because no one— whether donor or receiver—has incurred a cost. Another possibility is that both sender and receiver plants benefit, but at different times.[96]

Sheldrake's language here is noteworthy, as he views the idea of altruism with suspicion. He takes a myco-centric perspective in which 'brokers of entanglement [are] able to mediate the interactions between

---

[94] Suzanne Simard, *Finding the Mother Tree: Discovering the Wisdom of the Forest* (New York: Alfred A. Knopf, 2021), 175.
[95] Sheldrake, *Entangled Life*, 159.
[96] Sheldrake, *Entangled Life*, 161.

plants according to their own fungal needs',[97] in order to avoid what he sees as a problem. Sheldrake concludes:

> Overall, plants that share a network with others grow more quickly and survive better than neighboring plants that are excluded from the common network. These findings have fueled visions of wood-wide webs as places of caring, sharing, and mutual aid through which plants can free themselves from the rich rigid hierarchies of competition for resources.[98]

Whereas Sheldrake sees apparent altruism in nature as a problem to resolved in favour of behaviour that is ultimately, if not immediately, self-serving, Simard sees it differently.

In *Finding the Mother Tree: Discovering the Wisdom of the Forest*, Simard shares her discoveries that trees are social creatures that are able to communicate through mycorrhizal webs, nurture one another, heal themselves, their families and communities. She had learned from previous studies that different species grown in groups were capable of producing new mycorrhizal species that neither species was capable of producing on its own.[99] Thus, we return to the notion that an intersubjective relationship may produce a third thing with a distinctive identity or inscape.

Simard's further studies uncovered the dynamics of self-regeneration of old-growth forests through parental relationships wherein the young were nurtured by the old and eventually able to give back to the forest community. In doing so, she discovered the Mother Trees and mapped them to their offspring. She writes:

> But now we know Mother Trees can truly nurture their offspring.

---

[97] Sheldrake, *Entangled Life*, 162.
[98] Ibid.
[99] Simard, *Finding the Mother Tree*, 159.

Douglas Firs, it turns out, recognize their kin and distinguish them from other families and different species. They communicate and send carbon, the building block of life, not just to the mycorrhizas of their kin but to other members of the community. To keep it whole, they appear to relate to their offspring as do mothers passing their best recipes to their daughters.[100]

In this, there is a self-emptying or kenosis, especially towards the end of the Mother Tree's life. Simard concludes that trees 'cooperate, make decisions, learn, and remember— qualities we normally ascribe to sentience, wisdom, intelligence',[101] and suggests that, rather than humans saving trees, trees will save us by teaching us how to live in viable communities. Could this be a form of love and reciprocity? When does this behaviour evolve into love? Or is this the wrong question?

According to Delio, Teilhard held that certain characteristics of human love, such as attraction, irresistibility and union, are uncovered at the most fundamental levels of physical life.[102] For Teilhard, love energy, the force of attraction that holds together the universe, is there from the beginning. Informed by Henri Bergson's theory of creative evolution, Teilhard held that evolution is creative because there is 'an underlying impulse toward deepened unity. As life becomes more conscious and relational, love arises.'[103] Delio maintains that we awaken to that energy which is already there and call it love. And love, she contends, is the basis of all knowledge.[104]

Fiddes similarly argues that love is a form of knowing God; that God 'can be known through love as a kind of indwelling of God in the

---

[100] Simard, *Finding the Mother Tree*, 277.
[101] Simard, *Finding the Mother Tree*, 294.
[102] Delio, *Primacy of Love*, 16.
[103] Delio, *Primacy of Love*, 25.
[104] Delio, *Unbearable Wholeness*, 46.

lover.'[105] Human love and the experience of knowing divine love are inseparable—a reality that is revealed in the suffering of Jesus. Fiddes finds a connection between loving and knowing in the biblical tradition of *hokmah*/*sophia* (wisdom) and affirms that God is love and that love is God:

> God cannot be reduced to human love, while God can only be known through the phenomenon of human love. Created beings like us find that we are immersed into a web of relations where love is stronger, wider, more inexhaustible and more indestructible than our own.[106]

This inexhaustible 'web of relations' is, in Fiddes' understanding, the triune God. Both Fiddes and Delio thus bring trinitarian theology alive in fresh, rich and promising ways that open up the idea of love as the basic energy of the universe and point to the possibility that all loving relationships are part of the life of God. Aligned with contemporary science, their writings speak effectively to contemporary issues, thereby contributing to a theology of wholeness that is essential to the continuance of life on earth.

In *Participating in God, A Pastoral Doctrine of the Trinity* Fiddes writes, 'To participate in God means that there is the ever-present opportunity to be aligned with a movement of communication beyond ourselves which is pure love, and which is also a movement of the will.'[107] He sees God as working in this way in all of nature, 'guiding it patiently, offering innovation through the influence of the Holy Spirit, and calling out response from it.'[108] And, if human beings are capable

---

[105] Fiddes, 'God Is Love,' 23. Thomas Berry uses term 'incendence' to describe the idea of indwelling: Berry, *Dream of the Earth*, 208.

[106] Fiddes, 'God Is Love', 46.

[107] Fiddes, *Participating in God*, 53.

[108] Fiddes, *Participating in God*, 144.

of responding to God, then it is reasonable to think that all of creation can respond in some way to God.[109] Fiddes cites a scriptural basis for this understanding, reminding us that, after the flood, God makes a covenant with every living creature in Genesis 9:10, and in Romans 8:19–22 creation 'groans as if in the pangs of childbirth' (NEB), waiting with God's human children for freedom and redemption. Fiddes explains that this poetic language 'offers testimony to some kind of response which the natural world can make, or fail to make, to the purposes of God; it also hints that this response is implicated in some way in the human response.'[110] He proposes a 'trinitarian pan-en-theism', or the participation of all things in God, as 'interweaving movements of relational love' through which we are drawn bodily into the life of the triune God.[111] Fiddes thus sees the whole world as sacramental and the universe as the body of the Trinity, in the sense that God is eternally committed to materiality as the place of encounter with creatures.[112]

Like Fiddes' earlier work, Delio's theology of the Trinity finds God in the 'dynamic movement of love.' She reflects, 'God is self-creative love expressed in personal relationships of love which includes the dynamism of intersubjectivity and the community emerging from these relationships.'[113] As a process theologian, Delio sees this trinitarian relationship as emergent, as 'God and the world consummate their desire for one another in the marriage of heaven and earth, precisely because God and world are entwined in creative union.'[114] She continues:

---

[109] Ibid.
[110] Fiddes, *Participating in God*, 145.
[111] Fiddes, *Participating in God*, 292.
[112] Fiddes, *Participating in God*, 292, 299.
[113] Delio, *Primacy of Love*, 30.
[114] Delio, *Primacy of Love*, 32–33.

Each in its own way exists in itself and with the other, so that the creative movement of life is always toward the fullness of love, a movement that is at once divine, created and cosmic ... In Christ, God and cosmos are entangled in love and brought to explicit consciousness in Jesus of Nazareth.'[115]

Reframing these ideas in terms of the organizing principles of Swimme and Berry, one may think of the first trinitarian movement of 'self-creative love' as autopoiesis. The second movement of the Trinity is spoken into differentiation as the Word made flesh. And the third movement is the energy of bonding and uniting all into a sacred communion which is continually becoming more whole. Taking a cruciform view, one might imagine a space wherein the transcendent or vertical meets the immanent or horizontal—heaven meets Earth—and creates a verdant edge space at their intersection—a space of intersubjectivity that includes all of creation bound together with Christ in love; this invites us into new ways of being in relationship. In these cruciform spaces of creative tension, the power of the cross is amplified and extended in all directions as one empties oneself (*kenosis*) of a singular self-identity in order to become always more.

Intersubjective knowing, loving, and worshipping

Coming from the field of teacher education, Parker Palmer provides a vision of what this space of intersection might look like in the human learning community. Although written almost two and a half decades ago, Palmer's book, *The Courage to Teach* has something timely to say about systemic thinking that resonates with recent discoveries about the behaviour of natural networks. As an alternative to teacher-centered or student-centered classrooms, Palmer advocates for subject-centered

---

[115] Delio, *Primacy of Love*, 34.

education in which learners gather around 'a third thing' or 'great thing' that lies at the center of a 'community of truth'.[116] For, 'true community requires a transcendent third thing that holds both me and thee accountable to something beyond ourselves.'[117] The 'third thing' at the centre of the subject-centered classroom has a presence that is real, visceral and vocal. Palmer explains that in a subject-centered classroom the central task of the teacher is to give an independent voice to the great thing; an inscape, if you will. In such a classroom a teacher is able to 'invigorate those connections between our subjects, our students, and our souls that help make us whole again.'[118]

Palmer's model of community demonstrates an understanding of reality as a web of communal relationships that one can only know through entering into community with it, joining the knower to the known in a relational knowing. He first presents a diagram of 'The Objectivist Myth of Knowing' in which the 'pure' object of study exists in a conceptual space that hovers above the experts (teachers), who are trained to impart knowledge about the object in a detached and unbiased manner to the untrained and biased amateurs (students) at the bottom of the diagram. There are baffles at each point of transmission that only allow knowledge to flow downward. In this hierarchical and linear model truth flows only in one direction. It is a closed system.[119]

In contrast, Palmer offers a second diagram of 'The Community of Truth' that functions in a similar way to Sheldrake's mycorrhizal networks.[120] Unlike the object of study at the top of the first diagram, the 'subject' of exploration dwells at the center of a circular, interactive and dynamic community of truth and is available for relationships that

---

[116] Parker J. Palmer, *The Courage to Teach: Exploring the Inner Landscape of a Teacher's Life* (San Francisco: Jossey-Bass, 1998), 115.

[117] Palmer, *Courage to Teach*, 117.

[118] Palmer, *Courage to Teach*, 120.

[119] Palmer, *Courage to Teach*, 100.

[120] Palmer, *Courage to Teach*, 102.

do not need to be mediated. The 'knowers' are gathered around the subject, with lines connecting each of them to the subject as well as to every other member of the learning community, creating a complex web of relationality. The connective lines, which are akin to mycorrhizae, have arrows pointing outward at both ends, indicating an open system. In this community the knowers and the subject itself actively participate in the 'dialectic of knowing.'[121] Palmer reflects:

> the things of the world call us, and we are drawn to them—each of us to different things, as each is drawn to different friends. Once we have heard that call and responded, the subject calls us out of ourselves and into its own selfhood.'[122]

This model, while horizontal in design, offers the possibility of transcendence; a possibility made all the more powerful if the subject at the center is Christ, with love as the 'dialectic of knowing.'

Palmer is a Quaker and his writings on the Community of Truth are reflective of the dynamics of the Quaker Meeting, a form of worship in which 'Friends' gather together and sit in silence for long periods of time, held together in the heart of divine love, until the Holy Spirit moves them to speak and offer ministry. In *Invitation to a Deeper Communion* Quaker teacher Marcelle Martin writes of her experience during a Quaker prayer meeting: 'I discovered a powerful connection to the Divine within my own soul, in the form of the Inner Light, which permeates all of creation. Through this experience, I came to know this Light as the essence of my true self.'[123] She quotes Robert Barclay as he describes his transformative experience in a Quaker Meeting:

---

[121] Palmer, *Courage to Teach*, 105.

[122] Ibid..

[123] Marcelle Martin, *Invitation to a Deeper Communion* (Wallingford, Pennsylvania: Pendle Hill Publications, 2003), 12.

> When I came into the silent assemblies of God's people, I felt a secret power among them, which touched my heart. And as I gave way to it, I found the evil in me weakening and the good lifted up. Thus it was that I was knit into them and united with them.[124]

Martin also cites Thomas Kelly, who writes about 'The Gathered Meeting' in which the whole group gathered in prayer is collectively lifted to a new level of transcendence. The Quaker Meeting thus might be thought of as emergent whole-making, to use Delio's terms, whereby the group gathered has its own inscape or charism.[125] These testimonies offer a way to think about intersubjectivity among humans and God. And, although the natural world is not explicitly included in these narratives, perhaps its presence is implied (see Palmer's reference to 'things of the world'), or perhaps an awareness of it as the larger context for human life and prayer might be cultivated.

At another Quaker Meeting recorded by Martin, some members experienced God as a feminine, motherly presence and a sense of spiritual nourishment, reminiscent of Simard's Mother Tree, which brought one Friend to an understanding that 'This is Holy Communion. It was a direct communion with God that brought us all into communion with one another.'[126] The Catholic sacrament of Eucharist has the same end, although it may sometimes become a matter of personal piety rather than a gathering of the congregation into deeper communion. According to the Catholic doctrine of transubstantiation, through the words of consecration spoken by a priest, bread and wine become the Body and Blood of the risen Christ, whom we take into ourselves bodily and spiritually. Thus, one might say that Christ's indwelling in the Eucharist

---

[124] Martin, *Invitation*, 7.

[125] A collective experience of being lifted up also occurs in the Catholic practice of Adoration of the Blessed Sacrament, as well as in practices of other faith traditions, such as in group meditation.

[126] Martin, *Invitation*, 9.

is intersubjective, creating a third thing—'we.' As members of the Body of Christ, in communion with one another, we create multiple sites of 'we' that overlap in the edge spaces, connected together in networks of nurturance. This points to the sacramentality of food itself and the ecosystems of the soil, of which we are a part. Thus, through Eucharist humans and creation participate bodily and spiritually in Trinity.

While Quaker worship values private revelation, it is a knowing that occurs in the context of a larger web of intentional relationships, with silence serving as a conduit for intersubjectivity and indwelling love. One might think of it as an entangled knowing such as in Palmer's second diagram, as Friends gather around the Great Thing or truth in the centre, which is Christ. Whereas in much Christian worship the 'truth' of Christ is often thought to come through the clergy, who are gate-keepers, in Quaker worship it can come through any of the Friends gathered. All Friends, then, share equally in the role of mediating the divine directly and among one another.[127] The Quaker meeting might be seen as a conduit for intersubjectivity, with love at the centre and flowing throughout an open system. And, since humans are involved in many interlocking communities, we create ever wider networks of connectivity.

Conclusion: love and hope on the edge

This essay has explored the question of identity through narratives of intersubjective experiences, both at the individual and collective levels, and it has theologized the notion of intersubjectivity, leading to a fuller understanding of Trinity, informed by contemporary science. It has

---

[127] Catholics are moving more towards this model through synodality, in which laity and clergy alike, gather together in groups of various sizes to discern how the Holy Spirit is speaking to the Church. Other models are the 'church meeting' of Baptists, and the traditional 'class meeting' of Methodists.

reframed the question of knowledge from 'what do we need to know?' to 'how do we know?' and proposed that love is a form of knowing. It has looked at knowing and loving in community, which have implications for worship and sacramentality, since how we know and love directly impacts how we worship.

In *The Tao of Liberation: Exploring the Ecology of Transformation* Mark Hathaway and Leonardo Boff write of 'the pregnant void' as:

> a kind of vast sea of energy, seething with possibilities, in which space and time are intertwined in a dynamic unity capable of birthing new matter and even a new universe, so long as the matter is not annihilated by antimatter.[128]

The authors explain that:

> according to quantum field theory, what we perceive as "empty space" actually contains a huge "zero point energy," which arises from the combination of all the quantum fields it encompasses. The "empty" vacuum, not matter, is fundamental: matter is simply a small perturbation on an immense sea of energy.[129]

Some physicists see this as a kind of continuous-creation. Hathaway and Boff compare the pregnant void to the Tao; the whirling void that is the origin and guiding principle of all things.

In discussing the void, the authors cite Berry, who writes 'we are not lacking in the dynamic forces needed to create the future. We live immersed in a sea of energy beyond all comprehension. But this energy, in an ultimate sense, is ours, not by domination but by invocation.'[130] Hathaway and Boff respond to this idea by asking, 'Is it possible to

---

[128] Mark Hathaway and Leonardo Boff, *The Tao of Liberation: Exploring the Ecology of Transformation* (Maryknoll: Orbis Books, 2009), 181.
[129] Hathaway and Boff, *Tao of Liberation*, 181.
[130] Berry, *Great Work*, 175.

invoke the best energy present in the void to realize new possibilities? … there ways … to invoke it, to midwife new possibilities from the pregnant void?[131]

This opens up the idea that, although one may think of the pregnant void of potentiality as being 'out there' somewhere, it may also be within us and all of creation. Thus, our simple acts of invoking love in the edge spaces within our lives can affect the larger whole on behalf of the common good. Teilhard identifies the 'cosmic energy' to which Berry and others refer as love, and proposes that 'all we may well need is to imagine our power of loving developing until it embraces the total of [people] and the earth'. Again he reflects, 'Love alone is capable of uniting living beings in such a way as to complete and fulfil them.'[132] So we may actively participate in this fulfilment through creating ever-expanding intersubjective relationships of love.

Southgate writes that by fulfilling our role as mediator we 'help the world fulfill its destiny and be transformed by the light and presence of God.'[133] He draws upon the image of labour and childbirth in Romans 8:22 when he explains that this process of becoming is accompanied by an element of 'groaning', which is relieved through human participation in the divine transformation of the biosphere.[134] He continues, 'As priests, we are reverent-receptive contemplatives, but also co-redeemers, caught up in a process of transformation that will lead ultimately to the new creation in which there will be no more crying (Rev. 21:4).[135]

Delio similarly speaks of a rebirthing of consciousness and relationality. She argues that our dysfunctional closed systems need to

---

[131] Berry, *Great Work*, 182.
[132] De Chardin, *Phenomenon of Man*, 265–6.
[133] Hathaway and Boff, *Tao of Liberation*, 112.
[134] Hathaway and Boff, *Tao of Liberation*, 115.
[135] Southgate, *Groaning of Creation*, 113.

be transformed into open, holistic systems that engender an open consciousness. This paradigm shift is already underway and a new type of person—a new species—is emerging.[136] She urges us to wake up to a new consciousness: 'There's only now, and now is being invited.'[137]

Theologian John F. Haught explains that future hope is tied to creation, thus providing fertile ground for a theory of hope that is connected to environmental literacy and stewardship. Haught reminds us that Abraham stories in which ancient nomadic people depended upon green growth in the desert may have provided the original basis for biblical faith in the future, that:

> the first sparks of what would eventually flame out into the passionate, prophetic hope for the coming of God could have occurred in our remote biblical ancestors' encounter with the fragile thriving of life at the frontiers of their own wanderings.[138]

This image is evocative of natural edge spaces as well as the fragile edge upon which human life is precariously perched in our present time of climate change.

Informed by the science of edge spaces, William McCauley and I coined the term 'hope on the edge'[139] to describe a kind of hope that is born in the marginal, in-between spaces. We proposed that hope on the

---

[136] In *The Great Work*, 160, Berry devotes chapter 14 to 'Reinventing the Human', arguing that: 'Radical new cultural forms are needed. These new cultural forms would place the human within the dynamics of the planet rather than place the planet within the dynamics of the human'.

[137] Delio, 'Word Made Matter'.

[138] John Haught, 'Ecology and Eschatology', in Drew Christiansen and Walter Grazer (eds.), *And God Saw That It Was Good: Catholic Theology and the Environment* (Washington, DC: United States Catholic Conference, 1996), 55.

[139] Emily DeMoor and William J. McCauley, 'STREAM (STEM plus) and Hope: A Study of Teachers' and Students' Attitudes toward the Natural World,' unpublished paper, International Symposium on Educational Reform (ISER) conference, June 2012, Lexington, Kentucky.

edge is a both/and space that allows for the reintegration of matter and spirit, science and religion, immanence and transcendence, earth and heaven. Expanding upon this idea, hope on the edge creates open systems in which edge spaces of encounter are increased exponentially through multiple networked sites of intersubjectivity, each with its own sentient centre and inscape, wherein we awaken to ourselves as part of the one another, creation and the divine in a Christic whole. 'Hope on the edge' invokes and provokes love-energy into new possibilities, creating novel and distinctive lovescapes characterized by love, empathy, reciprocity and communion.

Underscoring the entangled nature of life, Berry prophesied that we will go into the future as one sacred universe-community, or we will not go into the future at all.[140] Hope on the edge creates intersubjective spaces in which, through *kenosis* and transformation, love begets more love and moves us forward towards ever greater trinitarian wholeness and generativity through, and with, our sacred and beloved planet.

---

[140] Berry, *Great Work*, 49.

2

Learning to Love Again: Rediscovering the Earth as Sacred

Celia Deane-Drummond

Far back in deep time, one of the earliest explicitly human moral emotions, remarkably evident even before *Homo sapiens* first emerged on the African savannah, was the ability to show compassion and love for others, including persistent and committed love for the weak, disabled and broken. These ancient close-knit societies were aware of their vulnerability in the face of extremes of climate change, threats from giant fauna and other dire risks to life. It was within that awareness of collective vulnerability that peculiarly human forms of pro-sociality and deep compassion emerged.

In a fascinating way, reflecting on the lives of our earliest human communities in deep time brings to the surface what could be termed the anthropological feature of committed love of neighbour that has persisted in human societies across millennia. This costly love for others surfaced within a close meshwork of relationships, including those with creatures, in a way that was crucial for human survival. Gradually a sense of something beyond mere utility dawned in the human imagination, leading to a strong sense that other creatures, both living and non-living, were participants in the human story. Eventually a sense of the sacred in all things was born, fuelled perhaps by a deep-seated sense of wonder and beauty that is, in accordance with Jane Goodall's observations, arguably present in nascent form among our closest primate cousins. It was only later in human history that these close interwoven relationships started to break down as societies became larger, and along with that, a disjunction in humanity's relationship to the earth, alongside a growing sense of a devastating crisis of breakdown between people and planet that is all too evident in our contemporary societies.

Drawing on the anthropology of the earliest hominin communities researched by archaeologist Penny Spikins and the anthropology of Tim Ingold, who has studied and immersed himself for years within contemporary indigenous societies across the globe, especially among the Skolt Sami in Finland, I argue in this essay that a non-dualistic way of understanding our humanity as embedded in a meshwork of relationships which embraces life as sacred facilitates genuine human love of the earth to be born. Such a position also reflects more accurately the holistic non-dualistic approach to the human person that agrarian societies assumed. That agrarian approach was presupposed in ancient biblical narratives and has largely faded from human consciousness in modern societies.

Our intimate relationship with other beings is also traced in physical bodily forms through mutualistic, symbiotic relationships which make up our microbiome, which quite literally are incorporated into all the cells of our bodies and enables all human beings to flourish. Belief in the earth as sacred is also resonant with Pope Francis' intention to develop an integral ecology, which aims to counteract the fixation on epistemologies shaped by a technological paradigm, incorporating an integrated multidisciplinary approach that does not rely just on technological fixes for resolution of global problems. Integral ecology is inclusive of knowing and loving the world fundamentally as God's creation, recognising its sacrality and accepting our creatureliness and vulnerability alongside that of other living beings.

This essay is also inspired by a close reading of the Thomistic understanding of the virtue of the love of God through friendship in charity. However, his own perception stopped short when it came to loving others, in that it was confined to God and restricted within the human community. I will argue, instead, that the uniquely human capacity to love God and neighbour requires special attention and tenderness towards our own woundedness and that of the earth, and, through understanding all life as sacred, begins to enable both humanity and the earth to heal.

Love in Deep Time

Models of human distinctiveness
Consideration of our early human origins often sparks our collective imagination, not least because an evolutionary narrative necessarily features in mapping out both how humanity came to exist and how, against the odds, humanity managed to survive. There are various evolutionary interpretations of human origins that are dominant in the publicly accessible scientific literature, with four options that are most dominant.[1]

First, there is a tendency to assume, especially if we are influenced by what we consider to be standard Darwinian theories that speak of nature 'red in tooth and claw', that the only way our early hominin ancestors managed to survive in such challenging circumstances of drastic climate change, predation by giant fauna and general vulnerability was through a strong dose of aggression, selfishness, and

---

[1] As summarized in Agustín Fuentes, *The Creative Spark: How Imagination Made Humans Exceptional* (New York: Penguin, 2017), 3–4. He has also discussed the importance of belief more broadly for human emergence and what he calls 'meaning making' in Agustín Fuentes, *Why We Believe: Evolution and the Human Way of Being* (New Haven: Yale University Press, 2019).

violence. The opposite possibility is that our distinctiveness is at the other pole—that is, self-sacrifice, service to the group and super-cooperation are all that mattered. A third possible explanation is that our evolved tendencies back in the context of the savannah have seeded strong inclinations to behaviours that are now maladaptive in current societies, so what was fit for purpose then, is no longer relevant, thus being the root cause of so much mental illness and general frustration with life characteristic of modern societies. A fourth explanation is that it was through our uniquely evolved intelligence that human domination of the earth ensued, but in a way that has now backfired, for through trying to mould the world to suit human purposes both ourselves and the planet are now at peril. Beyond these four interpretations, Agustin Fuentes favours a broader look at human creativity as crucial to early human survival, so, in his words:

> It's the epic tale of all epic tales: the story of a group of highly vulnerable creatures—the favoured prey of a terrifying array of ferocious predators—who learn better than any of their primate relatives to apply their ingenuity to devising ways of working together to survive: to invest their world with meaning and their lives with hope; and to re-shape their world, thereby reshaping themselves'. [2]

Empathy and compassion

Ingenuity (as highlighted by Fuentes) is clearly a crucial characteristic that can by mapped relatively easily in the material evolutionary record by demonstrating how humanity began to work and think together to cooperate in challenging circumstances and to create special tools to enable survival. Yet, the focus on working and thinking does not yet touch on another crucially important characteristic, namely, the fundamental ability to love, grounded in basic affective tendencies to

---

[2] Fuentes, *Creative Spark*, 4.

care for kin and close relatives that are also found in other social animals.

The abilities to show both compassion and love builds on basic capacities for empathy, but at the same time they are distinct from empathy. Empathy is a tendency to imitate another's emotional state and thus can include a variety of different dispositions, including pride, anger, sadness or happiness as well as compassion. Compassion, however, is other- regarding in a narrower sense, in that it is a response to another's suffering in a way that then leads to positive helping behaviour[3]. Empathic distress, on the other hand, instead of fostering compassion can also lead to avoidance of another's distress, or suppression, leading to callousness or apathy.[4] Empathic distress is associated with feelings of stress, while compassion is associated with feelings of love. There is some evidence to suggest that in order for compassion to become expressed, the initial feelings of distress on witnessing suffering in another need to be not just emotionally regulated, but also complemented by positive training in the ability to show compassion.[5] There are also a number of different motivational

---

[3] J. L Goetz and K. Peng, 'Sympathy and Responses to Suffering: Similarity and Variation in China and the United States', *Emotion* 19/2 (2019): 320–33.

[4] C. D. Cameron and B. K. Payne, 'The Cost of Callousness: Regulating Compassion Influences the Moral Self-Concept', *Psychological Science*, 23/3 (2012): 225–29; Nancy Eisenberg and N. D Eggum, 'Empathic Responding: Sympathy and Personal Distress', in Jean Decety and William Ickes (eds.), *The Social Neuroscience of Empathy* (Cambridge, MA, online edn, MIT Press Scholarship Online, 2009), 71–84; https://doi.org/10.7551/mitpress/9780262012973.003.0007.

[5] For a discussion of inhibitors to compassion and how these could be overcome, including tolerance of the feelings of distress when witnessing suffering, see Paul Gilbert and Jennifer Mascaro, 'Compassion Fears, Blocks and Resistances: An Evolutionary Investigation', in E. Seppälä, E. Simon-Thomas, S. Brown, M. Worline, C. Cameron, and J. Doty (eds.), *The Oxford Handbook of Compassion Science* (Oxford: Oxford University Press, 2017), 399–418. For neuroscience of compassion and how compassion training changes neurofunctions see Olga M. Klimecki and Tania Singer, 'The Compassionate Brain' in Seppälä et al. (eds.), *Oxford Handbook of*

reasons other than compassion that might lead to helping behaviour, such as desire to increase one's social status, gratitude, embarrassment,[6] or strong feelings of obligation.[7] Bearing in mind such qualifications, evidence for compassion in deep time among early hominins relies on finding persistence in caring behaviour towards those who are ill, disabled, and vulnerable in some way. The specific circumstances indicate that such expressions of devoted care are highly unlikely to be related to the more complex motivational reasons for such actions that are now characteristic of modern cultures and societies.

Care-giving in the Palaeolithic period[8]

Paleoanthropologist Penny Spikins and her colleagues at the University of York have done some fascinating work on the possible reconstruction of caring emotions in the pre-history of the *Homo* lineage.[9] The most

---

Compassion Science, 109–20.

[6] L. Kiang, E. A. Merçon-Vargas, S. E. Mendonça, A.Payir, and L. O'Brien, 'The Development of Gratitude and its Relation to Spending Preferences and Materialism', in J. R. H. Tudge and L. B. L. Freitas (eds.), *Developing Gratitude in Children and Adolescents* (Cambridge: Cambridge University Press, 2018), 154– 73); M. E. McCullough, R. A. Emmons, and J. A. Tsang, 'The Grateful Disposition: A Conceptual and Empirical Topography', *Journal of Personality and Social Psychology* 82/1, (2002): 112–27; S. B. Algoe, and J. Haidt, 'Witnessing Excellence in Action: the "Other-praising" Emotions of Elevation, Gratitude, and Admiration', *The Journal of Positive Psychology* 4/2 (2009): 105–27.

[7] T. Naito, and Y. Sakata, 'Gratitude, Indebtedness, and Regret on Receiving a Friend's Favor in Japan'. *Psychologia*, 53/3 (2010): 179–94; T.Naito, J. Wangwan, & M. Tani, 'Gratitude in University Students in Japan and Thailand', *Journal of Cross-Cultural Psychology*, 36/2 (2005): 247–63.

[8] While the Palaeolithic begins around 3.3 million years ago, the earliest evidence of care-giving is from 1.8 million years ago. See Penny Spikins, *Hidden Depths: The Origins of Human Connection* (York: White Rose University Press, 2022), 84. I would like to thank Penny Spikins for allowing me to read the proofs prior to formal publication.

[9] Penny Spikins, *How Compassion Made Us Human: The Evolutionary Origins of Tenderness, Trust and Morality* (Barnsley: Pen and Sword Archaeology, 2015), 60–

common attitude among anthropologists, Spikins claims, is to ignore all such emotions in human pre-history, on the basis that they are far too hard to detect, or at least could be confused with other possible motivations to act. What kind of evidence might point to changes in the inner mental lives of these very early humans? Spikins recognizes the socio-moral role of empathy, shame and remorse, but she believes that it is long-term *compassion* that is the most distinctly human characteristic that marks humans out from other primates.

Interestingly, wolves also have the capacity for long term compassion among their own kind in a way that seems to be analogous to that found in hominin societies, even if less well developed.[10] It is one reason why animal ethologists have argued for some time that emotional drives among social carnivores have even more resemblance to very early hominin communities than apes.[11] Further, as dogs became domesticated from wolves over millennia, they gradually took on even more characteristics of their human companions. Spikins and her collaborators argue that there are cognitive processes that are important to understand when considering how compassion evolved in earliest hominin societies. So:

> Understanding the evolution and role of compassion in past human species entails recognizing that compassion is more than just a *feeling* that we recognize as personal, but also in a wider analytical perspective it is a biological response, a 'motivation to act' whose roots lie in the hormonal and neuronal working of our

78. For further discussion of empathy and compassion see Celia Deane-Drummond, 'Empathy and the Evolution of Compassion: From Deep History to Infused Virtue', *Zygon* 52/1 (2017): 258–78.

[10] Penny Spikins describes consolation behaviour among not just apes and bonobos, but also wolves and otters. An injured lioness was provided with food by members of her group for nine months: Spikins, *Hidden Depths*, 28.

[11] Philip R. Thompson, 'A Cross-Species Analysis of Carnivore, Primate, and Hominid Behaviour', *Journal of Human Evolution* 4/2 (1975): 113–24.

mind.[12]

Like others who have studied the psychology of compassion, Spikins believes that compassion involves an initial step of empathy and then a strong motivation to help the other in distress.

A significant number of archaeological examples are indicative that long-term compassion first appeared in the *Homo* lineage far back in deep time. Spikins notes that:

> The most well-known early example of long-term support for an incapacitated individual comes from KNM- ER 1808, a female *Homo ergaster* dated to around 1.5 mya ... Examinations of the skeletal remains of this individual have led to suggestions that she was suffering from hypervitaminosis A, a disease caused by excessive intake of vitamin A.[13]

Symptoms of hypervitaminosis can be tracked in the human remains through reduction in bone density and the development of coarse bone growths. The symptoms for sufferers are known from contemporary medical studies to include 'abdominal pain, nausea, headaches, dizziness, blurred vision, lethargy, loss of muscular coordination and impaired consciousness'.[14] This pathology would have taken many months to develop, which shows that the care-taking in this case must have been over the very long term as the individual could not have survived on their own without the intensive care of others. The point is that this requires *long term* and *sustained* care of a type that has never yet been found in primates that are not in the *Homo* lineage.

This kind of evidence is not direct evidence for sustained

---

[12] Penny A. Spikins, Holly E. Rutherford, and Andy P. Needham, 'From Homininity to Humanity: Compassion from the Earliest Archaics to Modern Humans', *Time and Mind* 3 (2010): 305 (303–25).

[13] Spikins, 'From Homininity', 309.

[14] Spikins, 'From Homininity', 309.

compassion, which would be impossible, but is inferred; though it seems reasonable to make that inference. For example, an alternative explanation might be that long term care of such debilitated individuals was somehow forced through the hierarchical status of that individual in that society, rather than involving genuine caring emotions. But such a suggestion goes completely against what is known about the social structure of early human communities and their growing capacity to cooperate with one another in egalitarian societies, and the fact that children were also cared for and not just mature adults.

A second example comes from even further back in history, 1.77 million years ago from the well-known Dmanisi archaeological site in Georgia. As Spikins explains:

> This Dmanisi hominin, probably also a *Homo erectus*, had lost all but one tooth several years before death, with all the sockets except for the canine teeth having been reabsorbed. They must have had great difficulty surviving and could only have consumed soft plant or animal foods, leading the excavator, David Lordkipaidze, to conclude that they had been looked after by the others in the group. "[15]

A third example is relatively recent, and it is a Neanderthal lineage concurrent with the *Homo sapiens* lineage. Shanidar 1, also known as the 'Old Man of Shanidar', dated to around 60–80,000 bp is perhaps one of the best-known examples:

> This man suffered multiple fractures across his body, with the right side being particularly badly affected, the right arm has been described as completely 'withered,' with the forearm lost before death, and with degenerative deformities in both legs which is likely to have resulted in a painful limp. He had also suffered an injury to his skull, possibly causing blindness in his left eye, and

---

[15] Spikins, *How Compassion*, 68.

some have even hypothesised that there may have been some brain damage as a result of this injury. [16]

Yet, a close study of the bones revealed that the injuries happened during adolescence, with death at a relatively advanced age (for Neanderthals) of 35–50 years.

Evolutionary psychologist Robin Dunbar remains sceptical of the use of disabled individuals as evidence for early expressions of altruism, claiming that 'rather exaggerated claims about the altruism of Neanderthals on the grounds that someone so disabled could only have survived if they had been looked after by the group' are countered by 'plenty of examples of disabled monkeys and apes surviving in the wild without the help of their group members'.[17] Dunbar's speculation that such a severely incapacitated individual could indeed survive for so long as an isolated individual without support from the group seems extremely unlikely. In fact, work with hunter-gatherer societies shows that any rational assessment of cost in caring for others is unthinkable for such societies. Among the Baka, those with severe disabilities are integrated into the social group and become a social hub with social links to everyone within and indeed outside the group.[18] While it is important to recognize that hunter-gatherer societies are not necessarily representative of early hominins, they challenge contemporary assumptions about others and so provide some evidence that 'The wealth of grave goods associated with those with disabilities in the Palaeolithic might reflect that far from being seen as a burden they can be regarded as being particularly important'. [19]

Spikins compares this evidence for what she believes is a deep

---

[16] Spikins, *How Compassion*, 69.

[17] Robin Dunbar, *How Religion Evolved and Why It Endures* (London: Penguin, 2022), 152.

[18] Penny Spikins, *How Compassion*, 74.

[19] Spikins, *How Compassion*, 75.

commitment to care with cemetery evidence for abandonment of babies suffering from similar conditions in modern human societies. There are other examples of early upper Palaeolithic individuals suffering from conditions such as *acromesomelic dysplasia* that leads to severe disabilities. Spikins believes that compassion, which finds expression in the human ability to extend care and commitment in a sustained sense to others, can eventually include commitment to animals, or even objects and even ideas.

Spikins speculates that there were four stages in the evolution of compassion, the first stage being fleeting, that is still found in other primates; the second stage showing sustained investment in others; the third more deliberative and committed long term caring becoming more widespread. Finally, in the fourth stage from 120,000 years ago in Africa and 40,000 years ago in Europe, compassion started to be extended in a more abstract way to objects and more remote others. Her evolutionary model fits an older, commonly accepted, evolutionary account of human evolution in the literature, that poses a linear developmental trajectory, focused on an out of Africa origin model for hominin emergence with a later European expansion. This model has now been challenged by alternative theories that suggest a much more complex geographical origin and timeline for hominin evolution. There is also growing cumulative evidence of symbolic capacities that appear to come and then disappear at a range of geographical sites that show up in the hominin lineage earlier than the transition from anatomically to cognitively modern humans, which is often used as a marker for more so called 'advanced' capabilities such as symbolism. [20]

It is possible, therefore, to interpret Spikins' results rather differently. If long term compassion, like symbolic thought, is part of a

---

[20] Marc Kissel and Agustın Fuentes. 'From Hominid to Human: The Role of Human Wisdom and Distinctiveness in the Evolution of Modern Humans.' *Philosophy, Theology and the Sciences* 3 (2016): 217–44.

slow, more sporadic process that included *flickerings* of compassion rather than a single process, in an analogous way to complex cognition,[21] then it might be possible to track compassion alongside the tracing of symbolic thought in general. In fact, if symbolic thinking and long-term compassion are interrelated, then each would influence the other; since compassion for another encourages the accumulation of artifacts that act as proxies for the other and express symbolic thought, that in turn foster deeper longer-term compassion and so on. This would, further, be consistent with the thesis that the evolutionary lineage *Homo* was a slowly evolving community niche. This complex dynamic system included cognitive, social, emotive and ecological components interacting with each other and with the genotype in a complex feedback system. [22]

To understand more fully how compassion could be directed towards a range of others in community and objects associated with those others, some sense of how communities might be able to function in such a way to foster deep tenderness and caring towards others is important, especially as contemporary Western societies have tended to become more focused on individual success rather than community cohesion. So far, the dynamics of formation of communities of care in early hominin societies is poorly understood.

---

[21] Curtis W. Marean, 'An Evolutionary Anthropological Approach on Modern Human Origins', *Annual Review of Anthropology* 44 (2015): 533–66.

[22] Agustín Fuentes, 'Integrative Anthropology and the Human Niche: Toward a Contemporary Approach to Human Evolution', *American Anthropology* 117 (2015): 302–15.

Love in an age of planetary breakdown

Acknowledging the mutualism without and within[23]

Symbiosis is an important biological concept since it gets away from the idea, common in those influenced by Darwinian theories, that only focusing on individuals matters scientifically when considering change over time. Technically mutualism is a variety of symbiosis. Symbiosis means simply different organisms 'living together', while mutualism is living together in such a way to provide mutual benefit. Mutualism is analogous biologically to the moral aspect of compassion, in so far as it is mutually beneficial for the parties concerned. Historian Douglas Boucher has tracked the way in which mutualism has been appropriated within ecological thought, believing that the turning point was in the 1970s.[24] He uses the highly influential biologist Robert May as a case study. In 1973 May was dismissive of the importance of mutualism to ecosystems, arguing that the main reason for community stability lay in predator-prey relations. By 1976 he was prepared to suggest that mutualism was 'a conspicuous and ecologically important factor in most tropical communities'.[25]

Further back in time at the dawn of the emergence of eukaryotes, free-living cells engulfed bacterial cells, which then became integrated into their structure in a process known as endosymbiosis. These bacteria eventually became incorporated into what are now termed mitochondrial organelles, which have formed the primary basis for chemical energy for eukaryotic cells ever since. Given how far back in

---

[23] For further discussion of mutualism and evolution see Celia Deane-Drummond, 'Symbiotic Wisdom: Recovering a Memory of Deep Time', *Theology and Science* 18/2 (2020): 226–39.

[24] Douglas H. Boucher, 'The Idea of Mutualism, Past and Future', in Douglas H. Boucher (ed.), *The Biology of Mutualism* (London: Croom Hill, 1985), 1–28.

[25] Boucher, 'The Idea', 6.

time this must have occurred such a theory is speculative. However, there is good evidence that this was an integral part of evolutionary history.[26] Indeed, biologists Laura Katz and Laura Wegener Parfrey claim that 'one of the few certainties in the origin and diversification of eukaryotes is that mitochondria, found in many but not all eukaryotes, are derived from an endosymbiotic alphaproteobacterium.'[27] The scientific evidence for this is derived from the fact that the membrane structure and the genome of mitochondria have a close affinity to that of *Alphaproteobactea*. Mitochondria are also broadly distributed across the phylogenetic tree in all eukaryotes from 2.1–1.7 billion years ago, and those that seem to lack them carry organelles such as hydrogenosomes or mitosomes that seem to be derivative in a secondary sense from mitochondria. [28]

Eukaryotic life, which includes human beings, has at its origin a mix of different organisms which live together for mutual benefit. As time went on, humanity co-evolved with other species, each developing in step with the other and through interactions with the others in what is sometimes known as niche construction within an extended evolutionary synthesis theory of evolution.[29]

Discovering wonder in the world

A strong perception of the earth as sacred is unlikely to have arisen

---

[26] Laura A. Katz and Laura Wegener Parfrey, 'Origin and Diversification of Eukaryotes', in Jonathan B. Lasos, ed., *The Princeton Guide to Evolution* (Princeton: Princeton University Press, 2014), 136–42.

[27] Katz and Wegener Parfrey, 'Origin and Diversification', 137.

[28] Katz and Wegener Parfrey, 'Origin and Diversification', 137.

[29] Space does not permit full discussion of this theory, except to say that it puts more emphasis on the active importance of ecologies within the evolutionary trajectory of organisms. That ecology is not therefore simply a passive background on which the template of each individual becomes honed by adaptation. Rather, the system as a whole is dynamic, each organism influencing the other in an ecological system in complex ways.

completely *de novo* in human societies. Prerequisites for that sense, like empathy and prosociality that eventually becomes compassionate response in humans, can, arguably, be found by those who have spent many years living and working among primates and other social animals. Jane Goodall is a good example of how her close observations of chimpanzees blows away any prior conception that their mind is simply bent on basic survival behaviours. In a transcript of a video shown on the front page of the Jane Goodall Institute website she muses that:

> I can't help feeling that this waterfall display or dance is perhaps triggered by feelings of awe, wonder that we feel. The chimpanzees' brain is so like ours; they have emotions that are clearly similar too or the same that we call happiness, sadness, fear and despair and so forth; incredible intellectual abilities that we used to think were unique to us. So why would they not also have feelings of some kind of spirituality, which is really being amazed at things outside yourself. And it's the same with the start of the heavy rain ... Maybe it's defying the elements ... I think the chimpanzees are as spiritual as we are. But they can't analyze it, they can't talk about it. They can't describe what they feel. You get the feeling that it's all locked up inside them. And the only way they can express it is through this fantastic rhythmic dance. [30]

While it is difficult to come to the firm conclusion that the wonder experienced by chimpanzees is in a direct *evolutionary* relationship with the wonder that human beings experience, either way, there seems to be a convergence of a capacity for wonder in our nearest primate cousins.

---

[30] http://www.janegoodall.org/chimp-central-waterfall-displays, accessed November 15th, 2013. Unfortunately, this site is no longer available, but this is cited in Celia Deane-Drummond, 'Wonder and the Religious Sense in Chimpanzees', in Dale Peterson and Mark Bekoff (eds.), *The Jane Effect: Celebrating Jane Goodall* (San Antonio: Trinity University Press, 2015): 225–26.

Hagiographic accounts of the earliest Christian saints also regularly spoke of how other animals were responsive to God, often through the ministry of the saint who was prepared to spend time and pay close attention to them. Saint Cuthbert (634-687), for example, spent hours during the night in prayer submerged up to his neck in the sea. While clearly not literally true, he perceived otters as agents responding to his needs and through his prayers, while on a journey an eagle brought him fish. Later, as a hermit living on the island of Farne, ravens showed signs of remorse after eating his crops. He believed that these creatures were equally servants of God, like himself.[31] Prosocial behaviour is found in other social animals, but longer-term compassion is distinct to humans and a few social species. Scientists often prefer to use terms such as helping behaviour, consolation behaviour, caring or 'prosociality' to describe animal responses, but the brain regions which respond are homologous with those activated in humans.[32]

Living in a meshwork
Tim Ingold is an anthropologist who has spent many years conducting fieldwork among indigenous peoples, mostly in Canada and northern territories. He provides anthropological evidence to challenge the

---

[31] Bede, *The Life of Saint Cuthbert*, in *The Lives of the Saints*, trans. J . F. Webb (London: Penguin Books, 1965). See Chapter 10, 'How after he had spent the whole night praying in the sea, animals ministered unto him as he came out of the water'(84–85); Chapter 12, 'How on a journey he foretold that provisions would be brought by an eagle' (87–88) ; Chapter 20, 'How the ravens said their prayers and brought the man of God a gift to make up for the harm they had done' (97–98).

[32] C. Sue Carter, Inbal Ben-Ami Bartal and Eric C. Porges, 'The Roots of Compassion: An Evolutionary and Neurobiological Perspective', in Seppälä et al. (eds.), *Oxford Handbook of Compassion Science*, 173–88. For a discussion of prosocial behaviour in primates and other animals and its relationship to compassion see Celia Deane-Drummond, *Theological Ethics Through a Multispecies Lens: The Evolution of Wisdom Vol 1* (Oxford: Oxford University Press, 2019), 74–94.

dualistic mindset of modern Western societies, arguing, especially in his work, *Being Alive*, that 'meshwork' thinking characteristic of indigenous societies across the world is a 'way of being that is alive and open to a world in continuous birth', giving rise to 'astonishment' rather than 'surprise'.[33]

In the world of becoming, in contrast to the surprise of unfulfilled scientific predictions, astonishment is common even in the ordinary events of life. For those, unlike Ingold, with a religious conviction, a life suffused by astonished wonder is also resonant with a life attuned to sensing God's immanence in the world, where God's presence, as nature-mystics such as Francis of Assisi understood only too well, can become evident in the ordinary events of the everyday rather than just confined to the out of the ordinary or the surprise of the miraculous.[34]

Ingold criticizes what he calls the 'logic of inversion', whereby the essence of a person resides in an ethereal soul, enters the body at birth, animates it from within, but then exits the body at death, returning to an immortal heaven. Such an approach, influenced by Plato and Socrates, results in spiritualities that deny the importance of the material world and embodiment. The central problem with dualism is that it fails to appreciate the porous, dependent nature of flesh, what we might call the body's susceptibility to and need of a living world to constantly nurture it. Human beings are not self-contained or self-animating. They live in the mode that Ingold develops as the 'middle voice'—acting, but always being acted upon, moving, but always feeling the movements of others within themselves. The idea of a self-standing human being is a delusion that needs to be resisted because it simply is not true to physiological and ecological experience. For those who think theologically the

---

[33] Tim Ingold, *Being Alive: Essays on Movement, Knowledge and Description* [2011] (London: Routledge, 2022), 63.
[34] Celia Deane-Drummond, *Wonder and Wisdom: Conversations in Science, Spirituality and Theology* (London: DLT, 2004), 39.

elevation of the soul at the expense of the body also needs to be rejected since it denies the material world that God is believed to create and sustain in its unfolding. At the same time, Ingold's position is still based on the assumptions of materialism and emergence which is compatible with some forms of process philosophy, but it lacks proper appreciation of the importance of encounter with the divine Other and core theological beliefs such as the resurrection of the body.

Ingold's position is also subtly but importantly distinct from that of Bruno Latour, whose work remains very influential among theologians and philosophers. Actor network theory, proposed by Latour, is also a theory about community function, but each of the actors is considered as a discrete point, interacting with the others. The less discrete, tangled character of real life represents interaction between individuals as a tangled thread and pathway emerging along lines of perception and action. When applied to the focus on love, compassion arises spontaneously within tangled lifeways of those whose lives are in a meshwork with others and is best described in narrative form.

Ingold also rejects those tendencies to represent human life as uniquely symbolic, in so far as it implies a dualistic relationship with other beings that are perceived as meaningless. While the semiotics of C. S. Pierce can be rendered amenable to a more inclusive approach in anthropology[35] and theology,[36] and therefore is in this sense a useful bridging concept, Ingold rejects this move, even though admitting that he was initially attracted to it.[37] Influenced by psychologist James

---

[35] Marc Kissel, 'Becoming Wise: What Can Anthropologists Say About the Evolution of Human Wisdom', in Celia Deane-Drummond and Agustín Fuentes (eds.), *Theology and Evolutionary Anthropology: Dialogues in Wisdom, Humility and Grace* (London: Routledge, 2020), 69–85.

[36] Andrew Robinson, 'On the Origin of Symbols: Archaeology, Semiotics and Self Transcendence', in Deane-Drummond and Fuentes, *Theology and Evolutionary Anthropology*, 86–109.

[37] Tim Ingold, *Imagining for Real: Essays on Creation, Attention and Correspondence*

Gibson's theory of affordances, perception is direct rather than being mediated, as in semiotics, through a signifier. Meaning, therefore, is discovered through practice, rather than prior meaning being given to an object.

If we follow such an argument, then loving each other and the planet comes through direct immersion in practical care of other creatures, understood as caught up in a tangled meshwork, rather than deciding in advance that those creatures represent, for example, something worthy of loving attention and then acting accordingly. Rediscovering the sacredness of life, in this framing, means dwelling in the meandering path that makes up the movement within the meshwork of life.

Remembering the earth as sacred

Although Ingold does not use the language of the sacred in his work, theologians and biblical scholars find Ingold's critique of modern versions of the human—as autonomous subjects primarily defined by their cognitive capacities—of considerable help when recovering Hebraic characterizations of persons that are complex composites of flesh, thought, desire, and will. Jewish and Christian scriptures refer frequently to the *heart* as the central, visceral animating organ. Moreover, the individualizing tendencies of modern thought need to be counterbalanced with the strongly *communal* character of life as reflected in scripture. The aims of a faithful life are thus woven deeply within a broad community of life that includes the land, plants, animals, and fellow humans. Biblical scholar Ellen Davis[38] and theologian Norman Wirzba[39] are recovering the idea that God's covenant is never

---

(London: Routledge, 2022), 337–46.

[38] Ellen Davis, *Scripture, Culture, and Agriculture* (New York: Cambridge University Press, 2009).

[39] Norman Wirzba, *The Paradise of God: Renewing Religion in an Ecological Age*

simply with (a small segment of) humans, but with the entirety of the earth and its creatures, and that the scope of God's salvific aims is fully cosmic. Ingold's characterization of human life moving within a meshwork world opens multiple avenues for a theological reassessment and exploration of the ways of healing and redemption.

How far is the idea of the earth as sacred aligned with animistic beliefs? Ingold's description of animism provides insights on how to read ancient scriptural texts that include landscapes, vegetation, and non-human animal species within a moral/spiritual community of life.[40] For example, in Genesis 3 the soil witnesses against human wickedness, in Numbers 22–24, a donkey witnesses to the presence of God and acts as an agent of divine purposes, while in Isaiah 55 mountains break forth into singing and trees clap their hands. These are just some examples of how life, including importantly that in relation to God, is not reduced to solitary, self-standing beings, let alone only to human beings. Instead, creatures of diverse kinds participate in life's unfolding.

As Ingold says, agency is not a 'sprinkling' of some power of the mind added to beings that are otherwise inanimate. Instead, diverse kinds of beings are alive because they are 'swept up in the circulation of surrounding media that alternately portend their dissolution ... or ensure their regeneration. Spirit is the regenerative power of these circulatory flows'.[41] Animacy, in other words, is not the attribution of spirit to non-human beings. It is, rather, the recognition that creatures

---

(New York: Oxford University Press, 2003); Norman Wirzba, *This Sacred Life: Humanity's Place in a Wounded World* (Cambridge: Cambridge University Press, 2021).

[40] For further details on this and other aspects of how Ingold is important for theologians see Celia Deane-Drummond and Norman Wirzba, 'Belonging to this World and the Next: Why Tim Ingold Inspires Theologians' in Jan Loovers and Caroline Gatt (eds.), *Beyond Perception: Correspondences with the Work of Tim Ingold* (London: Routledge, forthcoming 2023), in press.

[41] Ingold, *Being Alive*, 29

altogether are continuously moving within the flows of a power that is not contained within any single creature. Mutualism echoes this pattern at the earliest stages of the emergence of life in a way that eventually becomes expressed in the life of all creatures and in turn flowers into helping behaviours and compassion that are fully developed in the *Homo* lineage.

To use the language of scripture, the power of God the creator and sustainer of life moves like the wind (in Hebrew the term for spirit—*ruach*—is also the term for breath) that then animates creatures from without and from within as the breath within each breathing movement. That same spirit inspires compassionate response and action towards those who are suffering, with a desire to promote their wellbeing.

Norman Wirzba explains the idea of the earth as sacred from a Christian perspective:

> To say that life is sacred is not to say that this world and its creatures are divine. It is, instead, to signal that places, ranging from wetlands to oceans to farm fields and city neighbourhoods, and creatures, ranging from earthworms and raspberry shoots to bees and people, are the embodied expression of a divine affirmation and intention that desires for them to be and to thrive … this means that this life is not simply the object of God's love; it is—in ways that remain incomprehensible to us—also the material manifestation of a divine energy that gives and nurtures and encourages diverse life without ever being exhausted or fully contained in the expression of any of its embodied forms. [42]

So, while recognising that the world is wounded and in need of healing, it is still the place of God's abiding attention and love.[43]

---

[42] Wirzba, *This Sacred Life*, p. xviii.

[43] This leaves aside the question of why a caring loving God might permit the world to become wounded and broken, though the responsibility of humanity rests with those actions that contribute to its woundedness, rather than what has sometimes been termed evolutionary suffering.

Pope Francis has opened an important new chapter in ways of being the Roman Catholic Church by putting much more emphasis on the need to engage in care for our common home and develop an integral ecology by listening to indigenous spiritualities in dialogue with diverse cultures and religions so that all branches of knowledge are included.[44] Moreover, his elevation of the goodness of Earth as our home, and nature as 'a magnificent book through which God speaks to us', signal a desire to restore material reality to the centre of theological reflection. This world is not absurd or a cosmic accident. Nor is it believed to be a mere play of material forces. It is rather *created* by God, and thus is the material expression of divine love. In his words, 'Every creature is thus the object of the Father's tenderness, who gives it its place in the world'.[45] His integral ecology has some echoes in Ingold's expansive approach to ecological anthropology that stitches people deeply within a meshwork world.

Acquiring and receiving the gift of love

Finding developing ways to live and paths of loving in community life can also draw inspiration from ancient Christian texts which speak of love and charity. Medieval theological scholarship, in so far as it was not indebted, to use Charles Taylor's expression, to modern conceptions of the isolated or beleaguered self, can give important insights about how to develop love and charity from a Christian theological perspective. Charity, at least in Aquinas' definition, focuses simply on the divine, so it is understood as 'the friendship of man (*hominis*) for God'.[46] For Aquinas, charity enables loving actions

---

[44] Pope Francis, *Laudato Si' : On Care for Our Common Home* (London: Catholic Truth Society, 2015).

[45] Pope Francis, *Laudato Si'*, 77.

[46] Thomas Aquinas, *Summa Theologiae, Secunda Secundae*, 1–91, trans. Laurence Shapcote, Volume 17 (Aquinas Institute: Green Bay, 2012): 2a2ae Qu. 23.1. Note the

towards others that are normally difficult and challenging to be, instead, conducted with relative ease, since their source is that which is mediated from the Holy Spirit, but that Spirit is discovered internally, rather than being an 'extrinsic' force. How this can be both integral to humanity and yet distinct from it arises through Aquinas' important idea of *participation in divinity*, so:

> The Divine Essence Itself is charity, even as it is wisdom and goodness (since the goodness whereby we are formally good is a participation of Divine goodness, and the wisdom whereby we are formally wise, is a share of Divine wisdom), so too, the charity whereby formally we love our neighbor is a participation of Divine charity.[47]

While the purpose or end of charity is that which 'attains God' as it 'unites us to God',[48] loving our neighbour is an experience marked by joy which then, through a kind of overflow, means that 'our neighbor is loved out of charity for God's sake'. [49]

Like Ingold, Aquinas uses the language of wayfaring, for there is a gradual becoming on the path towards participation in divine goodness. Yet, Aquinas' moral theology does imply a teleology that is distinctly lacking in Ingold's analysis. For Ingold humanity seems to be an aimlessly meandering, with no specific destination. For Aquinas, we may meander on the path to God, and indeed discover that path within a meshwork of relationships, but the journey still has a destination towards God. In this respect Aquinas is correct, but he still fails to appreciate adequately the importance of loving not just our human neighbours, but our creaturely ones as well, indeed the whole planet.

---

inclusive language used—all humans are capable of this friendship.

[47] Aquinas, *Summa Theologiae*, 2a2ae, Qu. 23.2

[48] Aquinas, *Summa Theologiae*, 2a2ae, Qu. 23.3

[49] Aquinas, *Summa Theologiae*, 2a2ae, Qu. 23.5

For Aquinas neighbourly relations can never include other creatures and friendship is only possible within the human community. Even though he puts a great deal of emphasis on love inspired by an affective relationship with God, for him right moral judgments are always based on reason, and his categorization of other beings as irrational therefore excludes them from an eschatological future, even if they can be loved for the sake of their usefulness to human beings.

Conclusions: learning to love again

I have argued in this essay that humanity's capacity to love and show compassion to the vulnerable goes back deep into our deep evolutionary past, is echoed in patterns of the emergence of life such as mutualism, and is arguably one of the core characteristics of human distinctiveness. Evolutionary narratives have tended to shy away from considering the inner mental lives of our earliest ancestors on the basis that they are too difficult to trace in the material record. However, there are good circumstantial reasons to suppose that early humans did show devoted and long-term care for the weak and sick in circumstances that were extremely challenging for human survival. Extending those feelings of compassion to other vulnerable creatures or showing devotion to objects associated with those loved ones was commonplace.

Modern Western societies have much to learn about fundamental aspects of our humanity from contemplating our hominin ancestors, as well as contemplating the lives of those living today in indigenous communities. Such communities have far less of a sense of separation from other beings, and instead perceive life as within an entangled meshwork of other beings in a world of becoming. A sense of the sacred, perhaps born from a preliminary sense of wonder common to other primates that is orientated towards that which humans find awesome or beautiful, emerges within rather than apart from the natural world.

Aquinas' notion of charity as friendship with God, and the ability to show love as dependent on participation in God, provide an important teleological thread to a theological perspective that stems from the idea of immersion within the world, rather than separated from it. However, his failure to extend the possibility of love towards other creatures is a fundamental mistake that jars in the face of our own human histories and the woundedness of both people and our planet which is the major challenge facing contemporary societies. At the same time his cosmic vision of God's activity at least softens his more anthropocentric eschatology and counters the historicism of modern theology, reminding his readers that if we are to learn to love again then humanity needs to pay attention to how this might be expressed in a way that honours the cosmos as a created gift of God.

3

Are Jews Commanded to Love the Planet?

Melissa Raphael

Between traditional and modern Jewish approaches to the natural world

Jewish tradition does not specify a commandment to love the planet, if it has a modern concept of the planet as a sphere of rock and minerals suspended in space at all. Yet despite the human, historical and national focus of its theological scheme, the tradition regards non-human animal and vegetal life as neither brute nor inert and meticulously legislates its care. Moreover, since the early 1990s, a small but steady and significant stream of scholarly and popular studies of Judaism and ecology have given Jews, especially in more progressive circles, every reason to support the a revision of the tradition's benign, but anthropocentric, welfarism into an approach that treats the natural world as holy in and of itself.[1] Although classical Jewish sources do not readily map onto

---

[1] For essays formulating a constructive Jewish theology of nature, see Hava Tirosh-Samuelson (ed.), *Judaism and Ecology: Created World and Revealed Word* (Cambridge MA: Harvard University Press, 2003). Other key studies include Jeremy Benstein, *The Way into Judaism and the Environment* (Woodstock: Jewish Lights, 2006); Ellen Burnstein (ed.), *Ecology and the Jewish Spirit: Where Nature and the Sacred Meet* (Woodstock: Jewish Lights Publishing, 2000); Aubrey Rose, *Judaism and Ecology* (London: Cassell, 1992; and Arthur Waskow (ed.), *Torah of the Earth: Exploring 4,000 Years of Ecology in Jewish Thought*, Vol 1, *Biblical Israel and Rabbinic Judaism* and Vol. 2, *Zionism and Eco-Judaism* (Woodstock: Jewish Lights Publishing, 2000).

the conditions of a contemporary global anthropogenic climate crisis and it is a mistake to ask 'what Judaism says' about 'nature' or climate change as these are concepts and possibilities foreign to pre-modern culture,[2] the Jewish eco-literature has presented a range of traditional texts–narratival and halakhic (legal)—setting out Jewish obligations that are directly, and now urgently, conducive to the flourishing of non-human living things.

This recent literature has rightly insisted that the sanctity of the natural world is thoroughly embedded in everyday Jewish life. The Hebrew Bible, for example, opens with a creation narrative whose first verses are virtually a hymn to biodiversity, and its subsequent narratives unfold on a notably earth-bound plane. Here, human beings, from the outset, are Earthlings: the first human being, Adam, shares his name with the soil or earth, *adamah*.[3] Neither agriculture nor war justify environmental destruction. As Evan Eisenberg has noted, a 'gust of country air' hits you when you open the Hebrew Bible, it smells of 'cedar, sheep-dung, sun-baked wheat, and olives bruised beneath one's sandals.' The Hebrew writers 'have dirt under their finger-nails'. Amos drove goats, David was leading sheep when Samuel discovered him.[4] Sabbath rest for humans and domestic animals, as well as periods of commanded rest for the land, suspend the processes of human creation and destruction and liberatively return the whole of creation to its primordial and eschatological integrity. Even a cursory reading of the classic Jewish sources would weaken or rebut the widespread critique of the Judaeo-Christian tradition, after Lynn White Jr,[5] as a mandate for

---

[2] Bernstein, *Ecology and the Jewish Spirit*, 13.

[3] See Arthur Waskow, 'Introduction. Earth and Earthling: Adam and Adamah', in Waskow (ed.), *Torah of the Earth*, vol. 1, vii.

[4] Evan Eisenberg, 'The Mountain and the Tower: Wilderness and City in the Symbols of Babylon and Israel', in Waskow (ed.), *Torah of the Earth*, vol. 1, 51 (18–54).

[5] Lynn White Jr,, 'The Historical Roots of Our Ecologic Crisis', *Science* 155 (1967), 1203-1207.

alienation from nature; for overpopulation and mastery of the earth in callous indifference to its sentience or worth. The tradition does not grant humanity a licence to crush or exhaust a nature that it fears or despises. The tradition may husband the natural world in the interests of humanity, but nature, in classical and modern Judaism, is holy on account of its being created by God. [6] It treated as neither brute nor inert.

That said, the climate crisis has not featured prominently in critical Jewish scholarship, including theology. [7] There has not, to my knowledge, been any attempt to correlate a Jewish theology of love with the tradition's evident valorization of care for creation. So too, if love of the planet is sometimes implicit it is not commanded, even by the numerous progressive contemporary Jewish eco-activist organizations that have arisen in recent years, perhaps being reluctant to alienate the secular and liberal Jews who form the majority of their members. The name of the New Jersey eco-activist group 'Shomrei Adamah', for example, means 'Keepers or Guardians of the Earth' in Hebrew, not 'Lovers'. The spiritual-political Jewish principles and themes informing groups such as Shomrei Adamah, the Coalition on the Environment and Jewish Life, Hazon (a faith-based environmental organization), the Jewish Climate Initiative, and, in Britain, Extinction Rebellion Jews, do not make any reference—at least in so many words—to standing under a commandment to love the planet.

Members of, and sympathizers with, these organizations instead activate a number of classic principles such as *hatzala*, which requires one to refrain from being a bystander when something is being harmed

---

[6] Michael Wyschogrod, in 'Judaism and the Sanctification of Nature', *The Melton Journal* 24 (1991), 5-7, describes the tradition as having a 'lower' ecology, as distinct from a pagan 'upper ecology' where nature is sacred in and of itself.

[7] Mara H. Benjamin, 'There Is No "Away": Ecological Fact as Jewish Theological Problem', *Religions* 13/290 (2022); https://doi.org/10.3390/rel13040290, 2 of 16.

(Lev 19:16). The traditional obligations to heal or mend a damaged world (*tikkun olam*), and *bal taschit* which proscribes laying waste to natural resources or even wasting them—and can include anything from proscribing taking more food than one can eat at a buffet to scorched earth military campaigns—are routinely invoked. Or again, the festival of *Tu B'Shvat*, the 'New Year of the Tree' has shifted from its original function as a Second Temple tithing celebration to a contemporary celebration of Jews' annual ecological reconnection with the earth.[8] Traditional Jewish texts are widely repurposed in support of the environmental cause. It is not unusual, for example, to see a line from the rabbinic commentary on Koheleth used as a strapline on emails: 'Pay heed not to corrupt and destroy my world 'for if you do, there will be no one to repair it after you'. Pre-modern *halakhot* that proscribe causing suffering to animals have created a compassionate modern Jewish sensibility of kindness to all creatures.[9] But, again, this may be more readily correlated to modern, pragmatic environmental principles than to a theology of love. There is, for example, an often-cited rabbinic opinion that if the messiah should appear while planting a tree, one must get the tree into the ground and watered before going out to greet him.[10] Arguably, even today, this expresses more a pragmatic recognition of the dependence of human life on trees than compassion for the tree itself.

Biblical and rabbinic perspectives on love and the planet

As Mara Benjamin has noted, while the tradition is polyvocal and some

---

[8] See Ari Elon, Naomi Mara Hyman and Arthur Waskow (eds.), *Trees, Earth, and Torah: A Tu B'Shvat Anthology* (Philadelphia: Jewish Publication Society, 1999).

[9] Lenn Evan Goodman, 'Respect for Nature in the Jewish Tradition', in Tirosh-Samuelson (ed.), *Judaism and Ecology*, 227-60.

[10] *Avot d'Rebbe Natan*, 31b.

of the more esoteric mystical Jewish traditions can support an immanentist theological reading, 'the vast majority of the exoteric tradition is incompatible with contemporary ecological knowledge'. Traditional Jewish thought, if it considers nature in the abstract at all, regards it as extra-historical, amoral or at least non-personal, seeing it as separable from a transcendent God whose will operates on the earth from outside it.[11]

Indeed, classical Judaism may not even *have* a category of planet—as opposed to the world (*olam*, also translatable as eternity) and land (*eretz*), which we are commanded to till and to tend (*l'vadah ul'shamrah*). Neither the world nor the land would equate to a planetary totality, including inanimate rocks, that could be considered the object of the same kind of interpersonal obligated love (*ahavah*) as that commanded for God, the neighbour and the stranger (*ger*) (Lev 19:34). The grace observant Jews recite after a meal in thanks for a sufficiency of food includes, for example, a blessing for the land. But here, as elsewhere in classical Judaism, the land is not so much the earth as planet but, more immediately, as 'the spacious, good' *Eretz Yisrael—* the Land of Israel—which is a theological inheritance more than it is a natural good.

Religious Judaism largely persists in a traditional positioning which might be paraphrased as, at most, a case of 'love God, love God's creation'. David Novak's suspicion of any Jewish environmentalism that blurs an onto-hierarchical distinction between God, humanity and the earth that is evident from the second chapter of Genesis onwards would be typical of most Jewish religious thought.[12] Without invoking the love commandment, it is sufficient for a specific range of earth-

---

[11] Benjamin, "'There is no Away'", 3–4, and throughout.

[12] David Novak, *Athens and Jerusalem: God, Humans, and Nature* (Toronto: University of Toronto Press, 2019); Novak, 'The Doctrine of Creation and the Idea of Nature', in Tirosh-Samuelson (ed.), *Judaism and Ecology*, 155–76.

related commandments to sanctify the land as God's property (Leviticus 25:23, 'The land shall not be sold forever; for the land is mine. For you are strangers and sojourners with me'). Here, to take or receive from the earth without a blessing is an offence of theft against God; creation may be a gift of divine love to humanity, but it is one that is held in trust.

Although the biblical covenants are various, and variously interpreted, the broad covenantal model that establishes an everlasting relationship between God, the Jewish people, and the land, sanctifies (marries, as it were) Israel to God, not to the land. The land broadly and effectively functions as collateral, pledged as security for loving obedience to its creator and may be forfeited in the event of default on the terms of the agreement. As such, the covenantal relation between the Jewish people, Israel, God, and the Land of Israel, explains how the Jewish obligation to love the human other can relate closely to the earth, but the earth is not, as it were, the third person of this trinity. For the prophets, it is a failure to love the stranger and neighbour, more immediately than a failure to love the land itself, that is punished with ecological catastrophe. Conversely, it is a practical love of neighbour that entails doing justly to him or her that fills the earth with God's loving-kindness.' (Ps 33:5.)   That is, God smiles upon human righteousness with a planetary flourishing that is a sign of his pleasure and favour. Here, the flourishing of the land is both a pragmatic good and an index to the vitality of the covenantal relation. When Israel conducts itself according to the laws of the Torah, the land is abundant and fertile. But when Israel sins: is idolatrous and unjust, its moral pollution literally sickens the land. The land becomes desolate and inhospitable, it vomits the people out (Lev 26:32; Deut 11:13–21).

Any Jewish answer to the question does God command us to love the planet?—a question now asked only in the urgency of its redemption—depends on what Judaism understands by love. As I observed in an earlier contribution to the current enquiry into love in the world religions, *ahavah* is an obligated love that shows little interest in love as a natural emotional state measurable by its intensity of feeling.[13] A*havah* is not so much an affective response to the other as an object of inordinate admiration or desire as it is a commanded responsibility to act with a daily, practical, loving kindness (*hesed*) that is conducive to their well-being. Love and observance are, as Shai Held put it recently, a virtuous circle. The love of God is a cause and consequence of observance.[14] Even God's love is expressed in practical remedial action: God commands us to show loving kindness to the suffering stranger— the fatherless and the widow—whom he himself feeds and clothes (Deut 10:19). Neighbourly love is exemplified by a set of specified acts of kindness such as a swift and humane execution of the condemned; visiting the sick; escorting departing guests to the door; comforting mourners; joining funeral processions; giving eulogies; burying the dead; or helping brides and bridegrooms rejoice.

The halakhic relation with any living thing, human or animal, assumes an obligation to treat it with loving kindness. Any particular commandment is always a function of the general commandment to love. To that extent, the earth is, necessarily, a material participant in practical love in so far as it is the site, occasion, medium and sometimes focus of the *mitzvah* (commandment). As the sum of all that lives on the thin crust of its surface, the planet would be covered by the commandment to love God its creator and all the living things that it hosts. But again, the planet is not, itself, a specified object of obligated love. It is not included as the direct object of the commandment to love God and neighbours and strangers. And even when commandments are

---

[13] Melissa Raphael, 'Judaism's Commandment to Love: "A Well-Tempered Banality" or the Messianic Trumpet's Blast?', in Paul S. Fiddes (ed.), *Love as Common Ground: Essays on Love and Religion* (Lanham: Lexington Books, 2021), 111–13.

[14] Shai Held, https://www.youtube.com/watch?v=WWVXInm4f3U, lecturing on the love of God in Jewish theology, 2021.

related to the flourishing of non-human living things, including the land, they are less concerned with cleaving to the earth itself than to its creator.

The early mediaeval Jewish philosopher and commentator R. Moshe ben Maimon (Maimonides) is, for example, well-known for his conviction that the proto-scientific study of nature is a means of achieving *ahavat Hashem* (love of God).[15] To ponder God's great and wonderful acts of creation as a oneness manifesting the oneness of God is to know an abundancy of divine loving-kindness (*hesed*) that is built into the Universe itself and bestowed upon us who have no claim on his kindness and in greater measure than is due to us. (*Guide* 3: 53, citing Ps 89:3).[16] Seeing in natural phenomena a creative genius that has no comparison, we will come to love—that is, praise and glorify—him. Because one cannot love someone one hardly knows, the greater the knowledge of God, the greater one's capacity to fulfil the commandment to love of God.[17]

That the earth, here, is primarily a contemplative, theocentric, occasion for love, owes much, of course, to rabbinic Judaism being in large part a product of diaspora. Broadly speaking, the trauma of exile unravelled and abstracted the relationship between God, the land, and the Jewish people, transposing their immediate practical ties into those mediated by the text. The Torah was now the tree of life. In *Mishna Avot* 3:7 Rabbi Shimon is perhaps more typical of rabbinic Judaism than Maimonides in his claim that a person who interrupts his Torah study while traveling, who stops, as it were, to look out of the window and appreciate the glories of nature, should be considered—hyperbolically and rhetorically, of course—someone who is *chayav mita* (punishable

---

[15] *Yesodei ha-Torah* 2:2.
[16] Moses Maimonides, *The Guide for the Perplexed*, second edition, trans, Michael Friedländer (New York, Dover Publications 1956).
[17] *Laws of Teshuva* 10:6.

by death).

Such texts suggest that a Jewish relationship with the earth is ultimately neither anthropocentric, ethnocentric, nor ecocentric, but theocentric. From biblical to rabbinic Judaism, the question of the earth's natural value probably has little meaning apart from that of God. So, for example, when nature sings, it sings praises to God, not itself. In Psalm 62, the whole planet praises God, but its song may be less a love-song than a triumphal witness to God's pre-eminence over the whole earth—creation bows down to a God who has lordship over all living things; not just over the Israelites, but over their enemies as well: 'Raise a shout for God, all the earth; sing the glory of His name, Make glorious His praise, Say to God, How awesome are Your deeds, Your enemies cower before Your great strength, all the earth bows to You...' In the light of such texts, the rabbis state that 'whatever God created, He created for His own glory (*Avot* 6:12; *Yoma* 38a commenting on Isaiah 43:7).

Of course, one can cite poetic textual exceptions to this general rule of rabbinic theology: trees converse with one another, they are companionable, providing fellowship for mortals (*Genesis Rabbah* 13.2). Or when a tree that bears fruit is cut down, its moan goes from one end of the world to the other, yet no sound is heard (*Pirke de R. Eliezer* 34). But perhaps more characteristic of the tradition is the moment when during the Sabbath prayers Jews affirm that 'the soul of every living being shall bless Your Name'. When Jewish mystics experience every blade of grass, every leaf, as singing praise to their creator, the earth witnesses not to its own own glory, but God's.

In short, it would seem difficult to claim that classical Judaism regards the planet, in its own right, as the direct object of commanded love. It does not fall into the personal category of neighbour or stranger. As a theistic, not a pantheistic, and only occasionally panentheistic tradition, the Earth is also categorically separable from the incorporeal

God Jews are commanded to love with all their might. The glory or sublimity of the earth awakens the praise due to God but is not itself an object of adoration. Halakhah consecrates human relationships with the natural order, but it is arguable that a disordered relation to nature is first and foremost a disordered relation to God. A world that is inhospitable to humans is a desecrated world that is thereby inhospitable to the holiness of divine presence. To damage the world is primarily and ultimately to damage the covenantal relationship with God. Such undoubtedly protects the planet from a good deal of anthropogenic harm, but it stops short of loving the planet as a quasi-personal entity with whom one can and should enter into an empathetically imaginative relationship.

Loving the planet as a turn to an immanent God

Insisting on the theological necessity of contemporary relevance, modern Judaism is necessarily both of its own moment and grounded in its past. A traditional account of commanded love as a commitment to practical care for the vulnerable other could therefore underpin the present essay's necessarily brief proposal that a contemporary, late modern, Jewish understanding of the commandment to love the stranger could include the planet as another, peculiarly modern, type of stranger.

Yet before the environmental crisis was so conceived, modern Jewish thinkers would not have considered the planet, as such, in special need of a redemptive love. Traumatized by the pogroms suffered by late nineteenth- and early twentieth-century eastern European Jewish communities and then by two world wars and the Holocaust, modern Jewish thinkers—even those Zionists in Palestine who, after the beginning of 'First Aliyah' in 1882, shifted their spiritual and cultural focus from the four holy cities of Jerusalem, Hebron, Safed and Tiberias to a productive agricultural settlement of the land[18]—could not have been expected to feel any pressing need to love the planet.

It was only by the late twentieth century, as the environmental crisis began to turn from a contested theory into an all too evident actuality, that a significant counter-cultural minority of Jews began to make their environmentalism a central focus of spiritual-political praxis. Many of these Jews did so under the auspices of Jewish Renewal (as much a mood as a movement) whose neo-Hasidic immanentism readily lent itself to the project of planetary healing.[19] Since the 1990s, Arthur Waskow, Michael Lerner, and David Seidenberg have, among others, been reading the biblical, rabbinic, and mystical tradition through the lens of modern Jewish relational philosophers such as Martin Buber and A. J. Heschel. They have presented a case for an earth-based spirituality that appeals to Jews whose denominational affiliations range all the way from Progressive to modern Orthodox.[20] Theirs is an environmental commitment that goes well beyond the traditional welfarism of biblically- mandated stewardship. It is an activism underpinned by a mystical-experiential reading of the tradition that authenticates loosely panentheistic claims for the non-instrumental, intrinsic value of the

---

[18] Ran Aaronsohn, 'Modern Jewish Agriculture in Palestine: "Indigenous" versus "Imported"', *Agricultural History* 69 (1995): 438–53 (438).

[19] Others at the forefront of Jewish environmental activism included Jewish feminists whose spirituality was variously inflected by Jewish Renewal, ecofeminism, and radical and cultural feminist neo-Paganism. See Melissa Raphael, 'Goddess Religion, Postmodern Jewish Feminism and the Complexity of Alternative Religious Identities', *Nova Religio* 1 (1998): 198–214.

[20] See, for example, Arthur Green, *Radical Judaism. Rethinking God and Tradition* (New Haven: Yale University Press, 2010); David Mevorach Seidenberg, *Kabbalah and Ecology: God's Image in the More-than-Human World* (New York: Cambridge University Press, 2015); Arthur Waskow, 'And the Earth is Filled with the Breath of Life', *CrossCurrents* 47 (1997): 348–63; Waskow, 'Prayer as if the Earth Really Matters', *Tikkun* 30 (2015): 31–35, and his two-volume edited collection, *Torah of the Earth* .

created world.   Here, we see the planet coming to life as a fully materialized manifestation of the immanent divine (sometimes feminized as She), and as a manifestation of the originary divine love present at and for creation.[21]

During a 2005 interview with Rabbi Burt Jacobson, Rabbi Zalman Schachter-Shalomi (Reb Zalman) the late leader of the Jewish Renewal Movement, interpreted classical Hasidism as having a panentheistic element such that God 'does not occupy a portion of existence over and against us, a divine territory in what we call existence or the universe'; God, quite simply, is 'all in everything': 'God so loved the world that She gave herself to it and became the Earth'. Jews must therefore 'love and care for the Earth because She is an embodiment of the Divine.' If humanity and animals and plants are one with the earth, and the earth is one with God, there are no ultimate boundaries between God, people, and the planet; nothing that would interrupt the flow of love. [22]

For both Reb Zalman and Michael Lerner—countercultural prophets of a 'love-ocratic' eco-social order—the creation of Earth as a living planetary intelligence of its own was an opportunity for the universe to manifest greater love.[23] As such, their contribution is to be celebrated. It has nourished the growth of a worldwide Jewish eco-praxis whose rituals, liturgies and causes unite the spiritual and the secular, the traditional and the contemporary, in ways that are exceptionally well-adapted and attractive to the moment.

Theologically, though, a Jewish immanentist turn is not unproblematic. If the commandment to love the planet cannot, as it

---

[21] Michael Lerner's *Spirit matters: Global Healing and the Wisdom of the Soul* (Charlottesville: Hamptons Road Publishing, 2000), is a significant exemplar of this Jewish eco-spiritual turn.

[22] 'The Jewish Roots of Kehilla's Values: Reb Zalman Schachter-Shalomi', https://kehillasynagogue.org/the-jewish-roots-of-kehillas-values-reb-zalman-schachter-shalomi-final-part/ posted by Maya Joshua, July 25, 2019.

[23] Lerner, *Spirit Matters*, 48.

were, come from a will and dimension that is external to it, and the historical and ontological nature and value of the planet is an undifferentiated whole, it is hard to see how one might be commanded to love it; after all, commandments assume a subject-object relation, even where they are critical of it. Obligated human care for the earth mirrors the relation between the transcendent God and the created world. [24] Moreover, relatively few Jews would want to over-blur the distinctions between God, nature and humanity. The distinction between immanence and transcendence prevents erroneous worship of finite material things (idolatry) and leaves open the possibility of historically interruptive messianic transformation; a restoration of the world under the operations of the commandment to love.[25] In a modern world characterized by the sins of estrangement, commanded love knows that love is not yet. Commanded love is not natural; most people's and polity's economies of love do not extend much beyond their biological, ethnic, and national family and their 'church'. To that extent, the love commandment must come from 'outside' the world and operate prophetically, dramatically, within the dynamics of a messianic-historical scheme in which the immanent and the transcendent may collide or interpenetrate, but are not the same.

A contemporary Jewish theological suggestion for loving the planet as a stranger

From an interruptive messianic perspective, the planet—smothered by concrete and tarmac, enslaved to and exhausted by the human project—stands in ever greater need of redemption. Perhaps, then, the moment

---

[24] See further, Hava Tirosh-Samuelson, 'Nature in the Sources of Judaism', *Daedalus* 130 (2001): 99–124.

[25] See Emmanuel Levinas, *Outside the Subject*, trans. M. B. Smith (Redwood: Stanford University Press, 1996), 58.

has come for the planet to be cared for rather more emphatically and personalistically than it is under the current auspices of either immanentism or welfarism. The welfarist language of stewardship, especially, does not have reach of the love commandment in a time of crisis, where industrialized modernity has rendered the human relationship to the planet one closely akin to that with a non-personal stranger in urgent need of obligated, practical love.

Broadly rhetorical, non-halakhic, cultural modifications of commandments are not, in fact, without recent precedent. At least two non-rabbinic, Jewish cultural commentators have rather boldly proposed new additions to the Ten Commandments. In 1979, Cynthia Ozick, appalled that the Torah's ethic had not been mobilized to countermand patriarchy, proposed the proscription of the dehumanization of women as an eleventh commandment.[26] Two years before his death in 2018, Amos Oz's eleventh commandment was 'Thou shalt not inflict pain, or to be more modest: Thou shalt try to inflict as little pain as you possibly can...'[27]

One way to at least initiate some discussion about modifying the commandment to love the stranger would be to re-read Emmanuel Levinas' well-known ethic of the face in the light of planetary suffering.[28] At first glance, though, Levinas' thinking would seem too anthropocentric a basis for a commandment to love the other-than-

---

[26] 'Notes Toward Finding the Right Question', in Susannah Heschel (ed.), *On Being a Jewish Feminist* (New York: Schocken, 1983), 126 (120-151).

[27] Amos Oz, The National Library of Israel, 3/12/2018, https://blog.nli.org.il/en/amos-oz-reveals-his-faith/

[28] The ethic of the face is presented throughout Levinas' work, most notably in his 1961 book *Totality and Infinity: An Essay on Exteriority,* trans. Alphonso Lingis (Pittsburgh: Duquesne University, 1979), especially sections I.A.4 and III. B. A useful essay that more briefly articulates the Levinasian ethic is 'Ethics as First Philosophy' (1984), in Seán Hand (ed.), *The Levinas Reader* (Oxford: Basil Blackwell, 1989), 75–87.

human other, let alone the planet as a categorical whole. As has often been noted, Levinas' account of ethical responsibility almost never extends beyond the realm of interpersonal relationships, namely, face-to-face encounters with the human other. His remarks on the moral standing of animals, for example, are notoriously undeveloped and largely confined to a 1986 interview with graduate students published under the title 'The Paradox of Morality'. When asked whether his ethic had room for an animal ethics, Levinas tentatively confirmed that 'the ethical extends to all living beings', and that 'one cannot entirely refuse the face of an animal.' Nonetheless, Levinas hesitated. Further analysis, he said, would be needed before he could say whether a specific animal (a snake, for example) has a 'face'.[29] Elsewhere, he regarded 'pure nature, when it does not attest to the glory of God, when it is no-one's, indifferent and inhuman nature', as being situated only 'on the fringes of this world (of the face)'. 'Pure nature', without conscience and intentionality, can be understood only 'on the plane of the human world of property'.[30]

Just one brief essay, 'The Name of a Dog, or Natural Rights', published in 1975, may give some Levinasian grounds for affirming a commanded love of the planet as akin to commanded love of the stranger. In this essay, Levinas shares a memory of how his experience of dehumanization in a forestry labour battalion of seventy French-Jewish prisoners of war expanded his understanding of relationship. In the camp hierarchy, and to those civilians they passed by, the Jewish prisoners had been 'stripped of [their] human skin'. They were no more than 'subhuman, a gang of apes.' Only a stray dog his battalion had

---

[29] Tamra Wright, Peter Hughes, Alison Ainley, 'The Paradox of Morality: an Interview with Emmanuel Levinas', in Robert Bernasconi and David Wood (eds.), *The Provocation of Levinas: Rethinking the Other* (London: Routledge, 1988), 169, 171–2 (168–180)

[30] Emmanuel Levinas, *Collected Philosophical Papers*, trans. and ed. Alphonso Lingis (Dordrecht: Martinus Nijhoff, 1987), 28–9 (25–46).

called Bobby recognized their humanity. Bobby would greet them with delighted barking when they returned to the camp, exhausted from their labours. Bobby's canine face and voice spoke the only language of welcome they heard in the camp: 'For him, there was no doubt that we were men'.[31]

It is poignant that in that time and place a mangy stray dog—a traditional metonym for the wretchedly subhuman—loved the stranger better than any human being. This homeless dog—'the last Kantian in Nazi Germany'—needed no commandment to come out and meet the persecuted other, as cast out from the sphere of ethical obligation as he was. It is not that Levinas wanted to equate the experience of Jews and stray dogs. Levinas' fond and grateful recall of Bobby does not promote Bobby to the standing of an honorary human being. It is rather that his essay can be read as suggesting that the operations of the love commandment include and exceed the other-than-human other; the suffering or wounding of the human stranger *and* the other-than-human stranger qualify for, and exemplify, different types of love within the same commandment.

Levinas' crisis was the abyssal horror of world war and the Holocaust. Now, in the contemporary climate crisis, we are again compelled to rethink our obligations to that which suffers and dies, and reconsider who and what has a face. To say that a face is not only and necessarily a human face need not so much anthropomorphize the other-than-human as suggest that it is not only or necessarily the human face that is made in the image of God. David Seidenberg has argued that a

---

[31] Emmanuel Levinas, *Difficult Freedom: Essays on Judaism*, trans. S. Hand (Baltimore: Johns Hopkins University Press, 1990), 152–3 (151–3). Compare Martin Buber's ruminations on his relations with non-human others, most notably his cat, but also vegetal and mineral entities in Buber, *I and Thou*, trans. Walter Kaufmann (New York: Charles Scribner's Sons, 1970), 144–5.

Jewish theology in a time of climate crisis must not confine the divine image to the human face. To do so would be to ignore the rabbinic view of animals, plants, land, rocks and so forth that sometimes ascribes them a moral standing of their own. And more, to say that only the human is made in the divine image would be to erroneously assume that only human beings have infinite value; that only human beings are beloved by God.[32] To confine the image of God to the human would be to ontologically and practically set apart or alienate the human from the rest of creation more than it is already, and in ways that would continue to justify its subjugation.[33] Above all, to limit the divine image to the human face would be an idolatrous domestication and exhaustion of divine being.

If both the human face and the face of the earth are both, differently, made in the divine image, then to witness and co-suffer the sufferings of the earth under climate change is to be drawn into a face-to-face relation with a different kind of other for whom we are obligated to care. If a face-to-face relation with an other-than-human animal 'face' is not necessarily an unduly anthropocentric extension of Levinasian thinking-of-the-other, [34] why not extend that relation to include the face of the earth? While Levinas regarded the human face as the sole or primary site of ethical revelation, if the face is, *and is not,* literally a human face, then the face of the earth, already known to the biblical text as a joyous,

---

[32] Seidenberg, *Kabbalah and Ecology*, throughout but esp. 39 and 95.

[33] Seidenberg refers us to Yosef Ashkanazi's kabbalistic claim that if Adam was created in God's image, and the Universe, in the form of Adam Qadmon, is made in the human image, then creation too is made in the image of God: Seidenberg, *Kabbalah and Ecology*, 241–65.

[34] For the formulation of a post-Levinasian animal and environmental ethic, see e.g., David Boothroyd, 'Levinas, Ecology, Nature', in Michael L. Morgan (ed.), *The Oxford Handbook of Levinas* (Oxford: Oxford University Press, 2019); Barbara Jane Davy, 'An Other Face of Ethics in Levinas', *Ethics and the Environment* 12 (2007) 39-65; William Edelglass, James Hatley, and Christian Diehm (eds.), *Facing Nature: Levinas and Environmental Thought* (Pittsburgh: Duquesne University Press, 2012).

expressive face that sings its praises to God, that is subject to the commandment, that is host to a sensate socio-natural order of plants, animals and people that are acutely vulnerable to agro-industrial degradation and nuclear apocalypse, issues (or is itself the summation of) a commandment to love *par excellence.*

The modern industrial alienation of nature has made the face of the earth another face of estrangement. It is a face on which the faces of all strangers under the threat of violence walk. The face of the planet is also that of a stranger to me. That is, the planet is not like me; it is not in reciprocal relation to the historical and ontological particularity that is me. It may at best have some local need of my ministrations, perhaps in the garden, where I might have caused a plant to suffer and die by inadvertent neglect, or where I could alleviate its suffering with water, liquid seaweed, re-potting, or picking off pests from its leaves by hand. But more generally, in modernity, nature, domesticated and enslaved to the human project, has lost its freedom and integrity. Even beyond the cities, nature has become the stranger who might lives among me as garden and woodland, but is more often outcast and homeless on the fringe of fields, roads, industrial estates and towns. So too, even if I am fortunate enough to live *amidst* nature as, say, a gardener or walker, I am still barely *of* nature; I remain a stranger to it. Even if the planet, as host to all living things, is granted some kind of consciousness, it does not know or welcome me as me.

Some might therefore object that the material totality that is the planet is, like the universe, so epistemically and experientially beyond my ideation that I cannot be commanded to love it. The face of the earth may seem too vast and unfathomable to be anthropomorphized into that of another stranger—another object to my subject. The face of the earth, which can be a resilient face, may contain my face, but its infinities of quantity, scale and time also obliterate my face.

And yet, after Levinas, it is precisely *because* the suffering face of the earth is a face that will always exceed itself as the object of my love, and *because* it is not containable as an image or idea, that it can be included in the category of the stranger we are commanded to love. We might, then, be commanded to love the planet precisely because it is inherently and eternally strange, absolutely irreducible to me and mine. It is precisely because commanded love demands radical transcendence of the egotism of familial or romantic love (which being for the other-as-same is little more than a natural self-love) that love of the planet must be non-naturally, that is, divinely, commanded.

Judaism traditionally understands humanity, made in the image of God, as ontologically and morally set apart from and transcendent of the planetary community of natural things. Contemporary eco-Judaism has rightly challenged the hierarchical anthropocentrism of this account of nature. But it is possible to steer a middle way between the traditional and the contemporary perspectives. This essay suggests that a prophetic ethic's concern for the exploited and the vulnerable should extend beyond defenceless people to include a planet that is defencelessly exposed to the extractive, depletive, pollutant forces of modernity. In this sense, a commanded love of the planet is cognate with the prophetic love that calls power to account and demands, for the powerless and disempowered, justice and protection from violence. Because the human is *of* nature but not *identical* to it, a commanded love of the planet is not the same kind of obligated love one might experience with a spouse or partner who is neither the neighbour nor the stranger, but a perfect 'match'. Love of the planet is not the intimate marital love (*yichud*) that is sealed within the circle of a gold ring. As Levinas puts it, 'The couple is a closed society'.[35]

By contrast, the face of the earth is a radically open, indeterminate locus of pure becoming, of pure possibility, without beginning or end.

---

[35] Emmanuel Levinas, 'The Ego and the Totality', in Levinas, *Collected Philosophical Papers*, trans. Alphonso Lingis (The Hague: Martinus Nijhoff, 1987), 32 (25–46).

It is, as Genesis 1 reminds us, a fathomless, formless, tehomic face: Deep Face.[36] It is at once the infinitely mysterious face of the stranger, and the face over which the creative spirit of God moves no less than over my own face. It is, in Genesis 1, a tehomic face that, no less than mine now, stands under the commandment to create a habitable world. Just as faces are both readable and mysterious, open and closed, the turbulent, wind/spirit-swept face of the earth labours under the same heavy hand of history as I do. As such, the strange face of the earth enters the sphere of what is knowable and, thereby, to be loved.

In particular, the face of the earth petitions or commands Jewish love because Jews too have known what it is to be a stranger infinitely and inaudibly vulnerable to harm; to be a stranger whose future hangs in the balance. Without making any facile comparison between ecocide and genocide, just as Jews are commanded to love the stranger because they too have suffered slavery and exile, so too should Jews feel themselves under a commandment to love a planet whose face is ravaged by drought, storm, wildfire, deluge, and pestilence. Its soil eroded, its forests cleared, the face of the earth is a face scarred by the lines of human and animal who traverse it; they travel as refugees from war, climate change, and ever-encroaching development, their populations harnessed for at least the last two hundred years to the modern colonial project.

It is possible that loving the planet as a stranger might come more easily to a Jewish woman than to a man. Traditionally, the Jewish woman has been cast as the silent inside-outsider, the stranger dispersed among men in a tradition founded on interlocution between men and a God who is masculine by default.[37] Even now, after Jewish feminism,

---

[36] On 'tehomic' theology' see Catherine Keller, *The Face of the Deep: A Theology of Becoming* (London: Routledge, 2003).

[37] Numerous Jewish feminist texts, especially those written in the second wave period when Jewish women had greater inequality of religious opportunity than Jewish men,

and with new permissions to study and lead communities if only as a kind of honorary man, a woman might still feel a certain empathy for the planet as a stranger—as nature—which (like her) has long been coded and sexualized as the merely chaotic feminine whose reproductivity must be owned and controlled by the masculine.[38]

Nonetheless, if gender inflects the idea of a stranger, and if responsibility for the causes and consequences of the climate crisis is socio-politically uneven, practical love of the planet in small ways and large is required of all, however and wherever they are economically and geographically situated. The face of the earth commands it. The Arctic, for example, is warming about twice as fast as the global average, the glaciers that polar bears depend on as habitat are melting away. Polar bears' main prey, seals, also need the ice on which to raise their young. Or again, recent years have seen the death of more than 61,000 koalas among 3 billion animals, including 2.46 billion reptiles, burnt, or injured by the Australian bushfires of 2019-20. [39] Now that, like everyone else, all Jews can see (and scientifically measure) the planet's suffering as a direct consequence of unjust human (masculinist) economic and political choices, they are ethically obligated to care for it in the disinterested, non-reciprocal, non-instrumental, justice-seeking

---

make this point. See e.g. Rachel Adler, 'The Jew Who Wasn't There: Halakhah and the Jewish Woman', in Heschel (ed.), *On Being A Jewish Feminist*, 12–18; Sheila Shulman, 'Worldly Jewish Women: A Possible Model', in *European Judaism: A Journal for the New Europe* 38 (2005): 80–94; Melissa Raphael, *Religion, Feminism and Idoloclasm: Being and Becoming in the Women's Liberation Movement* (Abingdon: Routledge, 2019), 156–68. More recent writing on gender and exclusion in Judaism would include the othering of the Queer, in some ways more of a collective stranger to the tradition than women.

[38] See further, Hava Tirosh-Samuelson, 'Religion, Ecology, and Gender: A Jewish Perspective', *Feminist Theology: The Journal of the Britain & Ireland School of Feminist Theology* 13 (2005): 373–97.

[39] https://www.theguardian.com/australia-news/2020/dec/07/devastating-more-than-61000-koalas-among-3-billion-animals-affected-by-bushfire-crisis

ways that are an expression of non-erotic agapeistic love by any other name.[40]

Levinas could write that 'The love of God for Man is the fact that Man loves his neighbour',[41] that God does not exist as another, if Supreme, Being, but is revealed as the inter-face relation through which God may pass. In the same way, a contemporary Jew might argue that love for the planet is commanded not because the Torah has specifically commanded it, but because it has a suffering face. Ethics is not the corollary of a theology of love, but a theology of love itself. 'To know God is to know what must be done.'[42] God is not a separate addressee of human love, and just as we love God by loving the human stranger, so too could we love God by loving the planet as a stranger—that is, by taking thankless responsibility for its well-being and demanding justice for the wrongs inflicted upon it.

Using a Levinasian account of love *as* ethics, commanded love of the planet is a disinterested, but radically empathetic, responsible, love of the other. For Levinas, love is something more demanding than refraining from doing something to your neighbour or kinsman that you would not have him do to you. It is not about loving the other as yourself. It is a practical alleviation of the suffering of what is *not* like you, without calculation or hope of reciprocity. Post-Levinas, a commanded love for the planet that cares for it irrespective of its yield or other return, and with no possibility of thanks or mutual empathy, can be a fully ecological, meta-anthropic love.

---

[40] See further, William Edelglass, 'Rethinking Responsibility in An Age of Anthropogenic Climate Change', in Edelglass et. al (eds.), *Facing Nature*, 209–28; Claudia Welz, *Love's Transcendence and the Problem of Theodicy* (Tübingen, Mohr Siebeck, 2008), 305, 311–12.

[41] Levinas, *Difficult Freedom*, 191.

[42] Levinas, *Difficult Freedom*, 17.

Conclusion

There are those who would regard any expansion of the commandment to love the stranger to include love of the planet as being yet another theological 'dominology' in which active, ethical, speaking human or divine transcendence 'lords it' over supposedly passive, amoral, silent (feminized), natural immanence. For those wanting to think and act in a deeper ecological register, there may be something amiss in applying the love commandment to the planet: it may appear to be little more than a variant of an older, if benevolent, condescension to the ecosphere on the personalist assumption that to love and be the object of love is the highest good.

The Jewish feminist theologian Judith Plaskow, for example, whose thought seems now to be heading in a post-theistic direction, would probably answer our question, 'are we commanded to love the planet?', as a series of category mistakes. Travelling with her partner Martha in the Amazon in the early 1990s, just after publishing her classic feminist theological work *Standing Again at Sinai*, Plaskow had an experience of planetary being that lasted over several days. Here, by the thundering waters of the Iguassu Falls, on the border of Brazil and Argentina, watching the sun rise over the Amazon where the Rio Negra and the Ariau River meet and the spider monkeys chatter and the vultures peck at the carcasses of crocodiles, she felt herself to be 'gazing at the well-spring of life in all its terror and sublimity'.[43]

Any commandment to love the planet might seem to re-establish a chain of command that she would reject in favour of an egalitarian, horizontal, self-regenerating web of organic connections. For her, an ethical obligation to the planet would arise not in any commandment to love it but in the interconnectedness and interdependence of all living

---

[43] Carol P. Christ and Judith Plaskow, *Goddess and God in the World: Conversations in Embodied Theology* (Minneapolis: Fortress Press, 106), 173–4.

things, which we have only a natural interest to nurture and conserve. If the planet is characterized neither by good nor evil, love nor hate, its God has no need to command anything. It is a creative energy or Ground of Being that, for no extrinsic moral or historical purpose, sustains all life. Rather than loving the planet, as I have suggested, as if it were another person, 'We are bound to one another only by the web of life and it is for the sake of the 'continual unfolding of the adventure of creation' that we must 'choose life'. [44]

It seemed right to end this essay by citing Plaskow's position as a significant contemporary Jewish theologian for whom the nature of the planet itself would raise a significant question mark over any commandment to love it. Yet her position has little by way of what may be considered to be characteristically Jewish. In Jewish thinking, the planet, or at least the earth and all its plants and creatures, comes under a clear and continuous—traditional and modern—ethico-halakhic, personalistic remit of care passed *l'dor v'dor*, from one generation to the next in their particular historical moment.

If revelation is cumulative and progressive, [45] it has seemed worth suggesting that, in the throes of a late modern crisis in the human relationship with the earth, Jews, as earthlings, as Adamah, are now commanded to love the planet, not just its creator or the rest of its human population. A degraded planet has pathos: it visibly suffers. It can be at least partially restored by human loving-kindness to lush, teeming health, although sometimes, as in extinction events, it cannot be revived. I have suggested that the climate crisis and its related ills call into question the traditional scope of the love commandment. We could use

---

[44] Christ and Plaskow, *God and Goddess in the World*, throughout, but esp. 174, 184–187, 237.

[45] On cumulative revelation in Judaism, see Tamar Ross, *Expanding the Palace of Torah: Orthodoxy and Feminism* (Lebanon, NH: University Press of New England, 2004).

the imperative of the love commandment to go beyond the trawl for Jewish texts, principles and festivals that have already done so much to authenticate a welfare-orientated ecological praxis. Only a face-to-face relation with the earth as stranger will let the earth speak intelligibly, compelling us to feel its pain and anger and act, in solidarity, in its defence. Human love might yet be the planet's best chance.

4

Nature as Beloved and Mentor: The Symbolic Representation of Nature in Persian Poetry

Amir H. Zekrgoo and Leyla H. Tajer

Introduction: nature, poetry and love[1]

Nature as a source of knowledge of existence has equally inspired philosophers, scientists, poets, artists, and people of faith. Art and literature provide a wide stage upon which intellect and emotion engage with the natural world. Throughout history, the fascination with nature's transitory and endless manifestations has inspired artists who have left behind works of art that adorn houses, museums and offices, adding to the quality of our lives. Lovers have viewed nature as a mirror that reflects their feelings, seeing the various phases of love in the ever-changing moods of nature. Nature has also been a medium of self-realization, an existential vessel in which different individuals can face their own selves; a testing ground upon which they can learn about their strengths and weaknesses.

People of faith look at nature as a path that leads to God-realization.

[1] The authors would like to express their gratitude to Prof. Paul Fiddes for his valuable comments during the final stage of preparation for this essay. A vote of thanks goes to Dr. Mahmoodreza Esfandiar's assistance in making available a few important Persian sources.

This is quite bold in Islamic teachings. For instance, the Qur'an introduces natural elements as divine 'signs' (*āyāt*). It is remarkable that many chapters of the Qur'an are named after natural phenomena. The Thunder (*al-Ra'd*, chapter 13), The Sun (*al-Shams*, chapter 91), The Moon (*al-Qamar*, chapter 54), The Bee (*al-Naḥl*, chapter 16), The Ant (*al-Naml*, chapter 27), The Light (*al-Nūr*, chapter 24), The Star *(al-Najm*, chapter 53), The Constellations (*al-Burūj*, chapter 85), The Dawn (*al-Fajr*, chapter 89), and The Night (*al-Layl*, chapter 92), are just a few so named. The nature-oriented Qur'anic oaths are also worth mentioning here. God takes an oath to the Heavens[2] and the Earth,[3] the Sun[4] and the Moon,[5] Night[6] and Day,[7] clouds,[8] wind,[9] and so on, and commands the believers to deliberate on *how the earth was outstretched* (Qur'an, 88:20) for ... *whatsoever is in the heavens and the earth ... are signs for people who contemplate* (Qur'an, 45:13). *How many a sign is there in the heavens and on the earth by which they pass; yet they turn away from them!* (Qur'an, 12:105). The Qur'an has been primary among sources of reference and inspiration in Persian classical poetry.

Nature has also been a means for expression of love. The 'Beloved's' identity in Persian poetry is often hidden behind a mystical mist, mainly because God is addressed as the ultimate Beloved. Hence nature, being the most comprehensive manifestation of the 'Beloved', demands love and respect. Poets' dealing with nature can therefore be seen as a form of romantic religiosity. A general overview of Persian

---

[2] E.g. Qur'an, 41:12; 2:164; 34:9; 2:29; 2:22.

[3] E.g. Qur'an, 2:255; 4:131; 22:65; 35:44; 34:9.

[4] E.g. Qur'an: 41:37; 6:96; 36:38; 7: 54; 16:12.

[5] E.g. Qur'an, 41:37; 84:18; 6:96; 91:2; 39:5; 16:12.

[6] E.g. Qur'an, 22:61; 57:6; 31:29; 84:17; 3:190.

[7] E.g. Qur'an: 3:27; 45:5; 28:73; 30:23; 7:54.

[8] E.g. Qur'an, 24:43; 2:164; 30:48; 24:40; 35:9.

[9] E.g. Qur'an, 10:22; 35:9; 38:36.

literature exhibits a bold and undisputed presence of such romantic, devotional material—phrases, sentences, paragraphs or even pages—before the beginning of the main texts.[10] This presence is evident even in legal documents, royal decrees, and marriage contracts. The language of such passages is Arabic, Persian or a mixture of the two.[11]

There are numerous giants in the world of classical Persian poetry who left their unfading impressions on the lives of many generations Many contemporaries followed their lead, while others took a new path and departed from the established forms of poetry while the contents and themes remained related.

This essay presents a survey of expressions of love for nature in Persian poetry, from classical times to modern era. In doing so, we touch briefly upon such expressions in selected couplets by a handful of poets: Rūdakī (twelfth century), Manūchehrī (eleventh century), Nezāmī (twelfth century), Rūmī (thirteenth century), Sa'dī (thirteenth century) and Vahshī Bāfqī (sixteenth century). Our main focus however is on two poets who lived some seven hundred years apart—Hāfez Shīrāzī (fourteenth century) and Sohrāb Sepehrī (twentieth century).[12] Hafez is among the historic, celebrated personalities whose love poems still comfort the hearts of readers today. Sohrab Sepehri, on the other hand, is a man of the modern age—the world of globalization—who, in his brief presence in the arena of literature, attracted many readers. In delving into the poems by Sohrab and Hafez, we hope to reach a better understanding of how much Persian poetry has evolved, and to what

---

[10] Such materials are mostly in prose, but examples of poetic introductory remarks are also extant.

[11] See Amir H. Zekrgoo, 'The Persian Tradition of Marriage Documentation: Pre-Islamic & Islamic Marriage Contracts', in *Al-Shajarah, Journal of the International Institute of Islamic Thought & Civilization (ISTAC),* International Islamic University Malaysia (IIUM), 12/2 (2007): 143–60.

[12] Henceforth, for ease of reading, the names of Hāfez and Sohrāb will be spelled without diacritical marks.

degree the modern version can be regarded as an extension to the old tradition.

For this purpose, we have selected relevant passages that reflect each poet's passion for nature as beloved and mentor. Fresh translations of the selected couplets are presented here for the first time. Our aim in doing fresh translations has been to maintain, as much as possible, the aesthetic values of the original couplets (such as rhyme and tempo), while remaining faithful—as much as possible—to the original text. Also, we feel that having a homogeneous translation produced by the same pen can contribute to the smooth reading of the essay. All English translations of Persian poems in this essay are therefore by Amir H. Zekrgoo.

Nature as reflected in the works of classical poets

Nature has a strong presence in Persian poetry. Natural forces such as wind and thunder, and natural elements such as plants, flowers and water streams have inspired poets and stimulated their imagination. Regardless of the type of appreciation for nature—its beauty, its usefulness, its life-giving force, or its inspirational values—almost all classical poets respected nature because they saw it as a revelation of the divine.

Sa'dī (d. 1291) is among the poets who masterly expresses this religious attitude towards nature. In one couplet he declares that he is in love with the natural world because it is a manifestation of God.[13] In other words, whoever loves God must have love for His creation. Sa'dī goes further in the same line by stating that the worshippers of God are not only the sons of Adam; that every nightingale that sings on tree

---

[13] Muṣliḥ al-Dīn Saʿdī, *Dīwān: Tayyibāt* (Tehran: Kānūn Maʾrifat Publishing, 1340 Sh/1961), 724.
For the original Persian couplet see Appendix 1.

branches is praising the Lord.[14]

Love for nature in a practical sense translates into taking care of the natural environment – a relevant issue in the contemporary world. Traces of such mentality are evident in poems by Nezāmī Ganjavi (d.1209) and Vaḥshī Bāfqī (d. 1583). Nezāmī refers to the force of life that is present in plants, and stresses that the life of life of birds and trees depend on it. He warns that the cutting of trees will shorten the span of life, and will bring about poverty.[15] Vaḥshī sends the same message by distancing himself from tree-cullers, as if it were a sin, and announces that: 'we are not tree cutters, they are others! although we possess a hundred axes, we will not break a single branch.'[16]

Rūdakī's (d. 941) expressions of nature are somewhat unique. Having been born blind, the poet extends his imagination far and wide, and provides vivid pictures of natural forces as if they are actively playing their roles in a cosmic drama. Each element is assigned a role in the epic stage of life. For instance, 'spring' represents human life; the 'cosmos' is a battle ground; dark clouds are armies that are moved by the force of wind; and roaring thunder is the army's drummer. The sound of thunder is also likened to moaning of a mourning man, while raining cloud is an expression of him shedding tears.[17]

Unlike Rūdakī whose expressions of nature are mainly imaginary, Manūchehrī (d. 1040) provides a tangible report of his first-hand

---

[14] Muṣliḥ al-Dīn Saʿdī, *Dīwān: Tayyibāt*, 17. For the original Persian couplet see Appendix 2.

[15] Nezāmī Ganjavī, *Khamsih-ye Nizāmī*, ed. Vahid Dastgerdī (Tehran: Agah Publishing, 1381 Sh/2002), 349. For the original Persian couplet see Appendix 3.

[16] Vaḥshī Bāfqī, *Dīwān*, ed. Parviz Babaei (Tehran: Negah Publishing, 1393 Sh/2014), 105. For the original Persian couplet see Appendix 4.

[17] Rūdakī Samarqandī, *Dīwān*, ed. Said Nafisi (Tehran: Negah Publishing, 1376 Sh/ 1997), 68. Also see: Muhammadreza Kadkani, *Ṣovar-e Khīyāl dar Shʿir Farsi* (*Imaginal Illustrations in Persian Poetry*) (Tehran: Agah Publishing, 1385 Sh/2006), 414–38. For the original Persian couplet see Appendix 5.

encounter with elements of nature. He paints a realistic picture of flowers, fruits, and birds in his poems.[18] When he speaks of a rainy day, one can sense that he is talking about his own unique experience of a certain day, which is different from other rainy days that he reports.[19]

Looking at nature as a beloved and a mentor literally means that nature is regarded as a charismatic teacher—a teacher well-versed in the subject of love who is also loved by his pupils. Rūmī (d.1273) applies the business of love to the cosmos itself and claims that the universe revolves around love:

> If the sky was not in love,
> It would not have so much clarity,
> And if the sun was not in love,
> There would be no purity in its beauty.
> Farm and mountain are both lovers,
> Or else plants wouldn't grow from their belly.[20]

Nature through the eyes of Hafez

Shams al-Dīn Muḥammad (d.1390), is mostly known by his penname Hafez (also spelled Ḥāfiẓ). The term *hafiz* literally means 'protector'. In religious terminology it is an attribute given to a person who protects the Qur'an by having memorized the entire holy book. Shams al-Dīn Muḥammad knew the Qur'an by heart and proudly used Hafez as penname. In his poems he admires his own poems by taking an oath to

---

[18] Kadkani, *Ṣovar-e Khīyāl dar Sh'ir Farsi*, 62–89.

[19] Manūchehri, *Dīwān*, ed. Muhammad Dabir Siyaghi (Tehran: Zawwar, 1388 Sh/2009), 64. See also Kadkani, *Ṣovar-e Khīyāl dar Sh'ir Farsi*, 501–25. For the original Persian couplet see Appendix 6.

[20] Ghazal 2673 in Jalāl al-Dīn Muḥammad Rūmī, *Kulliyyāt-i Diwān-i Shams Tabrīzī, bā taṣḥīḥāt va ḥawāshī*, ed. Badī' al-Zamān Furūzānfar, 4th ed. (Tehran: Sidāy-e Mu'āṣir, 1386/ 2007), vol. 2, 1054. For the original Persian couplet see Appendix 7.

'the Qur'an that is preserved in his heart', that he has not heard a more pleasant tune than that of his lyrics.[21] Hafez was born and died in his hometown Shiraz, a city that he loved and often praised in his *divan*.[22] He received a classical education in the Qur'an and Islamic theology, and wrote commentaries on religious classics. Although Hafez enjoyed the patronage of several rulers as a court poet, his poems are love-oriented with a strong sense of mysticism.

Ghazals of Hafez display an unsurpassed perfection in form. Unsurpassed does not, of course, mean absolute perfection; there are many giants in Persian poetry but the language of none has reached a degree of perfection that could not be improved! Hafez's poems are unique in the sense that words and phrases are so harmoniously bonded with the tune they carry that any change will only harm that perfect composition. The flawless form with a sublime content gave Hafez a most celebrated title—*Lisān al-Ghayb*, 'the tongue of the unseen realm'. In fact, many people today possess their own personal copy of Hafez, consulting it and seeking guidance from the unseen realm through his magical poetry. It would not be an exaggeration to claim that most Iranian households possess more than a single copy of the *Divan* of Hafez.

Love is the essence of Hafez's poetry. In his ghazals, *love, wine*, and *drunkenness* are prominent; they have been used symbolically to express ecstasy, enlightenment, and spiritual liberation. To express the joy and sorrow in the journey of love, the poet sometimes portrays the beloved as an extremely charming and seductive girl, and the lover as a grieving man whose life's mission is to pursue her in the hope of winning her heart. He repeats the same story in a language of symbols,

---

[21] Hāfez, *Dīwān*, ed. Mohammad Qazvini and Qasem Ghani (Tehran: Zavvar Publishing, n.d.), 312, Ghazal 447. For the original Persian couplet see Appendix 8.
[22] Hāfez, *Dīwān*, 189, Ghazal 279. For the original Persian couplet see Appendix 9.

using natural elements as characters performing on the stage of love. The poet uses elements of nature such as *cypress tree, rose, nightingale, spring season, day, night,* and *morning breeze* to express moods and emotions that are stimulated in the journey of love. They also represent the main wayfarers of the journey—lover and beloved.

The following couplets are examples displaying Hafez's symbolic treatment of elements of nature. Each passage is followed by a brief elaboration that might help the reader to connect better with the contents. To each group of couplets, we have added a title, using wordings from the ghazal.

I. *Stages of Spirituality*

[1] Last evening the nightingale, on a branch of a cypress tree,
Preached in melodious Pahlavi dialect, the stages of spirituality.[23]

II. *Love is Enough*

[2] In the rose-garden of creation, a rose-faced maiden is enough for me,
In the meadow of life, shadow of a 'gliding cypress' is enough for me.[24]

[3] Rest on the bank of a river, and watch how life passes by!
This hint to the fleeting nature of world is clear enough for me.[25]

[5] Relate the cash in the world's market to the world of pain it causes!

---

[23] Hāfez, *Dīwān*, 345, Ghazal 486. For the original Persian couplet see Appendix 10.
[24] Hāfez, *Dīwān*, 182. Ghazal 268. For the original Persian couplet see Appendix 11.
[25] Ibid. For the original Persian couplet see Appendix 12.

If this profit and loss isn't clear enough for you – it's enough for me.[26]

[6] The true Beloved is with us; what more should we desire for?
The treasure of presence of that soul-comforting one, is enough for me.[27]

[8] It's unfair to complain of the stream of fate, O Hafez!
Having a water-clear vision and ghazals that flow like stream, are enough for me.[28]

In the above couplets a number of symbols and metaphors have been adopted. [II.1] 'The nightingale' is presented as a mentor or preacher, who gives a sermon of spirituality using 'the cypress tree' as a pulpit. [II.2] The plane of creation is introduced metaphorically as a 'rose garden', while a 'rose-faced maiden' symbolizes the subject of love. Life is portrayed as 'meadow' and 'the shadow of cypress tree' suggests a state of tranquillity that the presence of the beloved offers. In all, the poet is announcing that if you are in love, the presence of the beloved heals the wounds and makes life easy and pleasant. [II.3, 5, 6] 'Running water of the stream' is a metaphor for life's transient nature. It indicates that change is essential to life, and that material or monetary earnings are but illusional glimpses of happiness. The poet concludes that relying on such insignificant matters will bring about pain and a sense of failure. A wise person will never invest his life in such a business. Wise investment would be the treasure of being in the presence of love, which comforts souls and heals injuries. [II.8] The most valuable treasures, the poet claims, are those that are within not without! He offers his gratitude for having talent to compose 'melodious poems' that flow like the

---

[26] Ibid. For the original Persian couplet see Appendix 13.

[27] Ibid. For the original Persian couplet see Appendix 14.

[28] Ibid. For the original Persian couplet see Appendix 15.

'crystal-clear water of a stream.' He further emphasizes that having this blessing is enough, and that complaining about the unpleasant turns of fate would be unfair.

III. *Tree of Friendship*

[1] Plant the tree of friendship, for the heart's desire is its fruit,
Uproot the bush of hostility that has immense pain at its root.[29]

[3] Cherish the night in the company of beloved ones; for after our time –
The planet will revolve countless times, with nights and days of dispute.[30]

[5] Seek 'Life's Spring Season', O heart! Otherwise in every year's spring –
A thousand nightingales sing, and a hundred rose-buds shoot.[31]

[6] In his old age in the garden of the world, Hafez asks the Almighty,
A stream-side rest, and embrace of a cypress-figure, that'll bring life to soothe.[32]

[III.1] Here two contradictory qualities, friendship and hostility, are given plant-like lives. Each of them can grow and expand if nourished. The poet lays emphasis on taking care of the auspicious tree of friendship for it bears sweet fruit, and stresses an uprooting of the ill-omened plant of hostility because it bears the fruits of misery. [III.3,5] The poet also contrasts two categories of experience of time. One is the linear time that is calculated by the passage of days and nights, and

---

[29] Hāfez, *Dīwān*, 78, Ghazal 115. For the original Persian couplet see Appendix 16.

[30] Ibid. For the original Persian couplet see Appendix 17.

[31] Ibid. For the original Persian couplet see Appendix 18.

[32] Ibid. For the original Persian couplet see Appendix 19.

another one is in the presence of the beloved which induces the experience of timeless joy. He mentions 'the spring season of life' as a state of being that one should desire. A contrast is portrayed between 'nature's spring season' and the 'life's spring season.' The former happens periodically as an outside event, while the latter is an inner state that one can evoke. [III.6] 'Old age' is presented as an elevated state where desires reach maturity throughout ups and downs of life. In each stage of life, a certain desire find manifestation. People, according to their capacity or limited vision, may regard those desires as ultimate. But, as time passes on and people become spiritually mature, true priorities unveil themselves. These priorities or mature desires are often simple. Hafez talks about the simple yet essential desire of a matured soul. He wishes to spend his remaining time in a quiet peaceful place at the bank of a river while the shadow of his beloved comforts him.

IV. *Breath of the Morning Breeze*

[1] The breath of the morning breeze, musk-spreading shall be,
And again, the old perishing world, fresh and young shall be.[33]

[2] The red 'arghavan' shall pass a ruby cup of wine, to the white 'lily',
The eyes of the 'narcissus', concerned for the 'anemone's' affair shall be. [34]

[3] The nightingale, tormented by the grief of separation,
Desperately crying – to the rose's pavilion shall flee. [35]

[7] The rose is precious – value its brief company,

---

[33] Hāfez, *Dīwān*, 111, Ghazal 164. For the original Persian couplet see Appendix 20.
[34] Ibid. For the original Persian couplet see Appendix 21.
[35] Ibid. For the original Persian couplet see Appendix 22.

For it came in the garden in one moment, out in another it shall be. [36]

[IV.1] 'Fragrance of the morning breeze' is a metaphor indicating that in every new day life begins with joy. [IV.2] The poet creates a scene in which four different flowers—*arghavan*, white lily, narcissus and anemone—are engaged in a human-like relation: the redness of the *arghavan* is compared to a cup of red wine that brings to life the pale face of the white lily. The narcissus, which in Persian poetry is often compared with the charming eyes of the beloved, looks at the bloody red colour of anemone with a sense of concern. This couplet reflects a worldview in which all elements of nature are regarded as conscious entities—an old trend in Persian poetry. A good example is Rūmī's famous couplets:

> Every small bit of the world,
> Whispers to you constantly days and nights.
> We listen, we see, and we are conscious,
> Yet to you strangers we are silent. [37]

[IV.3] The singing of the nightingale is compared to the moaning of a lover who is separated from his beloved. [38] The 'rose' is that beloved whose pavilion is a refuge for the heart-broken lover. [IV.7] The short life of the rose is used as an expression of alarm, reminding us that every moment of life must be treated as unique and precious.

---

[36] Ibid. For the original Persian couplet see Appendix 23.

[37] Rūmī', *Mathnawi*, III: 1018–19, in *The Mathnawi of Jalálu'ddín Rúmí*, ed. and trans. with commentary by Reynold A. Nicholson, 8 vols. (London: Gibb Memorial Trust, 1925–1940). But the translation of all lines of Rūmī's poetry in this essay is by Amir H. Zekrgoo. For the original Persian couplet see Appendix 24.

[38] In this essay we have used 'his' and 'her' to refer to lover and beloved respectively. The clear gender definition has its root in the body of Persian poetry where the lover is always introduced as male and beloved as female.

We can conclude that Hafez views nature as a book of wisdom, full of symbols and metaphors to be deciphered and learned from. For him creation is a 'garden' with all sorts of living beings that each have their own stories to tell. The rose is the most attractive feature in the garden of creation; it is the source of joy, though its presence in the garden is brief. The rose also represents the beloved's beautiful face—a medium of earthly love that could prepare the lover (a wayfarer on the journey of love) to get engaged in a more elevated love affair with the divine Beloved.[39]

The nightingale represents the passionate lover. For this love bird, the rose is equally the cause of joy and pain. In rare occasions the nightingale appears as wise preacher who gives sermons of spirituality from the top of a 'cypress tree'. The 'cypress tree', a very popular symbol in Persian literature, also represents the beloved's tall and graceful stature [see III.6]. Its shadow is the most pleasant place for the lover to rest under. Trees generally imply growth; even the feelings that grow within us are compared to trees. As such, we have 'trees of friendship' and 'trees of hatred and hostility'.

'Time', for Hafez is yet another important subject; it exists both on linear level and as a state of being. 'Day and night' are pulses that alert

---

[39] Love, in many spiritual traditions, is presented as a path that can lead seekers to the state of union with God. In Hinduism, for instance, the ways of unity with God are introduced in three categories: the path of love (Bhakti), the path of knowledge (Jnana), and the path of action (Yoga). Jalaluddin Rūmī emphasizes the interconnection between earthly and divine love in the following couplet:

Whether love is from this end or that end,

It will eventually lead us to that end.

(Rūmī, *Mathnawī,* I: 111). 'This end' refers to the earthly domain, while 'that end' is an indication of the heavenly realm. For the original Persian couplet see Appendix 25. Also see: Leyla Tajer, 'The Journey of Love and the Challenges of Self,' in Paul S. Fiddes (ed.), *Love as Common Ground: Essay on Love in Religion* (Lanham: Lexington Books, 2021), 54-57.

us about the fast disappearance of the moments of life. They carry with them the same message that the 'running water of stream' does. The 'Spring season', when discussed in the context of nature (the outside world) follows the same pattern of day and night, delivering the same message. However, some poems mention 'the Spring season of life' which refers to a state of being —a dimension that does not follow the rules of nature. When a lover and beloved are united, a timeless condition arises that is 'the Spring of life'. In order to maintain the Spring of life one must be attentive to its daily messenger, 'the morning breeze' with its charming fresh fragrance [IV.1].

Nature through the eyes of Sohrab Sepehri

Sohrab Sepehri (d. 1980) is among the most celebrated personalities in modern Persian poetry and visual arts. A painter and a poet, Sohrab's love and respect for nature was expressed in novel ways that have raised admiration among people of various social backgrounds. He regarded himself as a sincere worshipper who worshipped the creator through the sensible creation—the elements of nature. Addressed generally by his first name, Sohrab brought Persian contemporary poetry to a new state of consciousness. While sharing sentiments with the older generation and classical literature, Sohrab introduced a fresh child-like language that liberated him from the traditional formalism. Readers who are accustomed to classical poetry sometimes get shocked when encountering Sohrab's deconstructive engagement with established forms, but they are seldom offended because of Sohrab's innocent language. Reading Sohrab's poems is like viewing the world through the eyes of a curious intelligent child. Everything is fresh and interesting. Anything can mean anything. Through this perspective a language is born with new signs and symbols. Trees, insects, flowers, darkness, brightness, fragrances, come together to create a world of fresh meanings. In Sohrab's own words 'eyes must be washed; visions must be reformed.' The deconstruction in Sohrab's poetry comes from this very phrase. Sohrab 'walked the talk': he lived his imaginary world. He died from blood cancer at the age of 52 but left behind an ageless fresh poetry.

The selected passages that follow provide a glance into the world of imagination of a gifted painter-cum-poet. Each passage begins with a short introductory remark that may help the reader connect better with the contents. The titles provided for the poems are inspired by the content of the couplet.

V. *The Meaning of Life*

In the following passage Sohrab defines life with untarnished feelings that are aroused by encountering natural forces and elements. 'The ecstasy of plucking a fruit', 'the majestic look of a tree in the eyes of an insect', 'a moth's experience of darkness', 'the feeling of a migrating bird', 'the echo of a train's whistle', are among expressions that Sohrab uses.

> Life is the ecstasy of a hand,
> While plucking fruit.
> The first taste of a ripened black-fig –
> In the acrid mouth of summer.
> Life is the majestic look of a tree,
> In the eyes of an insect!
> It's a moth's experience,
> In the depth of darkness!
> Life is that strange feeling –
> That's felt by a migrating bird!
> The echo of a train's whistle,
> In the ears of a sleeping bridge! ...

Life is like viewing a garden,
From the sealed window of a plane!
And the exciting news of a rocket,
Being launched into space.
Life is touching the solitude of the moon –
And smelling a flower in another planet.[40]

VI. *The Magic of Sound*

In the following passage Sohrab builds creative expressions by using sound as a medium to connect with realities that are usually experienced visually. Expressions such as 'breathing sound of garden', 'coughing sound of light', 'sneezing sound of water', give a surrealistic edge to this poetic passage. And interestingly, all such expressions are in relation to natural phenomena.

I hear the breathing sound of garden,
And that of darkness, descending from a leaf.
And the coughing sound of light,
Heard from behind the trees.
I hear the sneezing sound of water –
From every crack in the rocks,
And the song of a swallow bird,
Dripping down from the ceiling of spring.[41]

VII. *Footsteps of Faith*

Sound, in the passage below, is again the main sense of communication with nature. Sohrab encourages his reader to face their surroundings through the vibration of air. 'Blowing whisper of matter', 'footsteps of

---

[40] Sohrāb Sepehrī, *Hasht Ketab*. Eight books (Tehran: Tahuri Publication, 1366 Sh/ 1987), 290. For the original Persian couplets see Appendix 26.
[41] Sohrāb Sepehrī, *Hasht Ketab*, 286. For the original Persian couplet see Appendix 27.

faith', 'melody of raindrops', 'sad tune of adolescence', 'song of pomegranate orchards', 'shattering sound of the glass of happiness', 'sound of papers shredded into pieces', 'resonating melody of wind', 'rhythmic pulse of flowers' are innovative expressions, a fresh departure from traditional symbolism used in classical Persian poetry.

> I hear the blowing whisper of Matter,
> And the footsteps of faith –
> moving in the alley of desire.
> And I hear the melody of raindrops –
> On the wet eyelids of love.
> I hear the sad tune of adolescence –
> Played over the song of pomegranate orchards.
> And I hear when the glass of happiness shatters –
> In the heart of night!
> The sound of the paper of beauty –
> That's shredded into pieces.
> And the resonating melody of wind –
> That constantly fills and empties the bowl of melancholy I am
> close to the beginning of the earth,
> The rhythmic pulse of flowers – I feel,
> And I'm aware of water's wet fate,
> And of tree's Green Habit.[42]

VIII. Hearing the Moon

Hearing is once again the medium by which Sohrab encounters nature. 'Remotest bird singing', 'loudest branches of the season', 'hearing the moon', are fresh and pleasant expressions.

> Listen!
> The remotest bird is singing!

---

[42] Sohrāb Sepehrī, *The Water's Footfall: Selected Poems*, Modern Persian Poetry, trans. Ismail Salami & Abbas Zahedi (Tehran: Zabankadeh Publication, 1382 Sh/2004), 35. For the original Persian couplet see Appendix 28.

The night is pure, plain and vast.
Even the geranium flowers,
And the loudest branches of the season –
hear the moon![43]

IX. *Being a Muslim*

Sohrab's imagination flies in a galaxy with no boundary. He presents tangible examples from nature to introduce abstract religious concepts, and substitutes natural elements for religious items and rituals. For instance, 'rose', which is a familiar symbol of the absolute grace and beauty of the beloved, is presented as the *qiblah*—the sacred direction in which all Muslims of the world face toward and pray five times a day. The 'prayer mat' is compared to a flowing stream that takes the worshiper on a journey of purification. The 'ablution' is metaphorically explained as an action of opening new windows to another realm. Prayer's ritual bowing (*rukū'*) that is supposed to show one's obedience to God is introduced as 'bowing to light'—referring to the Qur'anic verse that 'God is the light of the heavens and the earth.'[44] 'Prostration' (*sujūd*) is yet another ritual where the worshipper touches the forehead to the ground. Sohrab mentions prostrating on a grass field, an expression of being united with nature. This brings to mind another Qur'anic verse that 'whatever exists in the heavens and the earth glorifies the God Almighty.'[45] Furthermore, Sohrab compares pure and selfless worship to a clear surface or mass; he states that in his prayers 'the moon and rainbow flow', and 'rocks are visible', and that the 'particles of his prayers glow'.

---

[43] Sohrāb Sepehrī, *Hasht Ketab*, 231. For the original Persian couplet see Appendix 29.

[44] Qur'an, 24: 35.

[45] Qur'an, 62:1.

A Muslim, I am!
A rose, my qiblah,
A spring, my prayer-mat.
With the heartbeat of windows,
I take my ablution.
To light I bow,
And on the grass fields I prostrate.
And in my prayers –
Flows the moon, flows the rainbow!
And through my pure prayers –
Rocks are visible,
As all particles of my prayers glow.[46]

At a first encounter with Sohrab's poems, the reader can immediately sense a strong presence of nature—forces and elements alike. While some of his expressions are simple and child-like, other ones appear complex and sophisticated. In his poems, the mind of a philosopher and the language of a naïve artist are masterly combined, creating a surreal space full of fresh idioms that stimulates the imagination of the reader. Simple expressions such as 'tasting a ripened fig', as well as complex ones like 'coughing sound of light' and 'sad tune of adolescence' give his poems a contemporary edge.

In some passages Sohrab emphasizes a single sense—sound, for instance—and channels various senses through it. In another passage he introduces abstract concepts in visual terms. When Sohrab talks about his pure prayer, he presents himself as a man of faith; he resorts to a symbolic language rooted in nature to express religious devotion. Introducing 'the rose' as his meditative focus in worship, or expressing his devotion to Light in the ritual bowing, comparing the 'prayer mat' to a 'flowing stream', or explaining the ritual prostration as becoming

---

[46] Sohrāb Sepehrī, *Hasht Ketab*, 272. For the original Persian couplet see Appendix 30.

united with the grass-field shows how his imagination flew freely in the cosmos to find novel expressions.

Conclusion

A study of the nature in the works of Persian poets shows that the natural world is studied and respected as a book of wisdom. Nature helps the poets and their readers to reach a degree of self-realization that is believed, in a religious context, to be the corner-stone for God-realization. Appreciation for nature in Persian classical poetry has a language of romantic religiosity, perhaps because God—the Ultimate Beloved—presents Himself through natural forces and elements. Appreciation for nature's endless beauty has also a strong presence in Persian poetry.

Reading through love poems by the classical poets, one can be confused as to whether the poet is expressing his feelings for a charming, beautiful girl, or whether he using romantic language as devotional expressions addressed to God. The answer to this fundamental question is to be found in the perception of two realms: Love and Nature. On the one hand the experience of love was considered as a prerequisite for spiritual growth, and on the other hand, natural elements and forces were seen as conscious entities. We, the authors of this essay, feel that such expressions are not merely metaphorical. Life experience, supported by scientific experiments, gives proof of a reciprocal relation between human beings and the life that surrounds them—vegetable as well as animal. Human affection for nature transforms human actions, and nature's responses often appear in its manifestations. Gardeners and animal-lovers have their first-hand experience of this reality. The classical poets called this mutual relation Love. This very world-view has led to a sense of love and respect for, and protection of nature. And since the creation is regarded as a divine artefact, a profound love-affair with the natural world increases the human capacity to attain to the self-revelation of God through nature.

With the passage of time over a millennium, modes of poetic expression evolved alongside other aspects of life. From the twentieth century onwards, we come across a new trend of modern poetry that is very different from the classical, at least from a formalistic standpoint. Modern poetry is from one point of view an extension of the classical trend, and from another perspective a rebellious reaction to it. Deconstruction of the traditional forms along with fresh expressions have given contemporary poetry a new edge. While poetry-loving people have great admiration for their rich old heritage, they have also developed a taste for the new.

Hafez Shirazi and Sohrab Sepehri, while being seven hundred years apart, are inspiring poets that live side by side in the contemporary arena of literature. Hafez's poetry is nostalgic. It is like a treasure that carries the essence of classical poetry in a most refined language. In his metaphorical expressions one can sense a mystical interpretation of nature and love, in a language that is still adored. He has a macro-view of the universe and uses symbolic elements that have deep roots in Persian art and literature. The sun, the moon, fragrance of the morning breeze, cypress tree, rose and nightingale, are familiar metaphorical expressions used by Hafez that appeal to the almost every single reader of Persian poetry.

Sohrab's report of nature is, however, is very different from that of Hafez. He looked at the same nature, but in a different light. His love-affair with nature is very personal. The symbols and metaphors used by Sohrab are not only different from the classical poets, but even not similar to the poems of his own contemporary fellows. He breaks the boundaries of senses, talking about the sad music of adolescence, the heartbeat of a window, or the rhythmic pulse of flowers. He combines elements of nature in his own unique composition. His poems resemble, metaphorically speaking, abstract or surreal paintings. He arranges the content of an old treasure and displays it in a newly designed chest that appeals to the contemporary audience. In his symbolic language one can sense a strong individuality—a bold quality of the modern age.

A simple formalistic treatment of their poems may present Hafez as a representative of Persian poetry's glorious past, while Sohrab can be viewed as rebellious to traditional values, a man who broke ties with ancestral customs to establish himself as someone independent and different. Despite their formalistic differences, Sohrab can, however, also be studied as a poet who gave new forms to existing contents. He was a child of a new era, and displayed it with a great charm. Readers of this essay may see it as a brief account of nature-oriented expressions in Persian poetry played in fast-forward mode.

APPENDIXES

Appendix 1
به جهان خرم از آنم که جهان خرم از اوست
عاشقم بر همه عالم که همه عالم از اوست

Appendix 2
تسبیح گوی او نه بنی آدمند و بس
هر بلبلی که زمزمه بر شاخسار کرد

Appendix 3
از آن جنبش که در نشو نبات است
درختان را و مرغان را حیات است
درخت افکن بود کم زندگانی
به درویشی کشد نخجیربانی

Appendix 4

ما درخت افکن نه‌ایم آنها گروهی دیگرند

با وجود صد تبر یک شاخ بی بر نشکنیم

Appendix 5

چرخ بزرگوار یکی لشکری بکرد

لشکرش ابر تیره و باد صبا نقیب

نفاط برق روشن و تندرش طبل زن

دیدم هزار خیل و ندیدم چنین مهیب

آن ابر بین، که گرید چون مرد سوگوار

و آن رعد بین، که نالد چون عاشق کئیب

Appendix 6

فرو بارید بارانی ز گردون

چنان چون برگ گل بارد به گشن

و یا اندر تموزی مه ببارد

جراد منتشر بر بان و برزن

Appendix 7

اگر این آسمان عاشق نبودی

نبودی سینه او را صفایی

وگر خورشید هم عاشق نبودی

نبودی در جمال او صفایی

زمین و کوه اگر نه عاشق اندی

نرستی از دل هردو گیاهی

Appendix 8

ندیدم خوشتر از شعر تو حافظ

به قرآنی که اندر سینه داری

Appendix 9

خوشا شیراز و وضع بی مثالش

خداوندا نگه دار از زوالش

Appendix 10

بلبل به شاخ سرو به گلبانگ پهلوی

می خواند دوش درس مقامات معنوی

Appendix 11

گلعذاری ز گلستان جهان ما را بس

زین چمن سایه آن سرو روان ما را بس

Appendix 12

بنشین بر لب جوی و گذر عمر ببین

کاین اشارت ز جهان گذران ما را بس

Appendix 13

نقد بازار جهان بنگر و آزار جهان

گر شما را نه بس این سود و زیان ما را بس

Appendix 14

یار با ماست چه حاجت که زیادت طلبیم

دولت صحبت آن مونس جان ما را بس

Appendix 15

حافظ از مشرب قسمت گله ناانصافیست

طبع چون آب و غزلهای روان ما را بس

Appendix 16

درخت دوستی بنشان که کام دل به بار آرد

نهال دشمنی برکن که رنج بی‌شمار آرد

Appendix 17

شب صحبت غنیمت دان که بعد از روزگار ما

بسی گردش کند گردون، بسی لیل و نهار آرد

Appendix 18

بهار عمر خواه ای دل و گرنه این چمن هر سال

چو نسرین صد گل آرد بار و چون بلبل هزار آرد

Appendix 19

در این باغ از خدا خواهد دگر پیرانه سر حافظ

نشیند بر لب جویی و سروی در کنار آرد

Appendix 20

نفس باد صبا مشک فشان خواهد شد

عالم پیر دگرباره جوان خواهد شد

Appendix 21

ارغوان جام عقیقی به سمن خواهد داد

چشم نرگس به شقایق نگران خواهد شد

Appendix 22

این تطاول که کشید از غم هجران بلبل

تا سراپرده گل نعره زنان خواهد شد

Appendix 23

گل عزیز است غنیمت شمریدش صحبت

که به باغ آمد از این راه و از آن خواهد شد

Appendix 24

جمله ی اعضای عالم در جهان

با تو می گویند روزان و شبان

ما سمیعیم و بصیریم و هشیم

با شما نامحرمان ما خامشیم

Appendix 25

عاشقی گر زین سر و گر زان سر است

عاقبت ما را بدان سر رهبر است

Appendix 26

زندگی جذبه ی دستی است که می چیند.

زندگی نوبر انجیر سیاه، در دهان گس تابستان است.

زندگی، بعد درخت است به چشم حشره.

زندگی تجربه ی شب پره در تاریکی است.

زندگی حس غریبی است که یک مرغ مهاجر دارد.

زندگی سوت قطاری است که در خواب پلی می پیچد.

زندگی دیدن یک باغچه از شیشه ی مسدود هواپیما است.

خبر رفتن موشک به فضا

لمس تنهایی ماه

فکر بوییدن گل در کره ای دیگر!

Appendix 27

من صدای نفس باغچه را می شنوم

و صدای ظلمت را، وقتی از برگی می ریزد

و صدای، سرفه ی روشنی از پشت درخت،

عطسه ی آب از هر رخنه ی سنگ،

چکچک چلچله از سقف بهار

Appendix 28

من صدای وزش ماده را می شنوم،

و صدای کفش ایمان را در کوچه ی شوق.

صدای باران را، روی پلک تر عشق،

صدای موسیقی غمناک بلوغ،

روی آواز انارستان ها

و صدای متلاشی شدن شیشه ی شادی در شب،

پاره پاره شدن کاغذ زیبایی،

پر و خالی شدن کاسه ی غربت از باد.

من به آغاز زمین نزدیکم.

نبض گل ها را می گیرم.

آشنا هستم با، سرنوشت تر آب، عادت سبز درخت.

Appendix 29

گوش کن! دورترین مرغ جهان می خواند.

شب سلیس است، و یکدست، و باز.

شمعدانی ها

و صدادارترین شاخه ی فصل، ماه را می شنوند

Appendix 30

من مسلمانم:

قبله ام یک گل سرخ،

جانمازم چشمه، مُهرم نور.

دشت سجاده ی من.

من وضو با تپش پنجره ها می گیرم.

در نمازم جریان دارد ماه، جریان دارد طیف.

سنگ از پشت نمازم پیداست:

همه ذرات نمازم متبلور شده است.

5

Creation as a Divine Revelation in Judaism: Love of Nature as a Way to Love God

Naftali Rothenberg

Introduction

Sublime descriptions of nature abound in all canonical Jewish literature. This is particularly evident in the great book of faith, *Psalms*, which thrives in experiences of standing before God through admiration of the physical world. In the canonical love song, the *Song of Songs*, images of the beauty of the landscape, animals and plants serve as a background for the longing of its heroes to be united in their love. Descriptions of nature are also prominent in the book of *Job*, which discusses the relationship between the Creator and His creatures. Job's companions see creation as an expression of God's grace. These descriptions are intended to glorify the Creator through admiration for His actions, admiring creation itself. Rabbinic commentators expand on the importance of nature-knowledge, appreciation of creation and creatures, and studying the laws of nature as a way to know and love God. Nature is an expression of God, of His wisdom, power and beauty. It is an expression of God's virtues and above all His grace and love.

These are common starting points for mystical interpretation, especially for the foundations of panentheism within it,[1] but perhaps

---

[1] An approach that was founded in the Midrash and the Zohar but reached its maturity in the writings of Rabbi Shneur Zalman of Liadi. See Rachel Elior, *The Paradoxical Ascent to God: The Kabbalistic Theosophy of Habad* (Albany: State University of New

surprisingly they also appear in rationalist commentators, who hold a transcendental faith.[2]

The prevailing question in the various schools and theological streams is whether the love of God detached from nature is even possible. The main difference between the various approaches is the extent to which God and the divine can be identified with nature itself. This essay is an attempt to present the way in which different rabbinic schools of thought see the way to implement the commandment to love God and one's fellow through a deep observation of creation and creatures, and through love and responsibility for the environment. It is important to emphasize that these topics are to be found in numerous rabbinic sources in ancient, medieval and modern rabbinical literature. The intention is not to present, within this limited framework, a comprehensive analysis of the relationship to nature and the environment in the rabbinical works, but to describe and demonstrate the main points of their perception, especially in the context of the love of God, creation and creatures. The main discussion here is limited to sources from the Midrash and Talmud and some related key medieval commentators.

Our discussion is not only theoretical, since in rabbinical thought there is no place for a theology detached from actions, from the reality of life, from the *mitzvot* (commandments). To the question, 'How is love for God possible?' the rabbinic answer is: through keeping the *mitzvot*. Indeed, sages established an extensive set of rules defining human responsibility for the environment and its preservation. At the heart of this system are important commandments that can be called: the 'great balances' that moderate human involvement in nature: these are the

---

York Press, 1992), 49–57.
[2] E.g. in Maimonides, *Mishneh Torah, Foundations of the Torah*, 2:2, which will be discussed in detail later.

abstention from work on days of Shabbat (Saturdays) and holidays (two months a year!), the Shemita and Jubilee years, and kosher laws that drastically reduce the food consumption of animals on land and in water. The sages also established a set of rules designed to relate directly to the protection of the environment and nature: these include *bal tashchit* (a blanket ban on destruction), rules for keeping air free from diseases and bad smells, for preserving water sources, for noise prevention, and environmental urban planning in general. A large part of the rules between a person and the land are actually a person's duty towards another person and relationships between people. These rules detail the overall *mitzvah*, the great principle in the Torah 'love your fellow as yourself'.[3] The love of God, the love of nature and the love of one's fellow are united in the fulfilment of these commandments.

The next section in this article deals with the creation of the world. The focus is on the Creator's actions, on his relations with the entire creation and on the creation of Adam within it, while expanding on the complexity that this brings. The following section lays emphasis on God's requirement to 'observe' nature and creatures. Early rabbinical literature speaks of observing creation, admiring nature and appreciating the actions of the Creator. The question as to whether these actions are an expression of love for nature is not explicitly discussed by these sources. In this section, I present two directions of thought, which are not contradictory, for the clarification of this question. In the first, observing and studying nature is a way, indeed, a necessary step to reach love for God. In the second, the love of nature is equivalent to the love of God because the entire creation and every detail within it are identified to one degree or another with the divine Creator. These two sections, interpretive and theoretical, emphasize ideas in early rabbinic literature about the context of the place of the love of nature in the love

---

[3] Leviticus 19:18; Sifra, *Kedoshim* 2:12: 'love your fellow as yourself'; 'Rabbi Akiva says: "This is a great principle in the Torah".'

of God. The final section before my summary discusses the love of the environment and the love of God in practice, by preserving nature and relating its conservation to the *mitzvot* and rules established by the sages.

Creation: 'And God saw that this was good'

God is not revealed in the Hebrew Bible from a discussion or description of divinity itself but from the relationships that depend on Him. That is to say, God is known from descriptions of manifestations mainly in two contexts: God is the Creator, whose divinity is manifested in creation, in nature; and God, who is a Commander, instructs a person to live in the world according to His commandments, to fulfil what is proper and to avoid what is improper. The sages draw our attention to the fact that the mention of creation in the Torah precedes the mention of God's name: 'But for the Unique One of the universe, first He formed and then He was named' and also: 'only after He created the necessities of his world, then He recites His name: [which is why] (בְּרֵאשִׁית בָּרָא) "In the beginning he created" [comes first] and only afterwards (אֱלֹהִים) "God"'.[4] The rabbis[5] present the Creator as one who rejoices in creation as a whole and in the diversity of creatures of all kinds, from plants to living things and human beings, and we read about this in the verse from the Psalms: 'May the glory of the Lord endure forever; may the Lord rejoice in His works'.[6] The detail given to each element of creation, to each created species in itself, enhances its importance and its place in the world.

---

[4] *Bereshit Rabbah* 1:12. All translations from the Mishnah and from Maimonides in this essay, except where noted, are by the author of the essay, using various editions of the original text.
[5] BT *Hullin* 60a
[6] Psalm 104:31.

In the story of creation in Genesis chapter 1, the Creator refers to his actions seven times with appreciation or satisfaction. Six times we read 'and God saw that this was good' and finally, 'and God saw all that He had made, and found it very good' (v. 31). The reference to the Creator is not automatic upon the completion of every step, and it is not repeated at the end of every day during the days of creation. The creation of the heavens and the earth in verse 1 is not yet given the mark of divine appreciation. It only appears after the creation of light: 'God saw that the light was good' (v. 4). The creation of light turns darkness into a positive being by generating the balance between heat and cold that is necessary for the existence of the world and makes it possible to proceed with the rest of creation,[7] plants and animals, and to sustain them after they are created: 'And both (light and darkness) grow the plants and ripen the fruit.'[8] On the second day, the Torah is content with reporting the actions of the Creator without mentioning any divine appreciation. The creation on the third day is twice appreciated by the Creator: at the appearance of the land and the seas in their place and the creation of vegetation. For each of them separately we read: 'and God saw that this was good.' Also, about the creation of the lights on the fourth day it is said 'God saw that it is good'. The same is true of the creation of sea animals and birds on the fifth day and land animals on the sixth day.

To two of the groups of creatures, the Creator adds a similar, but not identical, blessing. With regard to the creatures of the sea, it is said: 'And God blessed them, saying, be fruitful, and multiply, and fill the waters in the seas.' And regarding Adam we read: 'And God blessed them, and God said to them, be fruitful, and multiply, and fill the earth'.

---

[7] The sages differ on the interpretation of the creation process. According to Rabbi Shimon bar Yochai and other sages, the actual creation was not chronological as described in Genesis 1. See: JT *Hagigah* 2:1:17

[8] Bahya ben Asher (1255-1340) on Genesis 1:4. His words are more appropriate for the creation of the lights on the fourth day, verses 14–19.

There is thus an increasing expression of valuation of creation throughout the passage, culminating in 'very good' (v. 31), which can be interpreted in several ways. To simplify the verse, it means that God here expresses appreciation for the entire creation upon its completion. In a more specific way it can be said that the appreciation is given to the creation of Adam. Nevertheless, human beings are complex creatures with other powers, and the sages associate with this phrase the ambivalence that the making of Adam adds to the entire creation:

> Rabbi Nahman said in Rabbi Samuel's name: 'Behold, it was good' refers to the Good Desire; 'and behold, it was very good' refers to the Evil Desire. Can then the Evil Desire be very good? That would be extraordinary! But without the Evil Desire no man would build a house, take a wife and beget children, and would not carry and give (for his living).[9]

This midrash well represents the position that holds that all the qualities and tendencies inherent in a person are meant to serve the appropriate positive action. Even seemingly negative qualities or tendencies have a good purpose, and without these qualities the goal of the entire creation implemented by human beings would not have been achieved: the settlement of the world. The language of the midrash is somewhat problematic, as it retains the negative concept of the 'Evil Desire' while attributing a positive quality to it. Yet, there is no doubt that the midrash expresses an apologetic attitude towards those who take a dichotomous position between qualities that belong only to evil and others that belong only to good. The desire for good and the desire for evil are united in the explanation of the commandment to love God in the Mishnah: 'With all your heart', in your two passions, in a good desire and in a bad desire.'[10] However, it should not be ignored that from the same impulse,

---

[9] *Bereshit Rabah* 9:7. See, for example, *Yalkut Shimoni* on Genesis 2:8.
[10] Mishnah, *Brachot* 9:5

due to the same mental and human strength, a person can act in creation for good or for bad. Perhaps in terms of preserving the environment, things are more complex: the same force that inspires person to build a house, start a family and work for his livelihood, may be destructive to the environment. That is why balance is needed in all human actions, even those whose beginnings are still good, which should be limited in such a way that the creation will not be spoiled, that the environment will be preserved.

In the description of the Garden of Eden in Genesis chapter 2, the scripture refers to the beauty of the plants and the blessing given by the fruits of the tree: 'And the Lord God caused to grow out of the ground every tree that is pleasing to the sight and good for food.' There is also reference to what includes the 'still' part of the creation: 'and the gold of that land is good; there is bdellium and the onyx stone.' Adam was entrusted with guarding the garden and its beauty: 'And the Lord God took Adam and placed him in the Garden of Eden to till it and keep it'. According to some of the main rabbinic thinkers, the Garden of Eden is not in the world to come, or in heaven, is not in a specific 'location' at all, but it is this created world in which we live. In the context of the story of the Garden of Eden in Genesis, it is the defined place where persons are found, since they are not present in the entire world. Hence, human beings' responsibility is for their immediate environment. The existence of the 'Garden of Eden' in this world depends on human behaviour. The human being, for whom the world was created as a paradise, may spoil it, as the Midrash says:

> Look at God's work—for 'who can straighten what He has twisted?' (Ecclesiastes 7:13). When the Blessed Holy One created the first Adam, He took him and led him round all the trees of the Garden of Eden and said to him: 'Look at My works, how beautiful and praiseworthy they are! And all that I have created, it was for you that I created it. Pay attention that you do not corrupt and destroy My world: if you corrupt it, there is no

one to repair it after you.'[11]

There are various references in the sages to the question of what kinds of human behaviour cause corruption and destruction to the world, and they are related to interpretations of Adam's first sin in the Garden of Eden. According to Maimonides,[12] Adam's first sin in the Garden of Eden was a lust for needs. This is the human behavior that is a major cause of the destruction of the environment. Adam was created in the image and likeness of God, perfect and intelligent,[13] and this can be concluded from God's commanding him not to eat from a tree of knowledge of good and evil, for there are no commandments except for those who have intelligence.[14] According to this interpretation, the tree of the knowledge of good and evil was not a specific tree or fruit, but any fruit or grain or vegetable that Adam did not need at that time. He was commanded not to consume anything that he did not need. When the driver for human action was according to his mind, that is, aligned to concepts of truth, the knowledge of good and evil was meaningless to him. As long as Adam chose in accord with truth, the question of good and evil could not arise. But he sinned, avoided listening to his reason, followed the advice of his imagination, and descended to the level of knowledge of good and evil: 'For the tree is good for food and how lustful it is for the eyes...'[15] There is no rational assessment here, but

---

[11] *Kohelet Rabbah* 7:13

[12] Maimonides, *The Guide for the Perplexed*, 1:2; *Eight Chapters*, 8; *Mishneh Torah*, Laws of Teshuva, 5:1; see Naftali Rothenberg, 'Maimonides on Love, Fear, Knowledge and Worship', in I. Refael (ed.), *Sinai* (Jerusalem: Rav Kook Institute, 1986), 56-74 (in Hebrew).

[13] Maimonides, *Mishneh Torah*, Laws of the Foundations of Torah 4:8.

[14] This is Maimonides' preferred view in *The Guide for the Perplexed*. But in *Eight Chapters*, 2 he talks about how the commandments are also related to other parts of the human soul such as emotions. This must be reconciled by distinguishing between the *purpose* of the practical *mitzvot* and the *actual* commandments.

[15] Genesis 3:6

imaginary lust.

From this moment on, there was a fundamental change in his position towards the environment, because it was no longer measured by the concepts of the intellect, or the truth, but by relative concepts of good and bad. After all, not everything that is good for one is also good for others, and different people see evil differently. The punishment is 'measure for measure'. As long as Adam lived under the rule of reason, all physical needs were within the scope of being necessary only for the existence of the body, and he did not consume more than he needed. Such a situation justified the reality of the Garden of Eden: freedom from worrying about physical needs—these were fulfilled automatically. But after he sinned, contrary to the dictates of reason, he lusted after what was not really necessary for his being, because he followed his imagination; thus, it was not appropriate that what he needed should be available to him without making any effort, and therefore there came the 'expulsion from Eden' which was a cancellation of the reality of the Garden of Eden, a reality of 'and eat and live forever'. According to this interpretation, Adam was not expelled from Paradise by God but actually expelled himself. The words of the Torah, 'And the Lord God sent him out of Eden to work the land that he had taken from there. And he drove out the Adam' (Gen. 3:23), can be interpreted as summing up the new situation created as a result of sin.

From then on, human beings must 'work the land he had taken from there'. He is required to make an effort to obtain his living needs, since he does not live according to reason, and in seeking to satisfy his needs, he is compared to the level of animals: 'Adam does not abide in honour; he is like the beasts that perish (Psa. 49:13).' Since Adam was once 'in honour', that is, in the Garden of Eden, but was unable to stay there, he has descended to the rank of beasts. The source of this interpretation, which links the meaning of the verse in the Psalms to the expulsion from

Eden, is in a well-known midrash:

> This is how Adam was compared (to the beasts) when the Holy
> One, blessed be He, said to him: 'Of every tree of the garden you
> shall eat. And from the tree of the knowledge of good and evil
> you shall not eat from it, because in the day you eat from it you
> will die.' Since he ate from it, he was lost. As it is said: 'Adam
> does not abide in honour; he is like the beasts that perish.'[16]

But even in the present situation, after sin and apart from the reality of
the Garden of Eden, not as in the parable of the beasts and in contrast to
the animals, the human being is still unique and special in this world:
'And the Lord God said, "Adam has become as one of his kind,[17]
knowing good and evil, and if he should put forth his hand, and take
also of the tree of life, and eat, and live forever... (Gen. 3:22).' Onkelos
interprets the first part of the verse as saying that the Adam is unique in
the world (in the sense that there is no other species like him), in that his
characteristic is to know how to distinguish between good and evil.[18]
Following Onkelos' interpretation, Maimonides explains that the
intellect is not taken from the Adam. He can still subordinate the
imagination to the mind, and in the world of the relative concepts of
'good' and 'bad' he still has a free choice to choose whatever he wills.
After all, he knows good and evil, and that is his uniqueness. He can
reach out his hand and take from the tree of life, 'and eat and live
forever.' Maimonides interprets the verse as an expression of hope, and
not as an expression of fear like other interpretations and most
translations. The hope is that a person might reach out and eat from the
tree of life, which will give to his or her needs and not beyond them.

---

[16] *Avot D'Rabbi Natan* 1:7; See BT *Sanhedrin* 38b, and other parallels.

[17] The translation here is according to the interpretation of Onkelos and Maimonides.
The common translation is 'as one of ourselves'.

[18] Onkelos on Genesis 3:22.

The expulsion from Eden in general and this interpretation in particular emphasize the connection between the two manifestations of divinity: God the Creator and God the Commander. Human persons are required to consume from creation, from nature, what is necessary for their needs and avoid what is not necessary for their needs. Every human being in this world should strive to return to the Eden, but the realization of this ambition, every step towards the goal, involves a great effort in which persons will consume what is required for their needs and no more than that.

The sages repeat and emphasize the connection between the two manifestations of divinity in the Bible, God as the Creator and God as the Giver of commandments, in the context of the act of creation. For example, there is this source in the *Mishnah*:

> With ten utterances the world was created. And what does this teach, for surely it could have been created with one utterance? But this was so in order to punish the wicked who destroy the world that was created with ten utterances, and to give a good reward to the righteous who maintain the world that was created with ten utterances.[19]

God created the world in utterances like this: 'And God said ...' In the verses about creation in Genesis, the sages count ten sayings of the Creator that bring about creation. The significance of this position is that every element of creation is an expression of God's word. When a person loses the world, harms nature, he harms the word of God and when he preserves the world, sustains it, he preserves and upholds the word of God. The Torah is therefore not satisfied simply with the *mitzvot* that God commands people and their duty to maintain. The Mishnah does not say: 'To be freed from the wicked who transgress the

---

[19] *Mishnah*, *Avot 5:1*, trans. Joshua Kulp, from Sefaria site, https://www.sefaria.org.il/texts.

commandments of God and to give a good reward to the righteous who keep the *mitzvot.*' Rather, it says: 'Who destroy the world that was created ... who maintain the world that was created ...'.

'When I behold Your heavens, the work of Your fingers': observing nature as a way to love God

> ... Examining the creatures and learning from them about the wisdom of the Creator is a duty for us because of the reason and the scriptures and the tradition [the oral Torah]. From what is written, here is what is written (Isaiah 40:26): 'Lift high your eyes and see: Who created these?' and said the devotee (Psa. 8:4): 'When I behold Your heavens, the work of Your fingers, the moon and stars that You set in place.' And the scripture said (Isaiah 40:21): 'Do you not know? Have you not heard? Have you not been told from the very first? Have you not discerned how the earth was founded?'[20]

Bahya ibn Paquda outlines in his book, *Duties of the Heart,* the path to attaining God's wisdom through a gradual process that should bring person to God's love. In the short paragraph quoted above, he summarizes a prevalent approach in the midrashim before him and in those written close to his time and after him, to the role played by the observation of nature in knowing God. It does not mean random exposure of people to the wonders of creation, when they pass by nature and landscape sites. It is about a duty imposed on a human being to study as systematically as possible the laws of nature and its phenomena, for as he put it: 'it is a duty for us because of the reason and

---

[20] Bahya ben Joseph ibn Pakuda (1120-1050), *Duties of the Heart,* Second Treatise on Examination, Chapter 2 (the discussion here is based on the version of the translation into Hebrew from Arabic-Jewish in Yosef Qafiḥ, Bahya ibn Pakuda *Torat Chovot HaLevavot (The Duties of the Heart), a Translation and Interpretation,* (Jerusalem: Yosef Qafiḥ, 1988), 94–103

the scriptures and the tradition.' This obligation stems from reason in the sense that possessors of logic have continually been engaged in observing and studying the laws of nature inherent in all parts and components of creation.[21] But this obligation is not only due to logic, but is also anchored in many verses in the holy scriptures such as the ones he quotes. And finally, he points to the 'tradition': there is nothing new about this duty since it was accepted by our ancient sages and they passed it on to the generations that came after them. For those who refrain from engaging in the wisdom of nature, and from calculations that must be calculated while following the changes in the celestial bodies and their influence on the climate, our sages read the words of the prophet: 'Who, at their banquets, have lyre and lute, timbrel, flute, and wine; but who never give a thought to the plan of the Lord, and take no note of what He is designing' (Isaiah 5:12). That is, they are people who spend their days in idleness and pleasures, ignore and do not see creation and creatures, the wisdom that must be learned from nature and the benefit that can be derived for humans from this wisdom. Our sages in the Talmud see this obligation as a real mitzvah that is considered a significant element in the service of God.[22]

The rabbis usually see this duty, study and practice of wisdom, as an end in itself. However, R. Bahya emphasizes that the purpose is not the attainment of wisdom for its own sake, but love for God. This should also be the motivation of the learner. Observation and study are the way to bond with God. Although the study of natural sciences is a necessary study from the practical point of view, at the same time it is a condition for studying at the higher level what he called the 'higher science' and the 'divine science' which should be studied with love according to the words of our sages in the Talmud.[23] As mentioned, this is the way to

---

[21] Qafiḥ, *Torat Chovot HaLevavot*, p. 99, note 49.

[22] BT *Shabbat* 75a; BT *Eiruvin* 100b.

[23] BT *Nedarim* 62a.

achieve the degree of God's love to which the *Duties of the Heart* outlines the path and which is the culmination of this book.[24]

Psalm 8, from which Bahya ibn Paquda quotes one verse (v. 3), opens and ends with the words: 'O God, our Lord, how majestic is Your name throughout the earth.' In the opening verse, the phrase continues, 'for which You bestow Your magnificence upon the heavens.' The earth, where human beings are, is indeed small compared to the 'heavens', that is compared to the entire universe and the infinite magnificence of God.[25] According to most commentators, the psalm is a call to know God and his greatness through nature, creation, the entire universe, together with a description of person's status as a result of this knowledge of God. As much as the psalmist observes and learns about the entire creation and all its components in detail (v. 3), so he feels how much he does not count, or how unworthy of mention he is (v. 4). And yet in the eyes of God, the human being is considered very important (v. 5): 'And you shall deprive him of a little of [being] God, and you shall adorn him with honor and glory.' The value of the human in the eyes of the Almighty is equal to the entire creation, to all creatures on land and sea. Through the observation and study of nature in its details, a person will be able to say: 'O God, our Lord, how majestic is Your name throughout the earth.'

The analysis of the psalm presented here succinctly, is repeated in many midrashim and in the words of commentators throughout the generations. From those that fell under the eyes of ibn Paquda in his lifetime to those that were written after his time, they continued and expanded the idea of knowing God and the way to love God through the observation of nature, creation and the creatures.

The sages describe a kind of oneness or overlap between the

---

[24] Bahya ibn Pakuda, *The Duties of the Heart*, in the introduction and at length in the Second Treatise on Examination.

[25] Commentary of rabbi David Kimhi (*Radak*) on Psalm 8:2.

created world and the Creator:

> 'And he (Jacob) came upon the place'[26]—Rav Huna says, in the
> name of Rabbi Ami: why do we substitute for the name of the
> Holy Blessed One and use 'Place'? Because God is the Place of
> the world, and the world is not the place of God ... the Holy
> Blessed One is the dwelling of the world and the world is not the
> dwelling of the Holy One.[27]

The world is identical or overlaps with God, but not the other way
around. For God is beyond the world, without attributing meaning to
this 'beyond' or trying to understand it. What is beyond the universe is
also beyond the limits of human understanding and perception. What is
left is for human beings to observe and study the natural phenomena,
the world that coincides with divinity. The ideas were reflected upon in
the Midrash in connection with the narrative of Jacob's ladder and the
revelation of God and the angels to Jacob in that 'place'. The meaning
of the Hebrew words *vayifga Bamakom*, (וַיִּפְגַּע בַּמָּקוֹם) 'and he came upon
the place' are interpreted by the midrash scholars as 'running into the
place' (like 'running into a wall'), and so 'praying to the Place' which
is a designation for God. The meeting with the world, with nature, with
'the place', becomes a meeting with God, who is called 'The Place'
(*hamakom*, הַמָּקוֹם). God's revelation in this verse is not expected and it
surprises Jacob: 'Surely God is present in this place, and I did not know
it' (Gen. 28:16). According to another description in the midrash, the
physical world changes in order to stop Jacob on his way to Haran and
bring him to divine revelation: 'He asked to pass, the whole world
became like a wall before him.'[28] Another interpretation attributes the

---

[26] Genesis 28:11.

[27] *Bereshit Rabbah* 68:9.

[28] Enoch Zundel ben Joseph, *Etz Yosef* (Warsaw, 1883), commentary on *Bereshit Rabbah* 68:9

change to an early setting of the sun that is not the way of nature. The darkness became a barrier on his way and it obliges Jacob to stop and experience the revelation in his dream. He also experiences a personal sunrise that causes him to wake up and complete the internalization of the prophecy with full awareness. Additional readings in the Midrash give nature an experimental dynamic: for example, the several stones he carried to make his bed (two, three, or twelve in number according to different versions in the Midrash) unite into one under his head. Further, the 'contraction of the road'[29] that happened to Jacob between Beer Sheva and Haran, together with Jacob's ladder itself, are said to extend over all lands. In all of these exegeses there is no distinction between the physical world, nature, and the manifestations of divinity in revelation, but they are integrated into each other.[30]

The images of the overlap between the divine presence and the world are not limited to place and time. They are permanent in the entire creation and according to a common concept in the Midrash and among many thinkers, it is God's permanent presence in creation that sustains the world:

> And what did David see in his soul to be giving praise to the Holy One, blessed be He? [David] said: this soul fills the body, as the Holy One, blessed be He fills His world. As it is written: (Jeremiah 23:24): 'Do I not fill both heaven and earth, declares the Lord.' Come, the soul that fills the body, and praise the Holy One, blessed be He, who fills the whole world.[31]

Just as the soul resides in the body and sustains it, God is the soul of the world and the source of its perpetual, unceasing life. Of course, the soul

---

[29] *Kefitzat Haderech* is a term, used in Jewish sources, referring to miraculous travel between two distant places in a brief time.

[30] BT *Sanhedrin* 95b.

[31] *Vayikra Rabbah* 4:8.

itself is also a divine presence in the human being, which is a small world.[32] King David exemplifies the reason for loving God through loving the creation out of praise and gratitude for His presence. A parallel in the *Zohar*[33] to the above quoted midrash establishes the phrase 'There is no space free from God' (Aramaic: לֵית אֲתַר פָּנוּי מִנֵּיהּ — *leit atar pannui minei*). The Zohar emphasizes that there is no place or object, or body or part of the body or any substance in which God is not present or is not connected to. So also, in the 'vacant spaces', or what appear to be so, between the material phenomena. This expression became very common in various schools of thought that developed later and formed the foundation of the theology of most Hasidic schools.[34]

Elsewhere, the Midrash[35] discusses the presence of God in the tabernacle, specifically in the small space between the two cherubim: 'There I will meet with you, and I will impart to you from above the cover, from between the two cherubim that are on top of the Ark of the Covenant, all that I will command you concerning the Israelite people' (Exodus 25:22). God's presence in the tabernacle is not exclusive and does not contradict the fulness of God in the entire world, but rather, it is drawn from it and connected to it. Pointing out God's presence in the limited place in the tabernacle, between the two cherubim, the Midrash expands his presence into the world in general and within humans in particular: 'And let them make Me a sanctuary that I may dwell among them' (Exodus 25:8), 'among them' means precisely 'not only in the

---

[32] *Tikunei Zohar* 101a.

[33] *Tikunei Zohar* 125b.

[34] The phrase *leit atar pannui minei* (there is no space free from God) was given other meanings by different thinkers. See: Joseph Ben-Shlomo, *The Mystical Theology of Moses Cordovero* (Jerusalem: Bialik Institute, 1965), 316–281; Elior, *Paradoxical Ascent*, 47-59, 90–95; Tsippi Kauffman, *In All Your Ways Know Him: The Concept of God and Avodah Be-Gashmiyut in the Early Stages of Hasidism*, (Ramat Gan: Bar-Ilan University Press, 2009), 27–162.

[35] *Tanhuma*, Vayakhel 7.

sanctuary'. The Midrash illustrates this presence in the parable of the cave: 'Like a cave that is on the shore of the sea, the sea raging, the cave is filled and the sea lacks nothing.' The tabernacle is a simile with a cave that is filled with sea water and does not detract from the fullness of the sea itself. The glory of God filled the tabernacle because 'I fill the heavens and the earth' and not the other way around.

These midrashic sources, and many others like them, laid the foundation for immanent, panentheistic, and some would even say pantheistic approaches in Jewish thought that developed over the generations.

The sages connect the worship of God in prayer to the cycles of nature, such as the blessing of the trees for the blossoming in the spring,[36] and to the transitions between day and night. At sunrise, there is thanksgiving for going from darkness to light. Towards the sunset appreciation is expressed for the day that has passed peacefully between sunrise and sunset. In the evening, there is a prayer and a request to pass the hours of darkness in peace.[37] Another popular interpretation attributes the ordering of the three regular daily prayers to the patriarchs, Abraham, Isaac and Jacob, who prayed in the morning, before evening and at night while going out into nature to a place of prayer. With regard to Abraham it is written, 'And Abraham got up early in the morning to the place where he had stood before the Lord' (Genesis 19:27). Regarding Isaac, a prayer is made while walking in the open air, 'And Isaac went out to walk in the field before evening' (Gen. 24:63). And regarding Jacob, 'And he (Jacob) came upon the place [at night]' (Gen. 28:11). Commentary on this verse is discussed at length above.

The Mishnah had already established a special blessing for many of the natural phenomena, for lightning and thunder storms, for seeing the open landscape of mountains, hills, seas and deserts and more:

---

[36] BT *Brachot* 43b.
[37] JT *Brachot* 4:1,7.

On comets, and on earthquakes, and on lightning and on thunder, and on storms, say: 'Blessed [be He] whose strength and might fill the world.' On mountains, and on hills, and on seas, and on rivers, and on deserts say, 'Blessed [be He] who makes the works of the beginning.' R' Yehuda says, 'One who sees the great sea says, "Blessed [is He] who made the great sea", if he only sees it occasionally. On rain and on good news say, 'Blessed be He who is good and does good.'[38]

The determination of these blessings by the sages of the Mishnah were intended to direct the reflective admiration of humans at the impressive sights of nature into praise and thanksgiving to the One who created all of them.

These ideas, which were greatly expanded and developed over the generations by various streams in rabbinic thought, connect the actual worship of God, standing before Him in prayer, with the unmediated presence of humanity and the whole of nature. As we know, this attitude received a practical expression in the ways of worshipping God in the Hasidic movements throughout the ages. An unmediated connection to nature, going out into nature itself, and paying attention to the changes that apply to it, are ways to hold to and love God.

The method by which the way to love God through observing and admiring nature was established in rabbinic thought can be learned from Maimonides' writings and especially from his great halakhic treatise, *Mishneh Torah*.

In his various books, Maimonides dealt extensively with the clarification of the gradual path to the love of God.[39] Sometimes he speaks of love in its highest degree as a quality that only virtuous individuals receive: 'And this virtue [love] is a very great virtue and not

---

[38] Mishnah, *Brachot* 9:2.

[39] For an extensive discussion on the subject in all of Maimonides' writings see: Rothenberg, 'Maimonides on Love', 1986.

every scholar deserves it, and it is the virtue of Abraham our father, whom the Almighty called His beloved, because he served Him out of love only'.[40] However, the commandment 'and you shall love the Lord your God' (Deut. 6:5) is also said to apply to everyone and is not a matter for virtuous individuals only. Maimonides ends the discussion of love in the *laws of Teshuva* with a halakhic conclusion:

> Love will be according to understanding: if [understanding] is slight, [love] will be slight, and if [understanding] is great, [love] will be great. Therefore, a person must set aside [time] for himself to understand and grasp the wisdom and understanding that his Creator provides him according to each person's ability to understand and grasp, as we have explained in *Laws of the Foundations of Torah*.

These words, 'Wisdom and understanding', are expressions which include observation of nature but also abstract study at the highest levels. In the *Laws of the Foundations of Torah*, Maimonides first presents love as an activating force arising from study of creation and its wonders and leading a person to yearn for knowledge:

> A. This God, honoured and mighty, it is our duty to love and fear; as it is said (Deut. 6:5): 'Thou shalt love the Lord, thy God', and it is further said (Deut. 6:13): 'Thou shalt fear the Lord, thy God'.
>
> B. And what is the way that will lead to the love of Him and the fear of Him? When a person contemplates His great and wondrous works and creatures and from them obtains His wisdom which is incomparable and infinite, he will immediately love Him, praise Him, glorify Him, and long with an exceeding desire to know His great Name; as David said [Psalm 42:2]: 'My soul thirsts for God, for the living God'. And when he contemplates these same matters, immediately he will withdraw frightened, and realize that he is a small creature, humble and

---

[40] Maimonides, *Mishneh Torah*, Laws of Teshuva 10:2.

obscure, endowed with slight and slender intelligence, standing in the presence of Him who is perfect in all knowledge. And so, David said [Psalm 8:3–4]: 'When I behold Your heavens, the work of Your fingers, what is man that Thou art mindful of him?' In accordance with these ideas, I shall explain some significant rules of the Works of the Sovereign of the Universe, that they may serve the intelligent individual as a door to the love of God, as our sages[41] have remarked in connection with the theme of the love of God: 'through this study you will know the One who said and the world was.'[42]

For the image of the desire and love that the contemplation of creation and the creatures evokes towards God, Maimonides quotes a part of a verse in Psalm 42. However, to understand the context, two verses must be read in their entirety: 'As the hart pants after the water brooks, so pants my soul after You, O God. My soul thirsts for God, for the living God. When shall I come and see the face of God?' The parable is the thirst of the animal that seeks to satisfy its thirst in the stream. This example is interesting because the verse does not speak of the spectacular sight of herds going down to the spring or stream and drinking from its waters. The parable of nature is not romantic or idyllic but presents drought, dryness, lack of water, and the wandering of the ram along the stream to quench his thirst for living water. This is a natural phenomenon of difficulty, and it is a metaphor for the suffering of human being, for the suffering of exile, and for the longing of sufferers 'for the living God', for the God of all living, for the Creator. This desire is a seeking to come into an unmediated relationship with God, like the actual contact between the ram and the water: 'When will I come and see the face of God?' In contrast to the harsh reality, the destruction and dryness in Psalm 42, the prophet Isaiah describes the redemption, the return of the exiles, the poor and the destitute, together

---

[41] *Sifrei* on Deut. 11:22.

[42] Maimonides, *Mishneh Torah*, Laws of the Foundations of Torah 2:1–2.

with the return of the water to the springs, valleys and rivers, and as a result the desert and the prairie become a blooming garden. All this 'so that they may see and know and do and understand together that the hand of God has done this and the Holy One of Israel has created it' (Isaiah 41:17-20). The future redemption is not only the redemption of exiled Israel, but the redemption of the whole of nature, and those who return to Zion see, know, internalize, and educate their new closeness to the Redeemer through the new life awakened in the universe by the Creator.

In these two paragraphs of the *Laws of the Foundations of the Torah*, the connection between love and fear is emphasized. Although each commandment stands on its own, a commandment to love God and a commandment to fear Him, they have a common origin: fear is the result of the same observation of nature and the same deep study that lead to love. And because one path leads to both love and fear, Maimonides presents them together. However, in these words, a fundamental difference between love and fear is also evident: love is seemingly disconnected from human's status vis-a-vis the Creator; it is an awakening caused by observing nature and marveling at the actions of the Creator, and it is a great desire for the knowledge of the great God. On the other hand, fear is related to human person's status and condition in the face of the power of creation: 'And when he contemplates these same matters, immediately he will withdraw frightened, and realize that he is a small creature, humble and obscure'. In the psalmist's words, 'Your heavens, the work of Your fingers' arouses the desire to know God, which means to love God, but at the same time teach the human being's smallness and nothingness[43]: 'what

---

[43] Rabbi Yosef Ibn Caspi (1340-1280), one of the most important commentators of the Maimonides, even goes further than Maimonides on the purpose of creation and the fact that every creature has a purpose for itself (as in Maimonides, T*he Guide for the Perplexed* 3:25). Ibn Caspi wants to see the human being as one creature among all

is man that Thou art mindful of him?'. It is possible that Maimonides' careful wording stems from his desire to go against naturalistic concepts that, according to him, could lead to idolatry. He also makes sure to explain that the fear of exaltation does not come from a comparison of the status of human with the status of God (an impossible comparison), but rather from seeing the status of humanity in the face of the greatness of the universe. Fear is therefore the result of a proper self-esteem of human beings and knowledge of their place in the world, first in relation to the natural world, and then, as their achievement develops along with the deepening of their knowledge, in relation to the metaphysical world as a whole, the world of abstract rational thought.

A few chapters later, Maimonides repeats and explains that love is the result of study, but here—unlike earlier—it is not study of nature and its manifestations, but study of the narrative of *Merkavah*[44] and the narrative of *Bereshit* (Creation), which are apparently, according to his method, high forms of metaphysical study. This study is, however, not completely abstract and not disconnected from the natural creation and its meaning. Such a high study brings love in its wake: 'He adds love to the Place (*Hamakom*, God), and his soul thirsts and his flesh aches to

---

the others, not as the ruler of nature but as part of the environment. See further: Hannah Kasher, 'For the Tree of the Field is Man: On the Ecology in the Thought of Rabbi Joseph ibn Kaspi', in Naftali Rothenberg (ed.), *Wisdom by the Week* (New York: Van Leer and Yeshiva University Press, 2011), 585–95.

[44] *Mase Merkava* ('The Work of the Chariot') is a term for esoteric literature, related to Jewish or universal secret teachings. Some interpreters connect with unique Jewish mystical literature, such as the Book of Creation; others connect it with literature and philosophy which deal with the essence of God. The word 'chariot' (in the sense of a 'seat') originally referred to the chariot of the cherubim from the Temple; the cherubim were considered to carry God above them. Later, the borrowed word refers to God's 'place' or throne. Maimonides, who did not use mystical terminology, mentions it as a superior form of metaphysical study, considering that who are skilled in it have a very high level of intelligence and education.

love the Place, blessed be He.'[45] Not only the soul but also the body, the flesh, expresses this strong desire. When referring to the midrashim, I dealt with the identification of God with 'the place' in the context of the story of Jacob's ladder. The presence of God in the world is imaged as being like the soul present in the body, and I mentioned the well-known assertion in the Zohar that God is everywhere in the material world. These sources show an approach that assumes a certain overlap between God and nature. God is present in all of creation and beyond. It does not seem likely to me that we should attribute such a view to Maimonides. He does use the phrase 'the Place' here, and he may be using it as one of the common pronouns that appear in the language of sages; nonetheless he does not go so far as to adopt the images of the midrashim. He sees physical manifestations of divinity to be the result of human perception and the inability to speak in abstract terms.[46]

In an attempt to understand the approach to the physical nature in the rabbinical thought, I have highlighted several main points:

1. God appears in the Hebrew Bible as a Creator and a Commander. The sages make a fundamental connection between these two appearances.

2. God expresses his love in the act of creation, appreciates every detail in the creatures and is joyful in the nature revealed in the universe.

3. Creation is the practical, present and continuous revelation of the Creator. According to a common concept in the Midrash, God fills the entire universe. Therefore, every manifestation of nature represents the divine or at least is related to God.

4. Observing creation and creatures and admiring nature is the way to know God and to love Him.

These principles are ideas, thoughts and beliefs. In their own way, the sages are not satisfied with thoughts, but offer a detailed practical framework of *mitzvot* and binding rules of conduct, which are supposed

---

[45] Maimonides, *Mishneh Torah, Laws of the Foundations of Torah*, 4:12.
[46] Ibid., 1:8–9.

to outline the relationship between human beings and nature. However, as with all other *mitzvot*, a person must follow these commandments and rules of conduct, regardless of whether he accepts the beliefs and ideas described in this part of the essay.

'To till it and to keep it': Preserving the environment in Halakhah

The practical expression of the love of nature, creation, as a way to love God includes an extensive set of *mitzvot* from the Torah as well as regulations and rules established by the rabbis.[47] Three broad areas in Halakhah are the 'great balances': Shabbat observance, Shemita and Jubilee, and the laws of kosher food. Observance of these *mitzvot* contributes to a constant, day-to-day balance between human actions to satisfy human needs and the preservation of the environment. Other laws and rules relate to the quality of the environment and its preservation: the planning of cities in Talmudic law, preventing air pollution, maintaining water quality, and finally an extensive prohibition from the Torah on desecration.[48]

Before proceeding to a more detailed explanation, I offer a preliminary observation. The move presented here is not inconsistent with those who oppose giving any reasons for the commandments. Those who believe that a 'utilitarian' presentation of the *mitzvot* harms

---

[47] The meaning of the Hebrew concept 'halakhah' is the Jewish religious law. It is based on the oral Torah and its interpretation of the *mitzvot* of the written Torah. The halakhic library begins with the works compiled during the Tannaim period (Mishnah, Tosefta, Midrash Halakhah and more), the Babylonian and Jerusalem Talmuds, the extensive halakhic literature that developed in their wake, mainly based on the rabbis' *responsa* from that time to the present day. This includes the customs and traditions established for generations in the various communities around the world.

[48] For an initial attempt at research on these topics, see: Manfred Gerstenfeld, *Judaism, Environmentalism and the Environment* (Jerusalem: Jerusalem Institute for Israel Studies and Rubin Mass Publishing, 1998), mainly 28-110.

the pure worship of God may criticize the argument that they contribute to the care of the environment. These are of course legitimate critiques. But it is still possible to relate environmental issues to the *mitzvot*, not as the *purpose* of the commandments and laws described here, but as a factual *result* of them.

At the centre was placed Adam: 'Everything I created, I created for you!'[49] In another significant source, the Sages express this concept in vivid images: 'The first Adam was from the end of the world to its end ...',[50] and 'The first Adam was from the earth to the sky'. Human beings themselves must be participants in this recognition: 'therefore, each and every person must say: "for me the world was created".'[51] However, one should not make the mistake of reading these rabbinical phrases as an anthropocentric position that stands on its own. The world remains the world of God: 'Let your mind not spoil and destroy *my world*',[52] says the Creator. It is as if God says, 'The fact that I created the world for you is not a privilege but a responsibility': 'And the Lord God took Adam and placed him in the Garden of Eden to *till it* [work] and to *keep it*' (Gen. 2:15). The meaning of Adam's central place in the world is his responsibility to creation and creatures, to nature.[53] He is to work six days a week while taking care of the environment. Beyond that, just as God created the world in six days and rested on the seventh day, so He gives human beings six days 'to till' whereas on the seventh day they will refrain from interfering with the physical world. According to the words of the Midrash, 'To till it, "six days you shall work" (referring to Exodus 20:8). And to keep it, "Keep the Shabbat day" (referring to

---

[49] *Kohelet Rabbah* 7:13

[50] BT *Sanhedrin* 38b; BT *Hagigah* 12a.

[51] *Mishnah Sanhedrin* 4:5

[52] *Kohelet Rabbah* 7:13.

[53] Naftali Rothenberg, '"To Till it and to Keep It". On Ecology and Everyday Life', in Sarah Hobson and Laurence David Mee (eds.), *The Black Sea in Crisis* (London: World Scientific Publishing, 1999), 147–51.

Deuteronomy 5:11): And likewise, it is to work on the six days of activity and to keep it on the Shabbat day on which there is no work.'[54]

To the six days of creation, the Torah adds the seventh day.[55] It is an unnecessary day in the context of the creation story. Creation is completed by 'the day after', the seventh day on which nothing was formed: 'And on the seventh day God finished His work which He had made; and He rested on the seventh day from all His work which He had made' (Gen. 2:2). Adam was created on the sixth day male and female. The world and everything created so far within it is under their control. Later, the Torah also gave to human beings the day on which creation was completed, the Shabbat, to sanctify it, and rest on it.

The Shabbat is mentioned in the Torah in two ways: as a social value on the one hand, and as a severe prohibition of work on the other. While the Shabbat social idea is quite acceptable, it is difficult for many to understand and accept the prohibitions of different actions or activities. As a day of social rest, a day of refraining from human work for a living without prohibitions that limit leisure and recreation, it is a very acceptable idea. This situation results from a deep gap between the social understanding of the Shabbat, with a perception of the weekend as an important element of 'leisure' on the one hand, and the essence of the Shabbat as the foundation for the prohibition of work on the other. This work is not *any* activity, but a creative skill that has an expression or projection onto materials, an action that creates a change through a material or in a material. The result of this distinction is that there are cases where an action that involves great effort is not prohibited, while an action that is done with no effort at all, but the result of which is physical intervention in materiality, will be prohibited. The practical

---

[54] Chizkuni version of midrash *Yalkut Shimoni*, on Genesis 2:15

[55] For more see: Naftali Rothenberg, 'Shabbat UMishkan: Melekhet Makhshevet Asrah Torah', in N. Rothenberg (ed.), *Potchim Shavua* (Tel Aviv: Yediot-Sfarim and Van Leer Institute Publishers, 2001), 243–55 (in Hebrew).

result of the halakhic position is the obligation to avoid, for example, the use of the vehicles, and the opening of factories and office buildings, on fifty-two Shabbats and eight more holidays, for a total of about two months a year. This is a kind of 'strike' of the biggest polluters. On the Shabbat and the holiday, every week, throughout the entire year, a Jew is required to cease his involvement with nature or at least reduce it to the minimum necessary for his existence. The prohibitions of work on Shabbat therefore create a great balance between 'to till it' and 'to keep it.' This illustrates the practical significance of preserving the environment in Halakhah, a praxis beyond the concepts presented in the earlier part of this essay.[56]

The Shemita and Jubilee years also meant to balance human involvement in nature. The Torah commanded a 'general strike' from field work every seventh year, which is the Shemita year, and for two consecutive years after seven Shemitas, in the forty-ninth year and in the Jubilee year, which is the fiftieth year (Lev. 25:1–13). There is no doubt that this is one of the most difficult commandments to implement and was a great and difficult challenge to maintain.[57] These difficulties were foreseen in advance and the Torah indicates the failure to observe the Shemita as one of the main causes of the punishment of the exile (Lev. 26:34-35).

The point of the Shemita does not only concern the reduction of work on the soil and less utilization of the fields. No less than that, its concern is the recession of competition, a deliberate slowing down of economic activity. In addition to the prohibitions of soil-work of all kinds, the Torah artificially sets a finishing line for the economic race:

---

[56] For a call by a Christian bishop for a re-examination of the Shabbat by the church, see: Richard J. C. Chartres, 'Sacrifice and Covenant, Prometheus and Noah', in Hobson and Mee (eds.), *Black Sea in Crisis*, 60–64.

[57] Tosefta, *Shabbat* 2:21: 'Israelites were suspected of [not keeping] the seventh year (Shemita) and not suspected of [not keeping] the Shabbats.' See also: BT *Gittin* 54a.

once every six years there is to be an expropriation of the concepts of ownership for one year. It is a year whose value-message calls us to live as human beings and as a society while taking into account the weak others who have not yet won the race for possessions. It is a year in which everyone has equal rights in obtaining their needs: rich and poor, Jew and Gentile. 'And there will be the earth-Shabbat. Even though I forbade it for you, I did not forbid it for eating ... but rather *that you shall not treat it as an owner*, but *all shall be equal in it.*'[58] To this must be added the *mitzvah* of withholding money,[59] a prohibition on the lender from collecting debts that are due but are not to be paid back because the Shemita has cancelled the debt. This *mitzvah* was also intended to reduce competitiveness in the economy. Although in practice the *mitzvah* did not achieve its goal and despite explicit warnings in the Torah (Deut. 15:19), people refrained from granting loans to the needy near the year of Shemita. To oppose this, Hillel amended the Prozbul regulation,[60] which allowed lenders to circumvent the *mitzvah* of depositing funds.

Excess competitiveness in the economy creates a rush of needs; people consume beyond what they need, and damage the environment beyond the necessity of human existence. The abstention from the use of land and money are commandments that were originally intended to contribute to the balance between 'to till it' and 'to keep it.'

The third group of laws within the framework of the 'great balances' between human needs and the preservation of nature concerns kosher food laws. The Torah permitted people to eat meat. Permitted, we note, not recommended (Deut. 12:20). The commentators explain that in the desert it was forbidden to eat meat except as part of the

---

[58] Rashi, Leviticus 25:6.
[59] Deuteronomy 15:2; Mishnah *Shevi'it* 10:1.
[60] Mishnah *Shevi'it* 10:3-8

sacrifices.[61] When they entered the land and settled there, the Torah allowed eating meat in moderation, not as the main meal but as part of it.[62] However, the greater restriction is on the species of animals and birds that allowed to be eaten. Only a very small part of the terrestrial animal world was allowed. That too, was to be under strict conditions for slaughtering the animals and preparing them. As for the millions of sea creatures, the allowed percentage is much smaller and only from fish and only from those that have fins and scales. Human intervention in nature as a result of what people were allowed to eat from the animal world is minimalistic. To this must be added the prohibition of cruelty to animals,[63] and of course the prohibition of eating an animal organ (when the animal is still alive).[64]

The effect of the commandments, called here the 'great balances' on the prevention of damage to the environment, is significant and wide. However, no less interesting, and perhaps surprising, is the group of laws developed by the rabbis concerning urban environmental planning. The principles underlying these laws are also true to a large extent for modern urban planning. The foundation is consideration for others, maintaining the quality of life and the health of the residents.

Already in the Mishnaic Halakhah, the Sages establish some clear principles for urban planning. The first principle is the removal of industry to a defined industrial area outside the city. This includes manufacturing processes that give off a bad smell such as leather processing (tannery),[65] and kilns for the production of lime and other

---

[61] *Sifrei* on Deuteronomy 12:20; BT *Hullin* 17b.

[62] *Sifrei* ibid; BT *Hullin* 84a

[63] Exodus 23:5, of which see the interpretations: BT *Baba Metzia* 31a; *Tur Shulchan Aruch* and *R'ama Hoshen Mishpat* 272:9.

[64] Genesis 9:10; see Maimonides, *Kedushah*, Laws of Forbidden Foods, Chapter 5; *Shulchan Aruch Yore Dea* 62.

[65] Mishnah, *Bava Batra* 2:9

materials that raise smoke,[66] cause damage to health and sometimes cause aesthetic damage, because the smoke blackens the walls of houses. The smoke removal range is set to a distance at which no suffering will be caused to people such as eye pain or other. The thresher must be kept away because the chaff flying from it will be carried by the wind and may cause breathing problems. These and similar factories cannot be located within the city but removed from it to a separate industrial area. The location of the industrial area should be on the side least exposed to the winds and not on the sides from which the winds blow towards the city. Also raising pigeons and beehives requires removal out of town.[67]

The sages established laws that limit the types of noises inside residential buildings and in the courtyard of the partners in the building.[68] They also forbade 'visual damage': construction that hides light and darkness or that infringes on privacy and allows a glimpse into private yards, balconies and inside houses.[69] These principles and others designed to create a cleaner and more pleasant urban environment. The process of implementing the laws concerns the preliminary stages for the construction of a city, back at the stage when only a few houses with a common yard have been built. The result was supposed to be that when the construction of the city was finished it would be free from hazards that had been prevented in advance.

One of the most important prohibitions in Halakhah for protecting the environment is the prohibition of vandalism and damages. Actions carried out by people in war are one of the biggest causes of damage to the environment, corruption and destruction. The Torah forbade the soldiers in battle to destroy fruit trees for the purpose of fighting:

---

[66] Tosefta, *Bava Batra* 1:7
[67] Ibid.; Mishnah, *Bava Batra* 2:9.
[68] Mishnah, *Bava Batra* 2:9.
[69] BT *Bava Batra* 59b; see also commentators and responsa.

> When in your war against a city you have to besiege it a long time
> in order to capture it, you must not destroy its trees, wielding the
> axe against them. You may eat of them, but you must not cut them
> down. Are trees of the field human[70] to withdraw before you into
> the besieged city[?][71]

The prohibition of destroying the trees also includes stopping the water
sources intended for watering them and harming them.[72] If during war,
the Torah forbade these actions of damage, certainly they are forbidden
in times of peace. According to this approach, the sages expanded the
prohibition to prevent the corruption of anything that has a benefit to
people, which includes a whole range of issues in the world, such as
killing animals, foods, corrupting utensils, clothes, and more.[73]

Summary: environmental responsibility

The halakhic sources therefore deal extensively and in detail with many
issues that have an impact on the quality of the environment and
sustainability. An attempt has been made here to briefly describe three
broad areas of Halakhah: Shabbat observance, Shemita and Jubilee
years, and kosher food laws. These three areas encompass complete
tractates in the Mishnah and Talmuds and a very extensive halakhic
literature. Observance of these *mitzvot* and rules may contribute to a
constant balance between human actions and the satisfaction of human
needs on the one hand, and the preservation of nature on the other. In

---

[70] For ecological interpretation see Kasher, 'For the Tree of the Field is Man', 585–95.
[71] Deuteronomy 20:19. See *Sifrei*.
[72] Maimonides, *Laws of Kings*, 6:8.
[73] BT *Hullin* 7b; BT *Shabbat* 140b; *Kiddushin* 32a. For a comprehensive overview of
this commandment see: Eilon Schwart, 'Bal Taschit: A Jewish Environmental
Precept', in Allen A. Thompson (ed.), *Environmental Ethics* 19/4 (1997): 355–74.

addition, the issues of urban planning and prevention of air pollution in Talmudic law, together with extensive prohibition from the Torah on vandalism have been mentioned. These halakhic positions, which express a practical approach beyond philosophical and theological theory, often arouse astonishment among those whose concern for the future of the planet is close to their hearts. Of course, an ecological study of halakhic sources should be welcomed, and at the same time, great caution and modesty is required not to err in anachronism and attributing meanings that the sages did not intend at all. We must be aware that the environmental concepts and challenges to sustainability faced by the sages in ancient times were different from ours. Still, it is legitimate to mobilize these sources for education in environmental responsibility in our time.

The connection between the earlier part of this essay, which deals with the love and joy of the Creator in his actions and the love of nature as a way to love God, and the later part which deals with the protection of the environment in Halakhah, is admittedly ambivalent. The latter is not required from the content of the former. The theoretical ideas in the first part and the practical guidelines in the second part stand, each on their own, seemingly independent of each other, and do not derive from each other. Even professional researchers dealing with these issues do not necessarily connect them. Rabbis dealing with Halakhah rulings analyze the halakhic precedents, study the changing reality and decide what the halakhic ruling is, but their conclusions are not required for biblical hermeneutics, philosophy or theology. Yet those who deal with these theoretical areas should also be familiar with the practice of the *mitzvot*. Love and admiration are not unconscious feelings but mental powers that are expressed in the act of the *mitzvah*. Persons who observe the commandments described above should be lovers of the universe who express their love in a practical way. Their love should manifest itself in great responsibility for the environment, avoiding destruction, avoiding actions that cause suffering and sorrow to others and damage to the health of others.

An appropriate conclusion to the review in this essay can be the story that the sages recount in the Talmud:

> The rabbis taught: A person may not take stones from his domain into the public domain. A story is told of a person who was clearing stones from his domain into the public domain, and a certain pious person found him. He said to him, 'Why are you clearing out a domain that does not belong to you into a domain that belongs to you?' He scoffed at him. After a time that person had to sell his field, and he was walking in that public area, and he stumbled on one of the stones. He said: 'That pious person spoke well when he said to me, why are you clearing stones from a domain that is not yours to a domain that is yours.'[74]

Private property, ownership of houses and fields, changes from time to time, and so it 'does not belong to you' for ever. The public domain— nature, the entire universe—remains in the domain of human beings and so 'belongs to you'. Creation and the created are the responsibility of human beings and they are commanded to protect them. Observation of nature, admiration and love for the environment, love for the Creator who gave all this to human beings, may give a reason for this responsibility.

Seeing creation as a divine revelation brings human persons closer to God. Everything that stands before their eyes, at any given time, is the revelation of God: 'I have set the LORD always before me' (Psalm 16:8). The literal meaning of the Hebrew text here (שִׁוִּיתִי יְהוָה לְנֶגְדִּי תָמִיד) is that people imagine God before their eyes, by finding the Supreme Reality in what they see. A person who adopts such an approach may experience the revelation through any element of the material world. More than that: there is not only a reference to the nearer or more distant

---

[74] BT *Bava Kama* 50b. See the Tosefta version *Bava Kama* 2:10.

environment, which is beyond the person, but to each of the person's own organs, to every breath of air which is inhaled into the lungs, to every sip of water swallowed. All these express the divine revelation in immediate proximity to the human. Most people are easily inclined to see the divine in special natural phenomena and beautiful landscapes. Babies born, children in their development, also inspire admiration attributed to the Creator. Expanding the experience of revelation to all instances of creation requires mental effort and may positively affect human behaviour. Taking responsibility for preserving the environment and having love for nature is the way to serve God and love Him.

6

Islamic Finance, a Green Economy and its Contribution to Loving a Greener World

Tareq Moqbel

Modern Islamic finance is regularly criticized for not fulfilling its stated objective of working toward a moral economy. Recognizing that the current state of the industry is in fact lagging behind the aspirations of its founders, this essay suggests that the story of Moses and the Servant of God in the Qur'ān can offer a framework for thinking about possible remedies to the present state of the industry. My approach will be to focus on two aspects: the ecological hermeneutics of the Qur'ān, which *should* form the basis of Islamic finance, and secondly reflections on the narrative of the Moses and the Servant of God, to serve as a corrective to the current practices of Islamic finance. By considering both these issues, I hope to be able to highlight the potential of Islamic finance for contributing toward the green economy.[1]

---

[1] This essay was researched and written within the framework of the H.M. King Abdullah ibn al-Hussein II of Jordan Fellowship for the Study of Love in Religion, Regent's Park College, University of Oxford, and the Project for The Study of Love in Religion, Oxford Centre for Religion and Culture. I am grateful to Professor Paul S. Fiddes and to Professor Mehmet Asutay for their comments, corrections, and useful suggestions on previous drafts of this essay. I am responsible for the flaws that remain.

Qur'ānic ecological hermeneutics

If Islamic finance were to be an effective moral player on the financial scene, then one condition would be to actualize the ecological mandates of the Qur'ān. Therefore, Qur'ānic ecological hermeneutics should be at the centre of any discussion on the Islamic moral economy. This consideration serves as the rationale for the present section—Qur'ānic ecological hermeneutics.

Ecological hermeneutics explores the interface between Scripture and environmental concerns. It uncovers the ecological potential for Scripture and provides general frames for analysing revelation with an eye on the environment.[2] In this section, I can only begin the task of outlining a Qur'ānic ecotheology. I will begin by offering some methodological remarks, after which I will sketch some ecological principles found in, or inferred from, the Qur'ān. Finally, I will present some possible challenges to an ecological reading of the Qur'ān.

To begin with, it is helpful to remember, when reading the Qur'ān within the context of ecology, that the Qur'ān's attitude to this debate does not easily translate into the conceptual framework of contemporary ecology and that, being a relatively short text concerned more with general notions, the Qur'ān offers no direct solutions to the current ecological concerns. That said, the Qur'ān just like the Bible, can potentially contribute—and in fact, has contributed—to ways of thinking about the environment. In particular, it prompts us to focus on the place of love in our approach to the natural world. An ecological hermeneutics is in fact inseparable from a hermeneutics of love.

Furthermore, my ecotheological reading of the Qur'ān appreciates

---

[2] For a useful overview of this topic, see the essays in Hilary Marlow and Mark Harris (eds.), *The Oxford Handbook of the Bible and Ecology* (Oxford: Oxford University Press, 2022).

that the Qur'ān is, unavoidably and necessarily, an open text that sustains a variety of readings, even to the extent of borderline contradiction. The Qur'ān is no easy read. In particular, my reading practice is grounded in the metaphysics of the seventh-century Yemenite-Andalusian mystic philosopher, Ibn 'Arabī. Scattered in his *magnum opus, al-Futūḥāt al-makkiyyah,* is an idea which he describes as *al-ittisā' al-Ilāhī* (divine plenitude or expansion).[3] I should like to think about it as an interpretive framework that respects the richness and multivalence of the Qur'ān and enables hermeneutical creativity.

As a final methodological remark, it is pertinent to highlight Norman Habel's approach to an ecological hermeneutics of the Bible which also informs my reading. He posits a reading that involves suspicion, identification, and retrieval.[4] As for the hermeneutics of suspicion, the element which concerns me is reading the Qur'ān with the suspicion that the *tafsīr* tradition reads it from an anthropocentric perspective. The second element, identification, enables us to connect to, and identify with, the actors in the Qur'ān, one of which is nature. The third element is a process that involves retrieving the voice of nature in the Qur'ān—to listen to nature, to hear what it says, and here the place of love becomes evident. Having briefly outlined my methodological ground, I now present some principles of Qur'ānic ecotheology.

Nature is an active agent.

Nature has a voice—it is articulate. The seven heavens, the earth, and everyone in them, we are told in Q. 17:44, testify to the glory of God. And this has its precedent in the Book of Psalms, Psalm 50:6, 'The

---

[3] See, for example, Muḥyī ad-Dīn Ibn 'Arabī, *al-Futūḥāt al-Makkiyyah,* ed. 'Abd al-'Azīz Sulṭān al-Manṣūb, 13 vols. (Sanaa: Wizārat ath-Thaqāfah, 2010), 2. 479.
[4] Norman C. Habel, 'Introducing Ecological Hermeneutics', in Norman C. Habel and Peter Trudinger (eds.), *Exploring Ecological Hermeneutics* (Atlanta: Society of Biblical Literature, 2008), 1–8, at 4–5.

heavens declare his righteousness'. In the same vein, and speaking of the fate of Pharaoh and the Egyptians in the 'Qur'ānic Exodus', Q. 44:29 reads, 'Neither heavens nor earth shed a tear for them, nor were they given any time', which suggests that heavens and earth, in principle, cry for the righteous.[5] Support for this idea is found in the Old Testament, Book of Job 31:38, where Job seems to be asking the earth to cry with him: 'If my land has cried out against me'.[6] The active agency of nature also makes clear that God speaks to, and instructs, it. We witness this in the Qur'ān's flood narrative: 'Then it was said, "Earth, swallow up your water"' (Q. 11:44). This imagery of the 'swallowing earth' resonates with a number of verses in the Bible, such as Exodus 15:12 where the earth swallows Pharoah's army. Conceiving of nature as an active agent has bearings on the idea of love, because it is only then that it can be truly loved. When the 'other' is active, one can engage in a mutual exchange of love. This case can be strengthened by considering an idea developed by Paul S. Fiddes that love is a type of 'participation'.[7] Humans and the rest of the created world are drawn to participate in love and this, I think, presupposes some form of active agency.

Nature is intrinsically beautiful.
The Qur'ān encourages a way of life that looks at creation as a work of God. All works of God are inherently beautiful as we learn from Q. 32:7,

---

[5] Not surprisingly, an alternative approach in the *tafsīr* tradition reads this verse metaphorically. See al-Ālūsī Maḥmūd al-Ālūsī, *Rūḥ al-maʿānī fī tafsīr al-Qurʾān al-ʿaẓīm wa-s-sabʿ al-mathānī*, 30 vols. (Beirut: Dār Iḥyāʾ at-Turāt al-ʿArabī, n.d.), vol. 25, 124–25.

[6] See Mari Joerstad, The Hebrew Bible and Environmental Ethics: Humans, Non Humans, and the Living Landscape (Cambridge: Cambridge University Press, 2019), 174.

[7] Paul S. Fiddes, 'God Is Love, But Is Love God? Towards a Theology of Love as Knowledge', in Paul S. Fiddes (ed.), *Love as Common Ground: Essays on Love in Religion* (Lanham: Lexington Books, 2021), 1–30, at 15–19.

'Who gave everything its perfect form.' Perhaps this aesthetic outlook is an indirect call for preserving this beauty. *The Study Quran* comments: 'This verse implies that the quality of "making beautiful" is something in which human beings can partake by beautifying the world around them and by beautifying their character.'[8] Much before that, the Bible attested to this notion: Ecclesiastes 3:11 reads: 'He has made everything beautiful in its time'.

Now, I understand that an aesthetic approach to nature may unsettle those who reject beauty as a valuational category (because, for example, it is a product of 'the male gaze'). In response to this I advance the argument that beauty in the Qur'ān is not necessarily a picturesque, symmetrical kind of beauty. Although not on the topic of ecology, Celene Ibrahim writes in her book *Women and Gender in the Quran*:

> With the exception of the beings in paradise, as discussed later, the Qur'an does not describe the physical beauty of any figure ... From the Qur'anic depictions of human beauty, we see that this is not primarily an aesthetic quality; rather, it relates, in a fundamental way, to virtue.[9]

I suggest that this argument can be extended to the natural world.

The intrinsic beauty of nature takes us to a comment on the relationship between beauty and love. The eminent theologian al-Ghazālī, drawing on the Prophetic tradition that 'God is beautiful, and He loves beauty', suggested that beauty, including the beauty of nature, is one of the causes of love:

> Every beautiful thing is deemed lovable in the sight of him who

---

[8] Seyyed Hossein Nasr et al., *The Study Quran: A New Translation and Commentary* (New York: Harper Collins, 2015), 1011.
[9] Celene Ibrahim, *Women and Gender in the Qur'an* (New York: Oxford University Press, 2020), 39–40.

apprehends beauty; that is due to the nature of beauty itself … no one can deny that beauty is intrinsically worthy of love.[10]

Human beings and nature are interconnected.
To begin with, Q. 20:55 reads, 'From the earth We created you' (Cf. Genesis 2:7, 'then the Lord God formed the man of dust from the ground'). Secondly, it has been suggested that Ibn ʿArabī's notion of the unity of being can be utilized in Islamic environmental discourses for rethinking the relationship between humans and the cosmos.[11] As William Chittick, the foremost Ibn ʿArabī scholar of our times, puts it: 'In the Islamic view of the cosmos … the natural and the supernatural blend and become inseparable'.[12] In another work, Chittick describes this as the 'anthropocosmic vision', writing:

> The Islamic philosophical tradition can only understand human beings in terms of the unity of the human world and the natural world. There is no place in this tradition to drive a wedge between humans and the cosmos.[13]

Correspondingly, Hilary Marlow notes this unity in a note concerning some verses from the Book of Isaiah. She writes:

---

[10] Al-Ghazālī, *Love, Longing, Intimacy and Contentment*, trans. Eric Ormsby (Cambridge: The Islamic Texts Society, 2016), 16–17. In the same vein, HRH Prince Ghazi Bin Muhammad, *Love In The Holy Qurʾan* (Cambridge: Islamic Texts Society, 2013), 11–13, 85, has shown the relationship between love and beauty.

[11] Richard C. Foltz, 'Islam', in Roger S. Gottlieb (ed.), *The Oxford Handbook of Religion and Ecology* (Oxford: Oxford University Press, 2006), 210.

[12] William C. Chittick, '"God Surrounds All Things": An Islamic Perspective on the Environment', *The World and I* 1/6 (June 1986): 671–678, at 674.

[13] William C. Chittick, The Heart of Islamic Philosophy: The Quest for Self-knowledge in the Teachings of Afḍal Al-Dīn Kāshānī (Oxford: Oxford University Press, 2001), 66.

Each of these texts from Isaiah 28–35 uses similar themes and motifs to demonstrate a fundamental interconnectedness within the created order. Abundant regrowth and rejuvenation of the physical world is accompanied by the physical and moral healing of its human population, and both result in rejoicing and renewed relationship with YHWH.[14]

This 'interconnectedness' has much relevance for the notion of love. Throughout the ages, one of the defining features of love has been the idea of 'love as union', whether this means achieving union with God or with any other being.[15] In view of this, it can be argued that the interconnectedness between humans and the cosmos, alluded to in the Bible and the Qur'ān, generates this aspect of love.

Moderation is promoted and consumerism is criticized
There are different ways through which the Qur'ān drives home this idea. I want to point out one of them, Q. 8:63, 'and [He] brought their hearts together. Even if you had given away everything in the earth you could not have done this, but God brought them together'. This verse addresses this topic in a subtle manner; it seems to show that there are things beyond materiality. Love and many other things cannot be bought and they should not be thought of in terms of money. This Qur'ānic verse parallels a verse in the Song of Songs 8:7: 'If a man offered for love all the wealth of his house, he would be utterly despised'. Fishbane comments on this verse: 'love cannot be purchased; it is not a commodity for exchange'.[16] In a way, I think these Qur'ānic and

---

[14] Hilary Marlow, *Biblical Prophets and Contemporary Environmental Ethics* (Oxford: Oxford University Press, 2009), 238.
[15] See on this idea, Vincent Brümmer, *The Model of Love: A Study in Philosophical Theology* (Cambridge: Cambridge University Press, 1993), 57–79.
[16] Michael A. Fishbane, *The JPS Bible Commentary: Song of Songs* (Philadelphia:

Biblical quotes are the antidote to materiality. Moreover, such moderation is an act of love toward the natural world as it attempts responsibly to preserve the 'beloved'. Through moderation, the 'object' of love is sustained, if only partially.

The preceding points from the Qur'ān show us how the Qur'ān creates a relationship between us, humans, and the natural phenomena. More precisely, the Qur'ān assumes an interconnectivity between God, humans and the natural world—and it is through this framework that Qur'ānic ecotheology works. But the Qur'ān also tells us that humans, who are regarded as God's trustees, are the cause for the devastation of the natural world: 'Corruption has flourished on land and sea as a result of people's actions and He will make them taste the consequences of some of their own actions so that they may turn back' (Q. 30:41).

Challenges to an eco-hermeneutic

So far, I have delineated positive principles of Qur'ānic ecotheology. I have also aimed to relate them to love in order to show that an eco-hermeneutic is also a love-hermeneutic. Now, attention should be given to some of the *potential* difficulties or challenges posed by the text of the Qur'ān vis-à-vis ecotheology. I will briefly highlight two issues and then provide a way of defending the relevant verses against anti-environmental readings, without claiming that these are airtight solutions.

The first set of challenges comes from Qur'ānic eschatology which depicts the destruction of the natural world at the end of days with violent language; for instance Q. 77: 8–10: 'When the stars are dimmed, and the sky is torn apart, when the mountains are turned to dust'. However, these and similar verses need not imply negative connotations

---

University of Nebraska Press, Jewish Publication Society, 2015), 212.

for ecology. For this imagery has been positively read as 'a symbol of man's relationship with and dependence on nature', and as a sign that this 'relationship is broken up on Doomsday.'[17] Alternatively, destruction in Qur'ānic eschatology can be taken as a reminder of the intrinsic worth of nature and thereby of the ethical responsibility of preserving nature. Yet, a third approach would be to understand destruction as transformation.[18] Another set of challenges comes from the verses saying that the earth was created for human beings (Q. 2:29) and that God made the cosmos subservient to the human race (Q. 31:20). Read at face value, this may imply dominance and hierarchy and thus open the door for exploitation. Nasr responds:

> Even when in the Quran it is stated that God has subjected (*sakhkhara*) nature to man ... this does not mean the ordinary conquest of nature, as claimed by so many modern Muslims thirsty for the power which modern science bestows upon man. Rather, it means the dominion over things which man is allowed to exercise only on the condition that it be according to God's laws and precisely because he is God's vicegerent on earth, being therefore given a power which ultimately belongs to God alone and not to man who is merely a creature born to journey through this earthly life and to return to God at the moment of death.[19]

An additional strategy to temper this implication of dominance is to factor in other verses in the Qur'ān which show that humans and nature work together, as in Q. 34:10, 'We said: "O mountains, repeat [Our]

---

[17] Soumaya Pernilla Ouis, 'Islamic Ecotheology Based On The Qur'ān', *Islamic Studies* 37/2 (1998): 151–81, at 172.

[18] Cf. David G. Horrell, 'Ecological Hermeneutics: Origins, Approaches, and Prospects', in Marlow and Harris, *Oxford Handbook*, 22.

[19] Seyyed Hossein Nasr, *The Need for a Sacred Science* (Albany: State University of New York Press, 1993), 134.

praises with him [i.e., David]'". Here, the relationship between King David and the mountains is that of identification.

Now, returning back to the theme of the essay, Islamic finance, I would like to ask whether Islamic finance, in practice, fulfils, or contributes toward fulfilling the ecotheological objectives of the Qur'ān.

The ethical state of Islamic finance

In its modern sense, Islamic finance emerged in the late 1960s and early 1970s as an attempt to develop an authentic system of ethical financing. Islamic finance is located within the Islamic moral economy, which, in essence, is a moral system based on considering the interest of all the stakeholders in decision making. This encompasses the love one expresses for other stakeholders including the natural environment. While the Islamic finance sector has demonstrated important transactional success and positive financial performance and expansion, it came at the expense of the social and moral aspirations of the Islamic moral economy.[20] So, what are the reasons for this alleged social and ethical failure of Islamic finance? Mehmet Asutay answers:

> The legalistic-rational method applied by the [Shari'ah] scholars should be considered as an important part of this observed social failure, which by definition ignores the 'substance' by prioritising the 'form.' While substance requires a consequentialistic approach in terms of outcomes, in the 'form' oriented approach, the entire emphasis is relegated to the process of constructing a product by

---

[20] For an introduction to Islamic finance, see Mahmoud El-Gamal, *Islamic Finance: Law, Economics, and Practice* (Cambridge: Cambridge University Press, 2006).

ignoring the outcomes of the product.[21]

In a more recent piece, Sencal and Asutay have argued that Islamic finance has not been able to achieve one of the basic objectives of Islam—the embeddedness of an individual with his or her surroundings. This has been driven, they argue, by the fact that the dominant methodology in Islamic finance is 'instrumental reasoning' which means prioritizing the *means* during the decision process. Furthermore, they argue that the current practices of Islamic finance have been legitimized by transforming the exception into the norm. In other words, the exceptional rulings in Islamic law, which are designed for limited applications, are extended and are made to justify the otherwise impermissible products and/or institutions. This has led to the transformation of the norm-based Islamic moral economy into what can be termed as an exception-based Islamic moral economy.[22]

Now, if these two intertwined problems—that is, the domination of instrumental, formal reasoning and the creation of an exception-based economy—are not resolved, Islamic finance will not be able to fulfil its objectives. In other words, the Qur'ānic ecotheology, which I highlighted at the beginning of the lecture will not be realized, as Islamic finance will continue to function as a profit-driven business, under the influence of the capitalist market system.

But before I move on, I should not fail to mention that Islamic finance has indeed contributed, in some sense, toward the idea of the green economy. In 2019, the Securities Commission of Malaysia and the World Bank Group published a report under the title of *Islamic*

---

[21] Mehmet Asutay, 'Conceptualising and Locating the Social Failure of Islamic Finance: Aspirations of Islamic Moral Economy vs. the Realities of Islamic Finance', *Asian and African Area Studies*, 11/2 (2012): 93–113, at 107–8.
[22] Harun Sencal, and Mehmet Asutay, 'The emergence of new Islamic economic and business moralities', *Thunderbird International Business Rev*iew, 61 (2019): 765–75.

Green Finance Development, Ecosystem and Prospects. The report concluded that there is a strong 'nexus between Islamic finance and green finance', and it also showcased a number of successful case studies on Islamic green finance which are worth considering. One example of success is Indonesia, which raised green bonds worth US\$ 2.75 billion. The proceeds have financed and re-financed projects in renewable energy, energy efficiency, sustainable transportation, waste management, as well as climate resilience for vulnerable areas.[23] Therefore, I would like to stress that the criticism of Islamic finance should not detract from the fact that Islamic finance has many good sides and positive contributions, as Abdal Hakim Murad writes:

> This is not to say that the experiment has been simply bogus, as claimed by some purists, a mere replacement of Western financial products with Arabic-sounding facsimiles. In our stressed global environment one is always looking for the least bad option. Sharia compliance is a matter of degree these days, and it behoves us to remember the religion's traditional realism, and the forgiving mercy of God. Utopians can be sure of nothing except disappointment.[24]

The 'Green Man' narrative as a proposed corrective for Islamic finance

I will argue in the remaining part of the essay that the Qur'ānic narrative

---

[23] Securities Commission Malaysia, 'Islamic Green Finance Development, Ecosystem and Prospects', available at:
https://documents.worldbank.org/en/publication/documentsreports/documentdetail/5
91721554824346344/islamic-green-finance-development-ecosystem-and-prospects.
Date accessed: 24 August 2022.
[24] Abdal Hakim Murad, *Travelling Home: Essays on Islam in Europe* (Cambridge: The Quilliam Press Ltd, 2020), 280.

of Moses and al-Khiḍr (also known as the Green Man) is a suitable framework which addresses both of the problems of Islamic finance outlined above, and that it could shed light, if we remove its particularities and allow a degree of abstraction, on how Islamic finance can be rehabilitated and thus contribute genuinely to the green economy.

In *Sūrat al-Kahf*, chapter 18 of the Qur'ān, we are presented with an elliptical story in which Moses and his accomplice travel to the 'meeting place of the two seas' to meet the unnamed character, whom the Qur'ān describes as 'one of Our servants—a man to whom We had granted Our mercy and whom We had given knowledge of Our own' (Q. 18:65). Moses asks this man to teach him what he knows, 'May I follow you so that you can teach me some of the right guidance you have been taught?' but al-Khiḍr warns that Moses will not have the patience to bear with him. Moses insists he will be a good student, agreeing not to question al-Khiḍr's actions, 'God willing, you will find me patient. I will not disobey you in any way.'

Next, and this is the core of the story, we are presented with three enigmatic episodes. The first riddle relates that the travellers embark on a ship, which al-Khiḍr proceeds to scuttle. Moses inquires how he could do such a thing, 'How could you make a hole in it? Do you want to drown its passengers? What a strange thing to do!', but al-Khiḍr warns him: 'Did I not tell you that you would never be able to bear with me patiently?'. Later on, as they walk along the shore, al-Khiḍr spots some boys playing and kills one of them. Clearly on moral grounds, Moses confronts al-Khiḍr saying: 'How could you kill an innocent person? He has not killed anyone! What a terrible thing to do!'. The third episode involves Moses and al-Khiḍr entering a village that refuses to receive them. Al-Khiḍr finds a broken wall in the town and fixes it. Moses tells him, 'But if you had wished you could have taken payment for doing that.' That is the last straw—Moses has used up all his chances, and al-

Khiḍr decides to explain his actions, but from then on Moses is on his own: 'This is where you and I part company. I will tell you the meaning of the things you could not bear with patiently.' The explanations which we will examine now assume that behind every inexplicable event, God has hidden reasons which are not apparent from a human perspective.

In the first explanation, al-Khiḍr tells Moses that he had scuttled the boat to prevent a wicked king who was seizing every [serviceable] boat by force. So, he did that to help the poor fishermen. Smashing their boat turns out to be a wise moral action. With respect to the second episode, al-Khiḍr tells Moses that he had killed the boy lest the child grieve his good parents by a wayward life, although this remains a troubling moral problem which has unsettled commentators. In the third episode he had rebuilt the wall so that the treasure that lay beneath would be safe until the two orphaned sons of the wall's owner could reach their majority and thus claim their inheritance. What concerns me for the purposes of this essay is the following question: what bearings does this narrative have on Islamic finance? To this I shall now turn.

The first implication has to do with the non-human creation. At the outset of the narrative, which I did not mention, we are informed, in an implied manner, that Moses and his servant have a fish, and that Moses will meet this most learned servant at the place where his fish escapes. When they lose the fish, Moses says: 'that was the place we were looking for' (Q. 18: 64). So, it is the fish that leads Moses to esoteric knowledge, and essentially, to God. The fish is actually central to the narrative. Second, the designated meeting place is *majmaʿ al-baḥrayn*, literally, 'the place where the two seas meet'. It seems that the non-human creation is vital to finding God—the way to God passes through the natural world. And if we accept this, then it is our responsibility to look after it. Third, it is relevant to mention here why the name 'The Green Man' is given to this figure in Islamic tradition. It has been related in some traditions that he was given this name because he once sat on a patch of dry pasture and it suddenly turned green. Alternatively, it has been said that whenever he prayed somewhere, that place would turn green.[25] Clearly, then, there is a symbolism and a strong connection between this figure and the 'green' of nature. In sum, this embeddedness with the natural world is a key lesson for Islamic finance if it genuinely aspires to be rooted in its core source; the Qur'ān.

The second theme addresses one of the key problems with Islamic finance—the focus on form at the expense of the substance. Norman Brown, in a fascinating article, entitled 'the Apocalypse of Islam', summarizes the thesis of this story:

> And the content of the folktale—the episodes of the ship, the youth and the wall—tells us in the most literal, even crude way, three times reiterated, that there is a distinction between "what actually happened," events as seen by the eye of historical materialism, and "what is really going on," events *sub specie aeternitatis*, as seen by the inward, the clairvoyant eye, the second sight. The form and the content of the folktale obliges us, as it has obliged all subsequent Islamic culture, to make the distinction between literal meaning and something beyond—in Islamic terminology between *zahir* and *batin*, between outer (exoteric) and inner (esoteric); between external-visible-patent and internal-invisible-latent; between materialist and spiritual meaning.[26]

Or, as in Martin Lings' words:

---

[25] See 'Abd ar-Raḥmān Ibn al-Jawzī, *Zād al-masīr fī 'ilm at-tafsīr*, ed. Zuhayr ash-Shāwīsh, 9 vols. (Beirut: al-Maktab al-Islāmī and Dār Ibn Ḥazm, 2002), vol. 5, 167–168. Ed.: the 'Green Man' in English folklore, and other European mythologies, similarly represents the world of nature within human life.

[26] Norman O. Brown, 'The Apocalypse of Islam', *Social Text* 8 (1983): 155–171, at 162.

It has at least given us a glimpse of the deviousness of the exoteric path and the extreme nearness of the Waters of Life. For we are already, if only we knew it, at the meeting place of the two seas—witness the miracle of Life which is always with us, both in us and about us, but which the powers of illusion persuade us to take entirely for granted, through inadvertence or distraction.[27]

Reflecting on Islamic finance, what seems to be going on is a reversal of the Green Man narrative. The literal is privileged over the substance. Islamic finance focuses on the legal as opposed to the ethical. If the moral of this story is observed in Islamic financial engineering, the industry will be able fulfil the higher objectives of *Sharīʿah*, the *maqāṣid,* which require jurists to penetrate beyond the outer layer of revealed texts.

My third reflection relates to the fact that Islamic finance has created an exception-based economy, that the exception became the norm. The story of Moses and the Green Man is also about exceptions, and this is very clear in the way Qurʾānic commentaries approach the story. For instance, the episode where the Green Man scuttles the ship is an exception from the normative rule that one should not trespass on someone else's property. So, I would like to argue that, through framing at least two of the episodes within the logic of exception, the story is stressing that exceptions should *remain* exceptions. Put differently, exceptions are not generalisable and their scope has to be limited. In fact, for one to exercise an exception they must acquire knowledge like that of the Green Man. Thus understood, the story addresses Islamic finance—it is a plea to confine exceptions to cases of necessity.

The fourth point relates to the character of the Green Man. He

---

[27] Martin Lings, *Symbol and Archetype: A Study of The Meaning of Existence* (Cambridge: Quinta Essentia, 1991), 76.

showed care for the poor fishermen, and he volunteered to safeguard the inheritance of two orphaned children. This inclusion of the poor and the willingness to volunteer are two principles that could guide the social responsibility of Islamic banks in terms of considering the salvation of the extended stakeholders namely the creatures of God so that the bounty of God can be made available to all the stakeholders.

Fifth, this story is about symbolism. The three episodes can be understood as symbols and as vehicles for the revival of symbolism. This revival is necessary for ecology as it imbues the natural world with meaning. Nasr writes: 'Symbolism, in the essential meaning of the term we have in mind, is concerned with the process of sacralization of the cosmos. It is through the symbol that man is able to find meaning in the cosmic environment that surrounds him.'[28] The symbolism embedded in this story is also captured by Cheetham as he writes:

> We have lived too long within a world of our own making. We have lived too long within a language of the merely human. To keep our internals open we have to learn to read and write ourselves out of ourselves, and uncurl ourselves back into the world. This is the task set to us by Khidr, the Green Man, the hermeneut at the meeting place of the two seas … Khidr is not a humanist. He is a messenger from far beyond. The world that he opens up to us is infinite. He announces that the cosmos itself is a "house of reading"—it is the Primordial Temple of the Word.[29]

Sixth, we noted that the Green Man was not named in the Qur'ān; rather,

---

[28] Seyyed Hossein Nasr, *Man and Nature: The Spiritual Crisis of Modern Man* (London: George Allen & Unwin Ltd, 1968), 131.

[29] Tom Cheetham, *Green Man, Earth Angel: The Prophetic Tradition and the Battle for the Soul of the World* (Albany: State University of New York Press, 2004), 113–14.

he was described as one who was given two qualities mercy (*raḥmah*) and divine knowledge (Q. 18:65). In fact, the word mercy occurs before knowledge in the verse. It follows that if we observe the order of words in the verse—in tandem with the fact that mercy and love in the Qur'ān are entangled—we can say that the basis of the Green Man's acts is love—his love for God and his love for creation. And love, as the verse implies, comes before knowledge.[30]

Finally, we may now relate the four principles of eco-hermeneutics I explored earlier to the story of the Green Man. The first principle, that nature is an active agent, can be seen in the third episode of the story where the Green Man finds a broken wall in the town and fixes it. The literal words of the Qur'ān read something like, 'they found therein a wall that *wants* (*yurīd*) to fall down'. Although this phrase is often understood metaphorically, I find it telling that the Qur'ān ascribes active agency to the wall—as if the wall is *desiring* to fall down. Once this active agency of the natural order is established, love can have a voice.

Second, there is the intrinsic beauty of nature. This seems to be implied, if only vaguely, in the meeting place of Moses and the Green Man. The place is designated as 'the place where the two seas meet'. A similar imagery is found in other places in the Qur'ān, for example, Q. 55:19, where it is invoked in the context of listing God's favours. It could be suggested, then, that the 'beauty' of this phenomenon—the meeting of the two bodies of water—is a divine favour. If this argument is accepted, it follows that by alluding to beauty, the Green Man story is pointing to one of the *causes* of love.

The third principle of eco-hermeneutics is that human beings and nature are interconnected. This, I think, is clear from a number of

---

[30] On the connection between love and mercy, see HRH Prince Ghazi Bin Muhammad, *Love In The Holy Qur'an*, 15–18.

aspects in the story, such as the connection it draws between the fish and Moses, as I noted above. I would also add here that the Qur'ān mentions that Moses and his accomplice, during their voyage, took rest beside a rock. The way the Qur'ān describes this is revealing; it says 'we took refuge at the rock'. The Arabic word *awaynā*—translated as 'we took refuge'—is, in my opinion, indicative of closeness and interconnectedness. Through establishing this relationship with the rock, the story internalizes one of the attitudes of love—interconnection.

Finally, I have maintained that moderation is one of the principles of ecotheology. This idea can be inferred from the fact that the Green Man attempted to prevent the unjust King from seizing the ship of the indigent people. In other words, he was prevented from excessive—and, in this case, unjust—consumption. Translated to the framework of love, which counters excessive consumption, the story reminds us that through moderation, a sustainability of the natural world is achieved, and this means that the 'object' of love is preserved.

This takes me to the major implication of this essay, which could be stated as follows: *for modern Islamic finance to achieve its objectives in an authentic sense, it has to fulfil its responsibility toward a greener world, as this will help to promote love, which is at the very centre of its moral economy model.*

The fact that love is scarcely discussed in the context of Islamic finance, and finance generally,[31] makes the plea to love within the financial context more urgent. This essay hopes to highlight this idea— that love (here manifested in mercy) can have and should have a role in financial decision processes, to enable working toward a greener world.

---

[31] Some exceptions are Patricia Marino, 'Love and Economics', in Christopher Grau and Aaron Smuts (eds), *The Oxford Handbook of Philosophy of Love* (New York: Oxford University Press, 2017), and Fiddes, 'God is Love, but is Love God? Towards a Theology of Love as Knowledge', 20–22.

7

'A Mirror of infinit Beauty': Contemplating Love in the Natural World with Thomas Traherne

G. P. Marcar

Introduction: thinking well and being grateful

Writing in the seventeenth century, the Christian poet and mystic Thomas Traherne (1636–74) gives an account of how and why the natural world should be loved which is striking for its eloquent and unambiguous affirmation of the world's essential goodness. To 'think well', according to Traherne, is to see and appreciate the goodness and beauty of the created world; it is to truly *enjoy* the things of the world, by considering their spiritual worth and value through the 'interior court' of the mind. This distinguishes human beings from other animals: 'Pigs eat Acorns, but neither consider the Sun that gav them Life, nor the Influences of the Heavens by which they were Nourished, nor the very Root of the Tree from whence they came.'[1]

By exercising its spiritual-cognitive capacities for beholding things according to their spiritual value, Traherne judges that the human mind is unique amongst animal faculties in being able to express gratitude towards God, *qua* Creator and Sustainer of a world that is given to

---

[1] Thomas Traherne, *The Works of Thomas Traherne*, V: *Centuries of Meditations and Select Meditations*, ed. Jan Ross (Cambridge: Boydell & Brewer, 2013), 15.

human beings for their enjoyment. If human beings were to exercise their powers of spiritual appreciation, it would become evident that even a single grain of sand 'exhibiteth the wisdom and Power of God ... Manifesting His Glory and Goodness to your Soul'.[2] Too frequently, however, this power fails to be used. Traherne thus bemoans the attitude exhibited by human beings towards the planet, proclaiming that '[t]he World is a Mirror of infinit Beauty, yet no Man sees it.'[3] Due to humanity's postlapsarian deviation from its original state of innocence and purity, the full extent of the world's beauty is neither apprehended nor appreciated by any person.

In order to illustrate this, in his Second *Century* Traherne asks his readers to imagine themselves to be the world's sole occupants and, from this position, to meditate upon all the sensory delights and other benefits that the world bestows upon them.[4] God has not only gifted human beings with their body and soul, but also with Heaven and the Earth itself, such that were persons to truly take stock of all they have received, the effect would be utterly disorientating. As Traherne exclaims during a similar thought experiment on the imperative towards gratitude in his *Christian Ethicks*: 'Where am I? Am I not lost and swallow'd up as a Centre in all these Abysses?'[5] Adjacent to this is a thought-experiment that Traherne posits, encouraging his readers to imagine how utterly transformed their experience would be if one of the world's central features—namely, the sun—were to be absent. Traherne proposes that if the sun were suddenly to disappear from the sky, the world would become something akin to a 'Dungeon of Darkness and Death', from which the present value of the sun's beams would become

---

[2] Traherne, *Centuries of Meditations*, 16.

[3] Traherne, *Centuries of Meditations*, 17.

[4] Traherne, *Centuries of Meditations*, 50–52.

[5] Thomas Traherne, *Christian Ethicks, or, Divine morality opening the way to blessedness, by the rules of vertue and reason* (Jonathan Edwin, 1675), 361.

more readily evident.[6]

Such a sobering reflection also highlights, for Traherne, how love for the natural world and love for oneself are, in fact, co-extensive, as without the world one's self could neither flourish, nor survive.[7] A transparent look upon nature would thereby lead the observer from love for one's self, to appreciation for the benefits bestowed upon the individual by the natural world, which in turn necessitates a relation of gratitude towards God. Indeed, Traherne goes as far as to posit that the door between heaven and hell has (in)gratitude as its hinge. To possess blessings and appreciate them is to be in heaven, while to possess blessings and be *ungrateful* for them is to be in 'Hell ... upon Earth'; a state, Traherne remarks, which in some respect is even more irrational than that of hell's inhabitants themselves, insofar as those in hell no longer possess blessings for which to be grateful.[8] Traherne appears to almost echo fellow poet John Milton's sentiments that 'The mind ... Can make a Heaven of Hell, a Hell of Heaven,' when he says that 'the World is both a Paradice and a Prison to different Persons', with the difference being whether one's mind is in a state of gratitude.[9] Proper contemplation of the world should, therefore, evoke loving appreciation towards nature and a profound gratitude towards God. Yet, as Traherne notes, although the world may be a 'mirror of infinite beauty', no individual has been able to bring themselves to fully apprehend this reality as they ought to.[10]

Traherne's context is one in which new technological lenses, such as the microscope and telescope, had resulted in the rapid expansion of humanity's epistemological horizons at both the atomic and celestial

---

[6] Traherne, *Centuries of Meditations*, 52.
[7] Traherne, *Christian Ethicks*, 358.
[8] Traherne, *Centuries of Meditations*, 23.
[9] Traherne, *Centuries of Meditations*, 19.
[10] Ibid.

levels. This essay will draw on Traherne's invocation of another, older visual technology in his *Meditations*—the mirror—in order to illustrate Traherne's Christocentric theology of cultivating an attitude of love and gratitude towards the world. I begin with an examination of the Christian mystical tradition represented by figures such as John Scotus Eriugena (815–877) and Nicholas of Cusa (1401–1464) on how the biblical affirmation that God is triune Creator of the world *ex nihilo* must inform how the Christian approaches the content of the natural world. From this, I will attempt to show how Traherne develops the theology of God being 'all in all' to construct a theological anthropology in which the human soul, by virtue of being in the image of God, is also capable of apprehending and appreciating all things.

Divine lights and universal workshops: Dionysius, Eriugena and Cusa on God being 'all in all'

The Catholic theologian and poet John Scotus Eriugena presents a striking theology of all creatures, *qua* creatures, being 'theophanies.'[11] Eriugena derives his theology from the Pseudo-Dionysius, a Greek Christian theologian whose writings emerged sometime in the fifth to sixth centuries. Due in part to a misattribution with the Athenian convert named 'Dionysius' mentioned by the apostle Paul in Acts 17:34, the Pseudo-Dionysius has had an almost unparalleled influence on Christian spiritual writers, with Eriugena being no exception. Indeed, Eriugena is credited with being among the first to make the Pseudo-Dionysius accessible to Christian theologians in the West, by translating his works from Greek into Latin. Eriugena's writings also include a Commentary on the Pseudo-Dionysius' *Celestial Hierarchies*, and it is here that we

---

[11] John Scotus Eriugena, *Periphyseon (division of nature)*, trans. John O'Meara (Washington: Dumbarton Oaks, 1987), 307-308 (681A-B).

find the theology of theophany which would later inform Eriugena's main work, on the division of nature (*Periphyseon*), as well as his homily on the Prologue to the Gospel of Saint John.

In his commentary on the Pseudo-Dionysius' first book of the *Celestial Hierarchies*, Eriugena first develops the theological concept which he finds within the Pseudo-Dionysius of created things as continuous theophanies. Beginning with the scriptural verse of James 1:17 that 'every generous act of giving, with every perfect gift, is from above, coming down from the Father of lights, with whom there is no variation or shadow of turning', the first chapter of the Pseudo-Dionysius' *Celestial Hierarchies* explicates how everything constitutes a 'divine illumination' according to its created goodness. The context of this is the Pseudo-Dionysius' affirmation, elsewhere in the *Divine Names* that, as a perfect Act which creates, sustains, and reconciles all things from nothing to itself, God's goodness 'actually contains everything beforehand within itself—and this in an uncomplicated and boundless manner.'[12] It is in this sense for the Pseudo-Dionysius, as well as for subsequent Christian thinkers, that God can be said to be 'all in all.'[13]

Eriugena's commentary on Pseudo-Dionysius' *Celestial Hierarchies* picks up on the Greek theologian's aforementioned utilization of James 1:17 in the first chapter. Eriugena exegetes this biblical passage to say that the light of the Father, which is also the triune light of the Son and the Holy Spirit, is 'diffused in all things that are, in order that they might essentially subsist; shining in all things that are so that all might be turned to the love and knowledge of its beauty... and thus all lights descend from the Father of lights'.[14] Seen thus, all

---

[12] *Pseudo-Dionysius: The Complete Works*, eds. and trans. Colm Luibhéid and Paul Rorem (New York: Paulist Press, 1987), 56.

[13] Ps-Dionysius, *Works*, 56.

[14] John Scotus Eriugena, *Commentary on the Celestial Hierarchy*, in Paul Rorem (ed.),

things are 'lights' which illumine and facilitate the turning of other things—including the human mind—towards the true source of all light in God.

Eriugena next anticipates an anthropocentric objection from his reader; how exactly, one might ask, are non-rational, wholly material parts of this world supposed to function as created 'lights' in relation to rational human beings? If one attends to a single stone, Eriugena says, several properties become apparent: these include independent properties of size, weight, and singularity, as well as its phylogenetic relation to other things in terms of species and genus.[15] Such properties are present in—or as Eriugena would say, *gifted to*—the stone in its singularity; that is, these characteristics exist in the stone 'without the participation of any [other] creature.'[16] The stone thereby 'subsists as good and beautiful', leading the person who truly perceives it to appreciate 'the cause of all things,' from which 'place and order, number and species and genus, goodness and beauty and essence, and other gifts and grants are distributed to all.'[17] Just as every constituent part of the created universe is a 'light' which is capable of illuminating and turning the mind back towards the transcendental creative source of *all* lights, so too, Eriugena points out, 'the greatest light is the universal workshop of the world' itself, which is 'composed of many parts (as it were, of many lamps).'[18] In even the basest, material and finite aspects of the natural world, therefore, the gratuitous creative activity of an infinite God is capable of being discerned.

In his *Homily on the Prologue to the Gospel of St. John*, Eriugena further develops this theological vision in seeking to explicate how 'all

---

Eriugena's Commentary on the Dionysian Celestial Hierarchy (Toronto: Pontifical Institute of Mediaeval Studies, 2005), 181–82.

[15] Eriugena, *Commentary*, 183.

[16] Ibid.

[17] Ibid.

[18] Ibid.

things were made [through the Word of God]' and 'without [*sine*; *chōris*] him was not anything made which was made', such that 'in Him was life' (John 1:3-4). Where the Vulgate Latin *sine* is usually translated as 'without' in John 1:3, Eriugena argues that a more apt rendering of the original Greek *chōris* is 'outside', such that the verse emphasizes that nothing was made 'outside' of God's Word.[19] This exposition, which is cited approvingly by Thomas Aquinas in his own commentary on John's Gospel (although he mistakenly attributes Eriugena's text to Origen),[20] serves for Eriugena to underscore John's message that 'there is nothing whatsoever that was not created in [the Word of God] and through him.'[21] This lays the ground for Eriugena's exegesis of John 1:4, which states that 'what was made in him was life.' Eriugena locates the meaning of this verse in the subsistence of all things in God as causes, prior to them coming into existence *ex nihilo* as effects.[22] This includes both corporeal and incorporeal creatures, 'heaven and earth, the abyss and whatever is in them'.[23] Even immobile objects, such as stones, subsist eternally in God, akin (Eriugena writes) to how light subsists within the sun, or how within the earth 'a great number of plants, shrubs, and animals are all contained at once in individual seeds.'[24] Eriugena's use of such analogies from nature here is instructive, insofar as it helps to underscore how each feature of the 'greatest light' and 'universal workshop' of the natural world manifests

---

[19] John Scotus Eriugena, *Homily on the Prologue to the Gospel of St. John,* in Oliver Davies (ed.), *Celtic Spirituality* (Mahwah: Paulist Press, 2007), 418.

[20] See Aquinas, *Commentary on the Gospel of John: Chapters 1-5*, trans. Fabian R Larcher and James A Weisheipl (Catholic University of America Press, 2010), 37 (para. 86).

[21] Eriugena, *Homily*, 418. Cf. George MacDonald's 'unspoken sermon' on the prologue of John's Gospel, in George MacDonald, *Unspoken Sermons: Third Series* (Grand Rapids, MI: Christian Classics Ethereal Library), 2–10.

[22] Eriugena, *Homily*, 418. Aquinas, *Commentary*, 38 (para. 90).

[23] Eriugena, *Homily*, 419.

[24] Ibid.

the presence of a triune creator God who is 'all in all.'

Another theologian within this mystical tradition, and whose work and influence was known to Traherne, is the proto-renaissance theologian Nicholas of Cusa. In *On Learned Ignorance*, Cusa describes how as 'the maximum', God, akin to an infinite and eternal circle, necessarily 'encompasses all things.'[25] As such, in giving himself to humanity in the figure of Christ, God also *gives* humanity all things. In the seventh chapter of his *Vision of God*, Cusa thus asks God in prayer, 'what is more absurd than to ask that You, who are all in all, give Yourself to me? How will You give Yourself to me unless You likewise give to me the sky and the earth and everything in them?'[26] The eternity of God contains and encompasses all particular things at once, while seeming to manifest one thing at a time to the temporal observer. Cusa gives the example here of a perfect clock: although the clock may be *heard* chiming six o'clock before seven o'clock at a particular time, ontologically speaking the clock includes both six and seven o'clock simultaneously; in other words, 'the Concept of a clock—a Concept which is eternity—both enfolds and unfolds all things.'[27] Cusa proceeds to conceive of God as 'Absolute Sight', which encompasses all modes of creaturely sight and, in beholding His creatures, constitutes and sustains them in existence. Consequently, Cusa writes:

> The one who looks unto You does not bestow form upon You; rather, he beholds himself in You, because he receives from You that which he is ...You bestow, as if You were a living Mirror-

---

[25] See Nicholas of Cusa, 'On Learned Ignorance', in Jasper Hopkins, *Nicholas of Cusa on Learned Ignorance: A Translation and an Appraisal of De Docta Ignorantia* (Minneapolis: The Arthur J. Banning Press, 1985, 1990), 7, 33.

[26] Nicholas of Cusa, 'De Visione Dei', in Jasper Hopkins, *Nicholas of Cusa's Dialectical Mysticism. Text, Translation, and Interpretive Study of De Visione Dei* (Minneapolis: The Arthur J. Banning Press, 1988), 692.

[27] Cusa, 'De Visione Dei', 700.

of-eternity, which is the Form of forms.[28]

As 'Absolute' or 'Maximum' sight and the 'Form of forms', God represents 'a mirror of eternity' from which all creatures receive their own finite (or 'contracted') mode of existence. Cusa here draws an instructive distinction between physical mirrors, in which the image of things is represented, and the divine 'mirror of eternity', in which the external creature *itself* is the image.[29] Cusa's emphasis upon sight, as well as his geometric language of infinite circles and his metaphor of divine reality being akin to an eternal 'mirror', all parallels the rhetoric and imagery of Traherne's own theological vision some two centuries later. A background appreciation of this theological tradition helps to inform our understanding of Traherne's theology, which we shall now return to.

The image of God: a mirror containing and loving all things

In *Commentaries of Heaven*, Traherne offers an explicit meditation on how God—and by extension, the human soul—is 'all in all.' God is simultaneously 'alone', Traherne observes, and, in a seemingly paradoxical way, 'all in all.' While being alone and having all things 'in his Company' may seem like contrary and mutually exclusive attributes, Traherne argues that they are in fact two sides of the same transcendental coin. From God alone all other things come into existence: He is therefore their 'Fountain', 'Cause', and 'End'.[30] A theological shorthand for this would be that God, alone, is Creator of all

---

[28] Cusa, 'De Visione Dei', 710.

[29] Ibid.

[30] Thomas Traherne, *The Works of Thomas Traherne*, III: *Commentaries of Heaven*, part 2: *Al-Sufficient to Bastard*, ed. Jan Ross (Cambridge: Boydell & Brewer, 2007), 15.

ex nihilo. It is also by virtue of this that God—as the Pseudo-Dionysius, Eriugena, and Nicholas of Cusa held—is 'in' all things. Just as God contains all things as their pre-existent, subsistent causes, so too God remains within all things once they have been actualized. As Traherne subsequently affirms in his discourse on 'Almighty', God 'includeth all Things and is All Things in Himself.'[31] Only in God, *qua* Creator *ex nihilo,* is it possible for anything to have value, wisdom or goodness.[32]

So far, one might say, so Dionysian. Unlike his Platonic mystical predecessors, however, Traherne draws upon this theology of God being 'all in all' in order to take an anthropological turn. As made in the image of God, Traherne observes, the human being too must be, albeit in a secondary and derivative sense, 'all in all.' Traherne begins by affirming the common scholastic sentiment, following Aquinas' commentary on Aristotle's *De Anima*, that the rational (that is to say, human) soul is wholly in the whole, as well as wholly in each part, of the body (*Anima est tota in toto,* and *tota in qualibet parte*).[33] This follows from the fact that, as the scholastics argue, the power of understanding exercised by the human intellect is both indivisible and immaterial.[34] Just as God, therefore, must be in the whole of the universe because He (as perfectly simple) has no divisible parts, so too the indivisible human soul, which is made in His image, subsists within the entirety of the body.

Traherne does not simply echo the scholastics' maxim or its underpinning theology, however. Instead, Traherne seeks to draw out the far more radical implications that he perceives as following from the soul being *tota in toto,* and *tota in qualibet parte* because of its status as the *imago Dei*. God created the human soul in the image of God so that it might perfectly enjoy him. While a soul's vegetative and sensitive

---

[31] Traherne, *Commentaries of Heaven*, part 2, 392.

[32] Ibid.

[33] See Thomas Aquinas, *De Anima*, Article 10.

[34] See for instance Aquinas in *Summa Theologica* I, q.75–79.

powers of 'Animation, Growth and Motion'—which it shares with plants and non-rational animals—may be confined to particular portions of the body, the rational human soul's powers of 'Sight and Love and Joy etc' entail that it is capable of attending to, and even being present in, external objects.[35] In exercising its spiritual powers, the soul can simultaneously 'be with the Sun wholly, and wholly with the Stars ... with GOD wholly, and wholly with his Creatures.'[36] Whereas Aristotle and the Christian theologies that drew upon his *De Anima* affirmed that the rational soul was not confined to any particular part of the body, therefore, Traherne goes significantly further,[37] and posits that the soul's reach need not stop at any particular part of the cosmos.

The soul's capacity to reach all in this way also entails its capacity to *love* all. Love is no less, Traherne insists in the Second of his *Centuries of Meditations*, than 'the Root and Foundation of Nature.'[38] From this standpoint, Traherne proceeds to reflect upon the centrality of love to human nature itself. Just as the sun, by its nature, shines, so too human nature has an innate propensity to love everything within creation. To be united in love with all creatures is humanity's *raison d'être*, by which human nature best aligns itself with God and His purposes in creating the world. Comprehension concerning the aptitudes, uses and powers of things is the cause of love and appreciation of them. If human beings were to comprehend the 'infinit Excellencies' possessed by a single drop of water or grain of sand—as God does— then they would love all things as they *ought* to be loved: that is to say,

---

[35] Traherne, *Commentaries of Heaven*, part 2, 14.

[36] Ibid.

[37] For Traherne's further comment and departure from Aristotle's *De Anima*, see Traherne, *Seeds of Eternity or The Nature of the Soul*, in *The Works of Thomas Traherne, I: Inducements to Retirednes, A Sober View of Dr Twisses his Considerations, Seeds of Eternity or the Nature of the Soul, The Kingdom of God*, ed. Jan Ross (Cambridge: Boydell & Brewer, 2005), 231–32.

[38] Traherne, *Centuries of Meditations*, 74.

in an infinite manner.[39] How, however, can something which is supposed to be finite exercise an infinite power to love? Central to Traherne's schema is the affirmation that the soul of human beings represents 'an Infinit Sphere in a Centre.'[40] Human souls, according to Traherne, are infinite in both their extent—that is, in having the potential to apprehend infinite treasures—and in their depth. In order to illustrate this, Traherne draws upon a thought experiment with parallels to Descartes' dreaming subject or Avicenna's 'floating man':

> Suppose a Man were Born Deaf and Blind...He thinks not of Wall and Limits till he feels them and is stopt by them. That things are finit therefore we learn by our Sences. but Infinity we know and feel by our souls.[41]

Just as Descartes had previously postulated that someone may doubt all things around them but nevertheless still affirm that they exist, Traherne observes that although a person may be able to 'unsuppose' all things around them, including heaven and earth itself, but 'the place where they stood will [nevertheless] remain behind.'[42] Once all sensory phenomena are disregarded, Traherne's deaf and blind man is left only with the immediate awareness of an infinite space. In a distinctly Augustinian tone, Traherne asserts that infinity is within each individual soul, 'for GOD is there, and more near to us than we are to our selvs.'[43] Seen thus, the human soul is an infinite abyss, an '[u]ndrainable Ocean' and an 'inexhausted fountain.'[44] While previous affirmations of the soul as *tota*

---

[39] Traherne, *Centuries of Meditations*, 79.

[40] Traherne, *Centuries of Meditations*, 82. This language of infinite spheres and centres clearly recalls that of Nicholas of Cusa noted above, in addition to other fifteenth-century Renaissance thinkers such as Marsilio Ficino.

[41] Traherne, *Centuries of Meditations*, 82.

[42] Ibid.

[43] Ibid.

[44] Traherne, *Centuries of Meditations*, 83. Cf. Augustine, *Confessions*, book III.

in toto, and *tota in qualibet parte* ground their position in the nature of rationality and other human faculties such as the will, Traherne's anthropology thereby grounds itself in the more explicitly theological claim that the soul is capable of 'seeing All Things' and being 'all in all' because it is made in the image of an infinite God.[45]

As God is infinite, it follows for Traherne that He cannot be loved with a finite or limited love; rather, the love that truly loves God must also extend to all of God's 'friends' and 'all His Creatures.'[46] The infinitude of God's nature therefore requires that the human soul 'lov all those whom He loveth' and 'receiv Him in all those Things werein He giveth Himself.'[47] To what does God 'give Himself'? God is infinite *in se,* and He is infinitely and endlessly *communicative*—enjoying in himself, Traherne goes on to state, 'infinite treasures' in a triune life of perpetually 'Giving and Receiving'.[48] In support of his vision of God's communicative, self-diffusive goodness, Traherne cites a paragraph of Gregory of Nazianzus's 'Oration on the Theophany,' just prior to which the Nazianzen had explained that 'God always was and is and will be—or better, God always is … For he contains the whole of being in himself, without beginning or end, like an endless, boundless ocean of reality.'[49] In alignment with this vision of God, Traherne describes how, in God, all things, from 'Beasts and fowles' to angels, are 'seen and Contemplated in His Bosom.'[50]

That the human soul is itself an '[u]ndrainable Ocean' images the infinitude of God—the truly endless, all-encompassing 'ocean of reality', in the words of Gregory of Nazianzus. The *imago Dei* within the human soul is therefore able to 'contain' the objects of its infinite

---

[45] Traherne, *Commentaries of Heaven*, part 2, 14.
[46] Traherne, *Centuries of Meditations*, 35.
[47] Traherne, *Centuries of Meditations*, 36.
[48] Traherne, *Centuries of Meditations*, 69.
[49] Gregory of Nazianzus, *Oration* 38, para. 7.
[50] Traherne, *Centuries of Meditations*, 124–25.

sight,[51] akin to a 'Mirror' that contains within its image that which it reflects.[52] Additionally, the human soul, as made in the Image of God, is capable of loving all that it contains, 'as a Mirror returneth the very self-same Beams it receiveth from the Sun.'[53] Just as the world, then, is a 'mirror of infinit beauty' because God is 'all in all', so too the human self is a mirror of infinite appreciation for this beauty. Indeed, as Traherne makes clear, the nature of the human soul means that its fulfilment requires that it loves God in all things, as it is only through this reciprocity of receiving and giving that 'Thou Expandest and Enlargest thy self.'[54] As made in the image of an infinitely giving God, the human self is most itself when, in mirroring the God who is 'all in all', it loves the all that God is in.

The cross of Christ: a 'Tree set on fire with invisible flame, that Illuminateth all the World.'

The focal point of Traherne's theology is God's love for humanity revealed by Christ dying on the cross. In meditating upon the Christ upon the cross, the soul encounters the 'Centre of Eternity.'[55] Speaking at length of Christ's crucifixion, Traherne explains that:

> There we may see a Man Loving all the World, and a GOD Dying for Mankind ... It is... the only Mirror, wherin all things appear in their proper Colors ... a Tree set on fire with in visible flame, that Illuminateth all the World ... In the light of which we see

---

[51] Cf. Traherne, *Centuries of Meditations*, 60. See also Maximus the Confessor, *Ambiguum* 41, para. 3.

[52] Traherne, *Centuries of Meditations*, 122.

[53] Traherne, *Centuries of Meditations*, 177.

[54] Traherne, *Centuries of Meditations*, 36.

[55] Traherne, *Centuries of Meditations*, 27.

how to possess all the Things in Heaven and Earth after His similitud.[56]

In willingly going to the cross while 'loving all the world', Christ reveals himself to be the heir *of* the world who dies *for* all of humanity. He thereby exemplifies how all things can be possessed and in whose light things are able to be apprehended as they truly are; that is to say, the 'only Mirror' in which the 'proper Colors' of things appear. One might perhaps recall Nicholas of Cosa's likening of God in *De Visione Dei* to a 'living-mirror-of-eternity', which is unlike any physical mirror not least because that which stands in front of it is actually the image, not *vice versa*. Among the true colours revealed by their mirror of the crucified God, for Traherne, is the nature of the human soul itself. To be the recipient of infinite divine love, to the extent that God was willing to sacrifice himself, entails for Traherne that the soul must be thought of as itself possessing an infinite capacity to receive such love: an infinite sea can only be fittingly directed towards, and received by, a correspondingly infinite vessel. Similarly, the infinite divine love embodied by God's self-sacrifice in Christ reveals the human soul to be something that God regards as possessing infinite value.[57]

Traherne's theology of loving the natural world thereby presents us with three interfacing mirrors: (1) the mirror of the God's self-revelation in the crucified Christ, which reveals the human soul to be of an infinite value; (2) the human soul, which is made in the image of God, and capable of attending, in true gratitude to God, to the natural world, which (3) is itself a 'mirror' of infinite beauty created by a God who is within all things. Traherne's theology is love all the way down, and mirrors all the way up.

---

[56] Ibid.

[57] Traherne, *Kingdom of God*, 442.

Conclusion

This essay has argued that Thomas Traherne provides a Christian theological vision of how and why the natural world should be loved which is striking for its eloquent and unambiguous affirmation of the world's essential goodness. I have further suggested that, by reading Traherne through the lens of a wider Christian mystical tradition, one can appreciate his theology of God, *qua* Creator *ex nihilo*, being 'all in all', and of human souls, *qua* bearers of the *imago Dei*, being thereby capable of possessing, appreciating or otherwise 'containing' all things within themselves. This theological anthropology further underpins Traherne's insistence upon both the capacity of the human being to express gratitude towards God for the natural world, and the ethical imperative of her doing so. Just as, according to Nicholas of Cusa, God is the only mirror by which things appear as they truly are, so too for Traherne the incarnate God's death upon the cross constitutes the 'the only Mirror, wherein all things appear in their proper Colors.'

We do not always love the natural world as we ought to, because we do not appreciate who we fundamentally *are*. God's initiative of love towards humanity illuminates the true nature and value of the human soul which, as the image of God, is equipped to properly attend in wonder to the 'mirror of infinite beauty' represented by the natural world. God being 'all in all' makes the world lovely; the soul being 'all in all' makes the human being capable of lovingly appreciating the world's loveliness—that is, loving all things in God, and God in all things.

8

Summing Up: Outlines of an Eco-Love-Theology

Paul S. Fiddes

What can it mean to love Planet Earth? Many people will profess casually that 'I love nature', but can that love make an actual impact on the life of our distressed and ravaged world? Is love a practical response to the ecological crisis into which the human and non-human world is plunged at the present time, or just an emotional extravagance? Further, is this love reciprocated by non-human forms of life and even by apparently inanimate objects—can the planet love back? And for religious belief, how does love for nature connect both with the act of loving God and with receiving the love that God bestows on all creation? Is love of God, not just love, any kind of practical response to environmental emergency? These are the fundamental questions that the essays in this book have sought to explore, from the perspectives of three world religions—Judaism, Christianity and Islam.

In this closing essay, I intend to draw upon those that have preceded, weaving threads together into a 'meshwork'[1] of thought that will, I hope, help us to participate more fully in the 'meshwork' of the planet.

---

[1] The term is coined by Tim Ingold as a more accurate description than 'network': see Tim Ingold, *Being Alive. Essays on Movement, Knowledge and Description* (London: Routledge, 2022), 79–80.. It is re-applied by Celia Deane-Drummond in her essay.

Loving the earth: divine revelation and divine immanence

Cutting to the heart of the issue, Melissa Raphael in her essay asks whether it is possible, from a Jewish perspective, to love the earth at all, rather than loving the God who is revealed through the world. According to Raphael's account, there is little evidence from the writings of the Rabbis that they thought the self-manifestation of God in nature meant loving the medium in which God is revealed. The basic question for a Jew is 'what or whom are we *commanded* to love?' *Ahavah* is an obligated love and there is little interest in love as a natural emotional state measurable by its intensity of feeling. [2] *Ahavah* then is less an affective response to others as an object of desire, and more a commanded responsibility to act with a daily, practical, loving kindness (*hesed*) that is conducive to their well-being. In the Torah and the Rabbis we find God's command to love the stranger—especially the fatherless and the widow—as well as the neighbour. Study of the natural world will lead to love of God, so that the earth is primarily a 'contemplative, theocentric, occasion for love', not an object of love in itself. To be sure, Raphael later develops in her essay a justification for modern Judaism to 'love the planet', but for the moment we should take note of her conclusion that from a Jewish perspective the fact that God is revealed through the world is not *sufficient* reason for loving it.

There appears to be a different tradition in Islamic poetry. Leyla Tajer and Amir H. Zekrgoo find that the self-disclosure of God in the natural world prompted the classical Persian poets to treat the earth as 'the beloved one'. They write about a 'love-affair with nature' in the verses of Rūmī and Hāfez Shīrāzī in the classical period, and also of

---

[2] See Melissa Raphael, 'Judaism's Commandment to Love: "A Well-Tempered Banality" or the Messianic Trumpet's Blast?', in Paul S. Fiddes (ed.), *Love as Common Ground: Essays on Love and Religion* (Lanham: Lexington Books, 2021), 111-13.

Sohrāb Sepehrī in the modern age. Since, following the Qur'an, the natural elements are signs of God, nature demands not only respect but love. Tajer and Zekrgoo show how classical poetry evokes this love through a stock of common images, and how the modern poetry of Sohrāb does so by using similar images more impressionistically, individualistically and unexpectedly. Nature is 'the beloved' because it cannot be separated from God as the ultimate 'Beloved'. In his essay, Tareq Moqbel gives a philosophical basis for this love by reference to al-Ghazālī's principle that beauty is lovable: 'no one can deny that beauty is intrinsically worthy of love.'[3]

However, we gather from the account of Tajer and Zekrgoo that love of the natural world is presented somewhat indirectly or obliquely. We cannot be sure in reading the poetry whether the love expressed is directed towards a beautiful woman, or nature, or God; there is deliberate ambiguity and blurring of reference which is entirely appropriate for poetry. Moreover, nature certainly teaches us about love, but in Hāfez nature is portrayed as being symbolic of human love-relations between lover and beloved, as if elements of the natural world are 'characters on a stage'. In the surprising, even disturbing imagery of Sohrāb, natural elements are substituted for religious objects and rituals, so that the feeling of devotion to God is evoked by encountering forces and aspects of nature. Love of the natural world is strongly implied in all this, but is rarely directly expressed.

One result from Raphael's analysis is to see that talk of loving the planet has a stronger basis if God is not only *manifested* through the world, but *immanent* in the world. The firmer the identification between God and the material world, the more love of God is identified with loving the earth. Raphael reviews some modern Jewish theology which takes this turn towards divine immanence. In these thinkers, the planet

---

[3] Al-Ghazālī, *Love, Longing, Intimacy and Contentment*, trans. Eric Ormsby (Cambridge: The Islamic Texts Society, 2016), 16–17.

comes to life 'as a fully materialized manifestation of the immanent divine (sometimes feminized as She), and as a manifestation of the originary divine love present at and for creation.'[4] Raphael quotes modern Jewish theologians who affirm that God is 'all in everything', and that 'God so loved the world that She gave herself to it and became the Earth'. Jews must therefore 'love and care for the Earth because She is an embodiment of the Divine.' Raphael commends such thinking for nourishing the growth of a worldwide Jewish eco-praxis, but cannot be comfortable with it herself. If love is 'commanded love' it must come from a will which is transcendent to the world, and she judges that the Jewish tradition stresses this separation between God and the world and is opposed to blurring distinctions between God, nature and humanity.

Raphael does admit that, while this hierarchical relation between God and creation is the majority opinion, 'some of the more esoteric mystical Jewish traditions can support an immanentist theological reading'. Naftali Rothenberg in his essay converges with Raphael in the judgement that that loving the earth is not *explicitly* called for among the early Rabbis, but he finds a belief in the immanence of God in the world to be rather more widespread than Raphael does. He quotes, for instance, *Bereshit Rabbah* 68 to the effect that 'the Holy Blessed One is the dwelling of the world and the world is not the dwelling of the Holy One', meaning that creation inhabits the being of God (an instance of panentheism). Again, he takes from the Mishnah the portrayal of God as the soul of the world, filling it like the soul in the body as the source of its perpetual, unceasing life. When this is combined with the actual command voiced by the Rabbis to observe and study nature, he argues that the result is two possible tracks of thought that are both present. First, admiring and pondering on nature is a necessary way to reach love

---

[4] Raphael cites Michael Lerner, *Spirit matters: Global Healing and the Wisdom of the Soul* (Charlottesville: Hamptons Road Publishing, 2000) as a significant exemplar of this Jewish eco-spiritual turn.

for God. Second, at least implicitly, 'the love of nature *is* the love of God', because 'the entire creation and every detail within it is identified to one degree or another with the divine Creator'.

This latter train of thought becomes more explicit in some passages in the Mishnah, and significantly where the noun 'the place' is used ambivalently both as a euphemism for God, and for a particular location in the earth.[5] 'Loving the place' thus equates loving God with loving the material world. While Raphael rightly warns that a doctrine of divine immanence *can* dissolve the difference between God and the world, Naftali maintains that a dwelling of creation 'in God' means that the world 'is identical with, or overlaps with, God', but 'not the other way around'.

The Christian contributions to this book affirm a deep immanence of God in creation, and base a human love of the planet on this reality. But they also affirm a participation of the world in God which does not simply dissolve God into the world. Celia Deane-Drummond portrays creatures of diverse kinds as participating in the unfolding of life, and so 'continuously moving within the flows of the Spirit'; she recalls here the view of Aquinas that created persons are enabled to love by the Spirit, 'because of participation in divine goodness'. Emily DeMoor draws from Ilia Delio the vision of God as the 'love energy' that maintains the physical structures of the universe (an idea ultimately deriving from Teilhard de Chardin),[6] and she affirms the kenotic (self-

---

[5] *Bereshit Rabbah* 68:9.

[6] Pierre Teilhard de Chardin, *The Phenomenon of Man* (London: Collins, 1963), 264–8; de Chardin, *Le Milieu Divin* (London: Collins, 1961), 135–8. Teilhard distinguishes between 'tangential energy' (energy of attraction associated with matter-to-matter interactions) and 'radial energy' (energy which draws the element in the direction of a more complex state, associated with consciousness), both divine: see Pierre Teilhard de Chardin, *The Human Phenomenon*, trans. Sarah Appleton-Weber (Brighton: Sussex Academic Press, 1999), 29–30. Delio identifies these with the Son and the Spirit within the Trinity: Ilia Delio, *The Unbearable Wholeness of Being. God, Evolution, and the*

emptying) presence of a loving God in all the 'inscapes' of nature. But at the same time she writes of love as the space for 'divine encounter', envisioning God as an Other to be met with, and portrays a human participation in the relational movements of the triune God. This appeal to the Trinity makes clear that, while all creation indwells God, God cannot be exhausted into the world, and she is indebted here to the thought both of myself and Ilia Delio. Later I intend to say more about loving the planet within what we might call a 'trinitarian panentheism'; this aims to be an 'immanent transcendence' which takes heed of Raphael's warning about losing the difference between the Creator and creation.

Loving the earth: three models of theological thought

On the foundation of God's manifestation in, and presence in, the world, essays have offered at least three theological models for loving the planet.

First, Raphael's own justification for loving the planet within a Jewish perspective reflects her suspicion of immanentist theology (while, of course, not denying God's various decisions to make God's self present in the world). She finds a command to love the planet—an obligated love—in extending the divine command to love the stranger so that it includes the natural world. She writes that 'The face of the planet is also that of a stranger to me. That is, the planet is not like me ... I remain a stranger to it. Even if the planet, as host to all living things, is granted some kind of consciousness, it does not know or welcome me as me.' With the use of the image of the 'face' she draws on the Jewish philosopher Emmanuel Levinas' thought, where the 'face' of the other makes an unconditional ethical demand upon us.[7] So, Raphael proposes,

---

Power of Love (Maryknoll: Orbis, 2021), 101.

[7] Emmanuel Levinas, *Totality and Infinity: An Essay on Exteriority,* trans. Alphonso

the face of the earth is strange and 'other' because it is vast, unfathomable and infinite, beyond our conception. It is a 'tehomic face', the 'face of the deep' that petitions love—and especially Jewish love since Jews know what it is to be suffering strangers—but it will always 'exceed itself as object of my love'. She also comments that loving the planet might come more easily to Jewish women who feel even more strongly the position of being treated as strangers, as outsiders to social life.

Raphael's approach entails, for her, a denial that human beings are in a reciprocal relation with the natural world, and here she diverges from other essayists, and indeed from my own proposal. We notice that she restricts love for the planet to what Anders Nygren called 'agape' love, or a love which is totally self-giving, and which does not satisfy desire and enhance the self in the way that is characteristic of 'eros'.[8] She writes that Jews are 'ethically obligated to care for [the earth] in the disinterested, non-reciprocal, non-instrumental, justice-seeking ways that are an expression of non-erotic agapeistic love.' We also notice that she is in accord with Levinas who denies reciprocity in all truly ethical relations between human beings; it is excluded by the absolute demand of the other upon us which means we cannot expect any return for our goodwill.[9] We must not assume that Raphael herself extends non-reciprocity to human relations, but as far as loving the planet is concerned, love consists of 'a practical alleviation of the suffering of what is *not* like you, without calculation or hope of reciprocity.' She claims that 'post-Levinas, a commanded love for the planet that cares for it irrespective of its yield or other return, and with no possibility of

Lingis (Pittsburgh: Duquesne University, 1979), 194–219.

[8] See Anders Nygren, *Agape and Eros*, Parts I and II, trans. Philip Watson (London: SPCK, 1982), 74–77, 94–5, 129–31.

[9] Levinas, *Totality and Infinity*, 194–201; Levinas, 'Meaning and Sense' in A. Peperzak, S. Critchley, R. Bernasconi (eds), *Levinas. Basic Philosophical Writings* (Bloomington: Indiana University Press, 1996), 49.

thanks or mutual empathy, can be a fully ecological, meta-anthropic love.'

As we explore other models of loving the planet, I hope it will become evident that Raphael's basic concept of loving the earth as a 'stranger' or an 'other' to us can be held together with a vision of erotic, reciprocal love, although we must recognize that she herself rules it out.

In an apparently complete contrast with Raphael, Greg Marcar gives an account of the Anglican Christian mystic, Thomas Traherne, who urges that we can and must love the world just because the human mind *can* embrace the world in its infinity. Exploring the background to Traherne's thought, Marcar recalls the relation of God to the created universe as held by Pseudo-Dionysius, John Scotus Eriugena and Nicholas of Cusa. In these theologians, there is a strong affirmation of divine immanence: everything manifests God as a divine light because there is a *mutual* indwelling between God and the world. All things subsist in God prior to coming into existence (Eriugena) and God as a maximum contains all things as a 'mirror of eternity' from which all creatures receive their finite forms of existence (Cusa). The Trahernian twist is to affirm that, since human beings are made in the image of God, the human mind or soul can also be present in all external objects and can expand to contain in itself all things in the natural world. Extending the image of Cusa, nature is a mirror of infinite beauty because it is created by God, and the human soul is likewise a mirror of eternity.

Now, love is at the centre of this vision. The human mind contains all things because it *loves* all things; the very capacity to be present in all is the infinite power of love. God cannot be loved with a merely finite love, but human beings *can* love God with an infinite love because they love God in all things. 'God's Nature requireth that Thou love all those whom He loveth. And receive Him in all those Things wherein He giveth Him self unto Thee ... Yea, by Loving Thou expandest and

Enlargest thy self.'[10] Comparing this account with Raphael's love of the earth as a stranger, it is apparent that there is a danger in Traherne's vision of allowing the human mind to dominate the rest of creation, subordinating it as an object to human subjectivity, and assuming it into the human self. This might encourage the human exploitation of nature which has proved so disastrous to the environment, despite Traherne's own injunctions to enjoy the world as a gift of God, and to make it an occasion not for human self-assertion but gratitude. Positively, however, Traherne stands in a long tradition of Christian thought in which the human mind and the cosmos are deeply intertwined, and his mystical way of expressing this situation roots it existentially in his experience of loving the world as a place of delightful wonders.

While Traherne does not use the word 'entanglement' he implies it, and this is the model which comes to the fore in the essays of Emily DeMoor and Celia Deane-Drummond, now enhanced by a modern scientific grasp of the processes of growth and development in the natural world. Loving the planet means exercising love within what Deane-Drummond calls a 'meshwork', taking the term from the thought of the social anthropologist Tim Ingold. She argues first that love in the sense of compassion, or caring-emotions, is unique to the homo-lineage of creatures. Something analogous to compassion, as a biological response to others, can be found in wolves and other social carnivores, but it is with the emergence of the human that we find evidence of long-term commitment to caring for another who is weak or in need. Such compassion, Deane-Drummond maintains, was gradually extended from other humans to animals, and finally to objects when it was accompanied by a sense of wonder, or the earth as a sacred realm. Thus

---

[10] Thomas Traherne, *Poems, Centuries and Three Thanksgivings*, ed. Anne Ridler (Oxford University Press, Oxford, 1966), *The First Century*, 72–73. I have modernized the spelling. For this expansion of the human being, compare Naftali Rothenberg's comments on Rabbinic ideas of Adam in his essay in this book.

it is possible to speak of a 'love of the planet', and Deane-Drummond stresses that extension of love arises in the context of exercising compassion in *community*.[11] This community, she then goes on to argue, has always been wider than human life. The phenomena of symbiosis (different organisms living together) and mutualism (living together for mutual benefit) appear at the very foundation of organic life, and take on the form of compassion with the evolutionary emergence of human beings.

Here she draws on the 'meshwork' thinking of Tim Ingold, the cultivating of an attitude which is open to the world in wonder and astonishment, and which resists dualistic thinking about the mind's control of matter. He affirms the sense that human beings are acted *upon* as they are wayfarers within a complex life in which we are entangled.[12] It is in realizing that we are immersed into this meshwork, stresses Deane-Drummond, that the sacredness of all life is rediscovered and love for the natural world is fostered, resulting in compassionate care for all creatures. Here she gives a religious dimension to Ingold's 'meshwork' and 'wonder'. Our astonished wonder is a resonance with the presence of God in the world. The community of life to which Ingold points can be understood as God's covenant with the whole earth and its creatures. Ingold attributes the sense we have of there being 'animation' in the whole world to the participation of all creatures in the unfolding of life, as they move within 'flows of spirit' which are larger than any individual.[13] This Deane-Drummond understands as moving

---

[11] In an important essay, Oliver Davies argues that a combination of the evolutionary science of the human with social neuroscience holds out the promise of a new depth of understanding of how community is formed: love is characterized by valuation and empathy, and so is a powerful kind of cognition at several levels of social organization. See Davies, 'Love as Belonging: Towards an Interdisciplinary Understanding of the Human', in Paul S. Fiddes, *Love as Common Ground. Essays on Love in Religion* (Lanham: Lexington Books, 2021), 287–310.

[12] See Ingold, *Being Alive*, 188–9.

[13] See Ingold, *Being Alive*, 35.

within the currents of the divine Spirit (*ruach*), and quotes Norman Wirzba on the impetus of 'divine energy'.[14] Aquinas is right. She thinks, to maintain that it is the interior force of God's Spirit that enables people to love, but he wrongly restricts this to love of God and neighbour, dismissing love of other beings as irrational.

Appealing to recent anthropology, Deane-Drummond shows that love of the natural world, and so giving of care to a distressed planet, arises when a sense of community is extended beyond the human arena, when we perceive the mutual 'entanglement' of all living things and objects. 'Entanglement' is also the argument of DeMoor, pointing to the phenomenon of symbiosis as a counterweight to Darwinian competition, finding—for example—a chemical 'call and response' in the life of truffles, and an altruism in exchange between trees through their complex interaction with fungi. Like Deane-Drummond, she finds this communal life to prompt a sense of the earth as sacred, and to be a self-revelation which leads us to the revelation and presence of God. She introduces, however, two significant elements into the vision of an entangled world which do not appear in this particular essay by Deane-Drummond.[15] One is the locating of human love for the planet not only in *realizing* our place within a network of life, but in a situation of 'intersubjectivity' which exceeds the human relation between subjects.

In the first place this means that there is a reciprocity between all entities in the natural world, as they express themselves in ways that are distinctive to their own nature and activity—using the language of the poet Gerard Manley Hopkins, DeMoor refers to the 'instress' and 'inscape' of their particular identities, unfolded outwards to others.

---

[14] Norman Wirzba, *This Sacred Life: Humanity's Place in a Wounded World* (Cambridge: Cambridge University Press, 2021).

[15] She certainly affirms a trinitarian perspective elsewhere: see Celia Deane-Drummond, *Christ and Evolution. Wonder and Wisdom* (London: SCM Press, 2009), 149–52.

Human beings can feel the 'allure' of nature which has an 'erotic' aspect to it, evoking and satisfying desire; DeMoor expresses this movingly in a poem of her own composition, and to this reciprocal relation I intend to return. There is a hint of this kind of interaction in Deane-Drummond's essay, but the notion of 'intersubjectivity' also appears to have a further dimension in DeMoor's thought. *In some way* the interaction between humans and their environment is the sharing of a common consciousness, which is a 'consciousness of love'. Here she is indebted to the thought of Ilia Delio, who affirms that consciousness is fundamental to all materiality, and that consciousness increases as things unite and new relations are formed through the 'radial energy' of love, until *self-consciousness* emerges in human beings.[16] DeMoor associates an 'empathetic' love with this kind of intersubjectivity, appealing to the idea of 'empathic fusion' between human subjects and the whole of nature. Deane-Drummond considers that love as compassion exceeds 'mere empathy' which she considers to be an '*imitation* of another's emotional state', but this difference with DeMoor appears to be a matter of definition, since DeMoor is writing of empathy as a *participation* in the emotions of another, within 'intersubjective spaces'. Love is a form of knowing, and the network of nature is a means of the mutual knowledge of created beings,

Another significant note in DeMoor's paper is her location of 'entanglement' in the interweaving relations of the triune God. This is the ultimate 'intersubjective space' in which we encounter God, other human beings and the whole of the natural world in love. While Deane-Drummond, in this particular essay, refers only to moving in the flow of the 'Spirit' of God (the biblical *ruach*), DeMoor writes that she intends to 'theologize intersubjectivity' in a vision of the Trinity. Following myself and Delio, DeMoor affirms that it is only possible to love God in our relations of love with others, since they participate in

---

[16] Ilia Delio, *The Primacy of Love* (Minneapolis: Fortress Press, 2022), 20–24.

the relational dynamic of the Trinity. This appears to be a more inter-personal version of Traherne's view that it is only possible for a human subject to love God in loving the many things of the world, and this is confirmed by the fact (though not remarked by Marcar) that Traherne himself roots this love in the Trinity. The human person can expand to include all things in love because the Trinity 'extends itself' in love, both within itself (in the traditional language of 'begetting' and 'proceeding') and *beyond* itself. So 'in all love the Trinity is Clear [. . .]. Love in the Bosom is the Parent of Love, Love in the Stream is the Effect of Love, Love seen, or Dwelling in the Object proceedeth from both'.[17]

These three accounts of what it means to love the world are not entirely in accord with each other, as we have seen. In a book like this, it is an advantage to be able to present readers with differing approaches for them to make their own judgement. Nevertheless, there is still a great deal of common ground between the three models. The potentially starkest contrast appears between Raphael's view that we love the natural world as a stranger to us, a mark of its strangeness being its infinity, and Traherne's concept (as related by Marcar) that we love the natural world by *encompassing* its infinity within our own minds. The vision of the entanglement or 'meshwork' of human and other natural life in Deane-Drummond and DeMoor further seems at odds with Raphael's approach. It also appears to depart from Traherne's focus on the capacity of the individual human mind, which verges on a particular kind of entanglement—one characterized by a dualism between mind and matter rejected by Ingold as well as our two essayists. However, Raphael's rightful insistence—with Levinas—that the earth is an 'other' face confronting us which we cannot subordinate to our own subjectivity can be heeded without the corollary that we should not look for a responsive relationship from the other, or develop a bond of sympathy. Feminist critics of Levinas, such as Luce Irigaray, have

---

[17] Traherne, *The Second Century*, 40. Spelling modernized.

commented that 'Levinas does not ever seem to have experienced the transcendence of the other which becomes an immediate ecstasy (*extase instante*) in me and with him—or her.' For Levinas, she goes on, love is an experience in which 'the distance is always maintained.'[18] The same critique might be transferred to a strictly Levinasian account of loving the earth as an 'other'. An 'erotic' love in which desires are fulfilled through relationships need not be be incompatible with an 'agapeic' love which does not *expect* any reward for loving. As many critics of Nygren's polarization of 'agape' and 'eros' have maintained, while no recompense is *demanded*, the result of true self-giving is in fact a deeper realization of our own identity.[19] In coming closer to the beloved, lovers come closer to themselves.

Traherne's account of loving the natural world is certainly more individualistic and anthropocentric than the 'entanglement' commended by DeMoor and Deane-Drummond. But there is nothing to prevent placing the human subject that Traherne describes in the context of *intersubjectivity*, first in human community and then in an extended community of created beings. Traherne's emphasis that the human mind is 'present' in all things rather than controlling all things from a superior position suggests a participation in the world which undermines a strict subject-object relationship. Moreover (as Marcar explains), the definitive mirror of eternity and mirror of infinite beauty is the crucified person of Christ, since in his self-giving we 'may see a Man Loving all

---

[18] Luce Irigaray, 'Questions to Emmanuel Levinas' in Margaret Whitford (ed), *The Irigaray Reader* (Oxford: Blackwell, 1991), 180.

[19] Eberhard Jüngel, *God as the Mystery of the World*, trans. D. L. Guder (Edinburgh: T. & T. Clark, 1983), 317–18, n. 13; cf. 298, 374–5; Werner G. Jeanrond, *A Theology of Love* (London: T. & T. Clark, 2010), 113–24; much earlier, see M. C. D'Arcy, *The Mind and Heart of Love* (Faber and Faber, London, 1945), 56-60, 185–93. Simon May makes the significant point, against Nygren, that *agape* and *eros* are both modes of attention to the loved one: May, *Love. A New Understanding of an Ancient Emotion* (Oxford: Oxford University Press, 2019), 112, 122.

the World'. This is the 'only Mirror, wherin all things appear in their proper Colors'. This mirror, continues Traherne, shows us 'how to possess all the Things in Heaven and Earth after His Similitude',[20] that is in the mode of self-sacrifice, not domination.

.

Love of the planet in a reciprocal relationship

Given that love of the planet is possible and desirable, how can love of nature make a difference to our treatment of it? Rothenberg points out the potential gap here; he admits that passages in the Mishnah which commend a love for God through giving loving attention to the natural world are not connected in Jewish tradition with passages in the Halakhah which are full of instances of practical responsibility towards the world. The latter display a sensitive balance between behaviour which is of benefit to humanity, and acts which foster the well-being of the earth, but they are not explicitly related to a theology of God's relation to humanity and the rest of creation. He proposes that modern Judaism *should* connect them, and follows this path in his own essay.

Now, it is easier to see the place of love in ecology if this love meets a response from the side of nature itself. If loving the planet is part of a reciprocal relationship with the natural world, possibilities of cooperation between humanity and the rest of creation within the 'meshwork' of life open up. At all levels of creation, including the human, there can be a symbiotic working together for the flourishing of life. Human acts of love are then not simply 'welfarism', bestowed with a patronizing superiority towards 'objects of concern'. In human relations, the lover must be open to receive benefits from the beloved, and to being changed by his or her response, or love simply becomes a cold charity. This is an integration between 'agape' and 'eros', where a person in the moment of self-giving (*agape*) is humble enough to allow

---

[20] Traherne, *The First Century*, 59–60.

the other to complete and fulfil his or her own desires (*eros*). In the same way, the very future of the planet may depend on a mutuality of giving and receiving in love.

As we have seen, Raphael explicitly rules out reciprocity in love, lest human beings exploit nature for the rewards and benefits that this kind of relation may bring, and we should remain sensitive to this danger. She is, of course, well aware of other contemporary Jewish theology that takes a different path, and which affirms that 'We are bound to one another only by the web of life', and it is for the sake of the 'continual unfolding of the adventure of creation' that we must 'choose life'. [21] But her own approach reminds us of the unconditional 'command' to love the stranger, and the ethical demand that the face of the other lays upon us. Levinas rejects the reciprocity in relations generally which is advocated by another Jewish philosopher, Martin Buber, dismissing it as a 'comfortable give-and-take.'[22] But Buber is clear that reciprocity is not a symmetrical 'give and take'; there is an element of being 'overwhelmed' by the other person in any personal relationship, as the core of the subject is broken open by the ethical demand which the other makes.[23] The essence of the I-Thou relation lies in the space 'between' persons, not in an exactly matching and equal response of each person,[24] and yet there is a genuine mutuality as each treats the other as a 'thou' rather than an 'it'.

The Islamic tradition of poetry gives us a picture of what a respectful reciprocity between human beings and nature might look like. If nature and God are both known as the 'beloved', and God actively

---

[21] Carol P. Christ and Judith Plaskow, *Goddess and God in the World: Conversations in Embodied Theology* (Minneapolis: Fortress Press, 106), 173–4.

[22] Levinas, 'Meaning and Sense', 49.

[23] Martin Buber, *I and Thou*, trans. R. Gregor Smith (Edinburgh: T. & T. Clark, 1937), 51–54, 111–12.

[24] Martin Buber, *Between Man and Man*, trans. R. Gregor Smith (London: Collins/Fontana, 1961), 19–22, 32–33.

loves, then it follows that nature too is loving. Tajer and Zekrgoo, reviewing classical and modern Persian verse, find that the experience of love is necessary for spiritual growth, and that in the Islamic tradition 'natural elements and forces were seen as conscious entities' within this spiritual process. They quote, for example, verses from Rūmī in which sky and sun are portrayed as 'in love', and where 'Farm and mountain are both lovers/ Or else plants wouldn't grow from their belly'.[25] They cannot dismiss such expressions as 'merely metaphorical', and believe that life experience, supported by scientific insights, 'gives proof of a reciprocal relation between human beings and the life that surrounds them—vegetable as well as animal'. They write that 'human affection for nature transforms human actions, and nature's responses often appear in its own manifestations'.

Tareq Moqbel also invokes a reciprocity between human beings and the natural world, basing this firmly on the Qur'an. In the first part of his essay he develops an 'ecological hermeneutics', which he parallels by a 'hermeneutics of love', and together these provide tools for reading the Qur'an. The very first principle of an ecological interpretation is that nature is an 'active agent'. As an example, nature has a voice: the seven heavens, the earth, and everyone in them, we are told in Q. 17:44, testify to the glory of God, and here Moqbel draws attention to precedents in the Hebrew Bible (such as Psalm 50:6). This leads us, he suggests, to recognize a reciprocity between human beings and nature, since the activity of what is other to us offers the possibilities of a 'mutual exchange of love'. Other principles of interpretation are the realization that human beings and nature are interconnected, the union between them being love; that nature is intrinsically beautiful, and so 'loveable'; and that moderation is needed in consuming the products of

---

[25] Ghazal 2673 in Jalāl al-Dīn Muḥammad Rūmī, *Kulliyyāt-i Diwān-i Shams Tabrīzī, bā taṣḥīḥāt va ḥawāshī*, ed. Badī' al-Zamān Furūzānfar, 4th ed. (Tehran: Sidāy-e Mu'āṣir, 1386/ 2007), vol. 2, 1054.

the world, which is an attitude of love. In the present environmental crisis key players in developing a 'green economy' will be those who handle Islamic finance, and he believes that the system has drifted away from its supposedly Qur'anic base, especially in failing to recognize that individuals are embedded in their natural environment. He commends his hermeneutic to those who hold the levers of the Islamic economy, and bids them give attention to one particular narrative in the Qur'an, that of the 'Green Man'.

Thus the second part of his essay develops an exegesis of the story of the Green Man, in a passage where this un-named character teaches lessons to Moses (Qur'an 18). The narrative places non-human creation at the centre of life, and offers, Moqbel suggests, symbols of what is hidden beneath the surface of nature, beyond mere appearance. This constitutes a rebuke to Islamic finance which is often concerned with form—using the tool of 'exceptions'—rather than substance. What is hidden is mercy and love which is prior to knowledge, and which must shape financial systems. Further, he suggests that through the symbol of *al-kidr*, the man immersed in nature, the narrative assumes that this love is, in some mysterious way, being exercised by natural elements themselves as well as by God.

In her essay Deane-Drummond moves at least tentatively towards an idea of reciprocity when she locates a 'mutualism' at the foundation of organic life, developing into 'prosociality' or 'helping behaviour' at a high level of animal life, which finally emerges as compassion in human life. Just as Moqbel appeals to a piece of what Norman Brown calls 'folk-lore',[26] so Deane-Drummond cites hagiographical stories of animals being responsive to God and to the needs of the saints, legends which are not to be taken literally and yet which point to some kind of agency. But it is DeMoor who gives reciprocity a central place in her

---

[26] Norman O. Brown, 'The Apocalypse of Islam', *Social Text* 8 (1983): 162, as cited by Moqbel in his essay.

account of loving the planet, focused on a vision of *intersubjectivity* between human life and the natural world. Like Moqbel, she quotes the Hebrew psalms as giving agency to elements of the natural world: 'their voice goes out through all the earth' (Psa 19:6). Leaning on the thought of Teilhard, DeMoor finds that love is both the energy that sustains the universe and the 'unitive force': so the allure which is exerted by all things in their own way and through their own bodies is a 'propensity to unite'. When she writes in her poem that 'the sky/ made love to me' she is echoing, probably unconsciously, the poet Rūmī as cited by Tajer and Zekrgoo: 'If the sky was not in love/ It would not have so much clarity.'

From a theological perspective, the universe is to be seen as sustained by the energy of divine love, and all created beings and things within it are understood to be not just passive vehicles of that love (mere channels through which the divine agape passes), but active partners in it. Is it possible to be more precise about the nature of this agency and reciprocity in the light of scientific accounts of evolution? Our essayists who subscribe to this picture of 'what is really going on' (to quote Moqbel) tend to find something *analogous* at non-human levels of creation to the love and compassion which emerge at the end of the evolutionary process with human beings. DeMoor follows Delio in quoting Teilhard's view that 'the *characteristics* of human love such as attraction, irresistibility and union, can be found on the most fundamental levels of physical life.'[27] Other terms essayists use for these analogous characteristics are 'symbiosis', 'mutuality', 'call and response', 'allure', 'impulse towards unity', 'helping behaviour', and 'prosociality'. Deane-Drummond remarks that, with regard to 'social animals', scientists observe that 'the brain regions which respond are homologous with those activated in humans.'[28] Essayists avoid the

---

[27] Delio, *Primacy of Love*, 16; cf. Teilhard de Chardin, *Phenomenon of Man*, 264. My italics.

[28] See also Celia Deane-Drummond, *Theological Ethics Through a Multispecies Lens:*

rather homogeneous notion in process theology that all entities in the world have a mental as well as a physical aspect, although DeMoor comes close to this with her adoption of a universal 'consciousness' from Delio.[29]

If we take the approach of analogy rather than pan-mentality, it may be asked whether it is proper to use the same word, 'love', of the nature and self-expression of God, human beings, other animals, vegetable life and inanimate objects. Is it just loose talk to say that human love of the planet is met by the planet's love of humanity? Here several essayists show it is indeed appropriate by placing the analogy in a larger context; behaviours analogous to human love are part of a larger whole of which we *are* confident to use the word 'love'. They do not just mirror love but *participate* in love. They exist in the 'field' of divine love, or share in the 'flow of the Spirit', or are part of 'the unfolding of life', or they are part of a larger 'consciousness' which loves (a notion to which I shall return). Above all, DeMoor affirms that they participate in the inexhaustible, interweaving currents of love that Christians call the 'Trinity'.

The implications of reciprocal love

DeMoor writes, as a Christian thinker, that intersubjective attraction at the collective or systemic level can be understood as happening within the loving relations of God as Trinity. I suggest that it is essential to clarify that this is an intersubjectivity *within* the Trinity and not an intersubjectivity *of* the Trinity. God, as the only uncreated reality, cannot be conceived in a literal way by created beings. As the Mystery of love which cannot be categorized in human terms, we can only use appropriate analogies and metaphors for God. This means that God

---

The Evolution of Wisdom, Vol. 1 (Oxford: Oxford University Press, 2019), 74–94.

[29] Delio, *Primacy of Love,* 20–22; *Unbearable Wholeness of Being,* 39–40, 170–5.

cannot be reduced to an object of human examination, but no more can God be reduced to a *subject* or a community of three subjects. It is appropriate to speak, by analogy, of loving *relationships* within God because in actuality we find ourselves *participating* in relations which are wider and more inexhaustible than our own; from the perspective of the Christian story of Jesus Christ we can say that these relations are *like* a father sending out a son on a mission of healing, a son who is responding in obedience to a father, and a spirit who is opening up these relations to a new depth and a new future.[30] These relations of love can also be experienced and spoken about in terms of relations between a mother and a daughter, since God as the ultimate Reality cannot be restricted to a particular gender, and because there are many contexts in which feminine language is more suitable.

When talking about God we cannot, then, appropriately speak of subjects who *have* relationships. If we speak, in the traditional Christian language, of three divine 'persons', we can only mean that these 'persons' *are* themselves relations.[31] All we know is that we are immersed in differing currents or movements of relationship that are always 'more' than our own. Moreover, we only experience these 'transcendent' relations by engaging in relations with other created beings, whether other human persons or other entities in nature. The transcendent is always immanent. We find ourselves immersed in the love of God only when we love others.

This is the reciprocity in God that eternally makes room for the reciprocity of created beings. Our intersubjective relations are held and

---

[30] Cf. Karl Barth, *Church Dogmatics*, trans. G. Bromiley and T. F. Torrance (T. & T. Clark, Edinburgh, 1936-77), I/1, 372.

[31] For earlier versions of persons as relations see: Augustine, *De Trinitate* 5.6; Aquinas, *Summa Theologiae* 1a.29.4. For a full exposition, see Paul S. Fiddes, 'Relational Trinity: Radical Perspective', in Stephen Holmes, Paul Molnar, Thomas McCall and Paul Fiddes, *Two Views on the Doctrine of the Trinity* Counterpoints: Bible and Theology (Grand Rapids: Zondervan, 2014), 159–206.

nurtured in networks of relations in God, so that there is intersubjectivity *in* God, but God in God's self cannot be an intersubjective community. I am proposing, then, what may be called a 'trinitarian panentheism'— everything created is 'within' the triune relations of God. That is, God in creating makes room in God's own being for everything, because there is a space for everything between the interweaving and dynamic relations of love that are God. As Ilia Delio puts it simply: 'the world is in the heart of God from all eternity'.[32]

DeMoor follows quite closely the thought of Delio, as she makes clear in her essay. Delio herself does not seem to maintain a difference between intersubjectivity *in* God and *of* God. She writes that 'to say God is Trinity is to say that God is always in the dynamic movement of love. God is self-creative love expressed in personal relationships of love which includes the dynamism of intersubjectivity and the community emerging from these relationships.'[33] This appears to imply that the intersubjectivity and community are of *God*, and not only of the *world* in God. But she also treats divine 'persons' as relationships rather than a community of subjects: 'God is creative and dynamic, a triunity of love relationships energizing the heart of creation.'[34] If we do decline to talk about God as an intersubjective community in God's self, and limit our talk to a web of divine 'relationships' as I suggest, then there is more possibility for common ground with strictly monotheistic religions. I am not, of course, being so presumptuous as to conscript other religions into the Christian vision of the Trinity, which has its origin in what Christians want to say about Christ, but there can at least be an overlap when Jewish and Muslim scholars want to affirm that loving relations

---

[32] Delio, *Primacy of Love*, 33.

[33] Delio, *Primacy of Love*, 30–31.

[34] Delio, *Primacy of Love*, 41. Cf. *Unbearable Wholeness of Being*, 101–2: 'The Trinity is not a separate divine community of Persons into which creation must fit; rather, the whole cosmotheandric process is Trinity'.

in creation are held within the life of God. Raphael, for example, quotes Levinas to the effect that 'The love of God for Man is the fact that Man loves his neighbour',[35] and she comments that 'God does not exist as another, if Supreme, Being, but is revealed as the inter-face relation through which God may pass'.[36]

It is in these terms that we might be able to affirm DeMoor's suggestion that every part of nature shares in a larger whole which is a loving 'consciousness'. Rather than supposing that every element of nature is itself conscious, we can envisage that it participates in a 'meshwork' of life in which consciousness gradually emerges. While there is then a created consciousness larger than any individual which is held in the relational life of God, there is no need to postulate that God *is* that consciousness as a kind of cosmic mind. Categories such as 'subjectivity', 'consciousness' and 'mind' belong to created realities, and God cannot be shrunk to fit them. All things have 'subjectivity' in that they express themselves outwardly, or as the poet Hopkins put it, each thing 'deals out that being indoors each one dwells;/ Selves—goes itself',[37] and at higher levels of nature this subjectivity deepens into consciousness. It is right to call the 'attraction', 'allure' and 'mutuality' at every level of creation 'love', since it shares in this larger context.

Reflecting on the reciprocity within the natural world, another issue arises. We have been assuming that the elements of the world are not expressing and communicating the energy of divine love which sustains them in a merely passive way. They are not merely the channels for a greater love, simply inactive conduits for the powerful stream of God's love. They contribute, in suitable ways, their own characteristics in a movement towards unity, and the love to which we respond is thus a

---

[35] Levinas, *Difficult Freedom*, 191.
[36] Cf. Levinas, 'Meaning and Sense', 65.
[37] 'As kingfishers catch fire', in *The Poems of Gerard Manley Hopkins*, Fourth Edition, ed. W. H. Gardner and N. H. Mackenzie (Oxford University Press, London, 1967), 90.

cooperation between uncreated and created love. If this is so, then the elements of nature must have their own responsiveness to God as well as to each other and to human beings. They will have the capacity to 'go with the flow' of God's purpose to make a more flourishing life, and this means that they will also have the potential to *resist* the movement of God's creating Spirit. This would be a complex response to God, entangled with accident, randomness and contingency, and only becoming free-will in personal beings, although it would have a family-likeness to freedom in human beings who have emerged from the natural world

There have been attempts to describe this ability to cooperate or resist in scientific terms: process philosophy, for instance, envisages the basic building blocks of the physical world as microscopic 'entities' which have objective and subjective aspects, analogous to the body and mind with which we are familiar. In the process vision, these dipolar entities occupy a vast network of mutual influences in which they relate and grasp ('prehend') each other, forming the large-scale objects we perceive. God is immersed into this process as 'the great companion—the fellow-sufferer who understands',[38] being affected by the whole and moving it through the 'lure' of persuasive love towards fullness of value and beauty. Because there is an aspect of 'feeling' in every entity, all can accept, modify or even reject the divine aims that are offered.[39]

While I want to affirm the mode of God's action in the world as persuasive love, I doubt myself whether we have as yet a scientific language adequate to describe the phenomenon of the responsiveness of all creation to its creator. We do have the poetic images of Hebrew,

[38] Alfred North Whitehead, *Process and Reality. An Essay in Cosmology* (New York: Macmillan, 1929, repr. 1967), 532.
[39] See Whitehead, *Process and Reality*, 27–39, 163–6, 373–5, 519–33; Lewis S. Ford, *The Lure of God: A Biblical Background for Process Theism* (Philadelphia: Fortress Press, 1978), 82–5; Charles Hartshorne, *The Divine Relativity: A Social Conception of God* (New Haven: Yale University Press, 1948), 134–8.

Christian and Islamic scripture to portray it, as various essays in this book show, and to which we may add the image of 'covenant' between God and every living thing.[40] I suggest that the influence of God on the growth of every created thing may be seen in an 'environmental way': in a trinitarian panentheistic account all created beings dwell together in the triune God, and so their growth and development is shaped by immersion into the interweaving movements of love and justice that are God, and their response and lack of response takes multiple forms. Other useful language for this responsiveness includes the 'plasticity' of organisms, and John Polkinghorne's proposal that God offers 'informational' input to shape patterns of growth holistically, which may or not be adopted.[41]

Now, if we accept that all created entities have some capacity to respond to the lure of God's love, and to express it outwardly, we must also take seriously the potential for resistance to this love. Essays in this book have presented—rightly—the natural world as suffering as a victim of human greed and exploitation. 'Love for the planet', in a reciprocal relation of love, is seen as a way of rectifying human despoilation of nature and learning from nature about the way to develop more healthy forms of life. But we cannot ignore the stark fact that there is a suffering within the natural world itself, which becomes especially acute among 'social animals' who have existed *prior* to the emergence of humanity. There is a problem of pain outside the sphere of human life. If we love the natural world because is it 'loveable', we must admit that there are aspects than are hard to love. Not only is predation built into the survival of living beings, but the story of evolution is one of

---

[40] Gen 9:16–17; Hos 2:18; Rom 8:19–22.

[41] John Polkinghorne, *Belief in God in an Age of Science* (Yale: Yale University Press, 1998), 56–9; see Paul S. Fiddes, *Seeing the World and Knowing God. Hebrew Wisdom and Christian Doctrine in a Late-Modern Context* (Oxford: Oxford University Press, 2013), 164–5.

waste and involuntary sacrifice.

There has been a recent surge of discussion about this issue among Christian theologians, wanting to reconcile the 'disvalues' in creation, as well as its values, with a good Creator. Some have asserted that there is simply no other way for the development of complex forms of life, and ultimately the emergence of human beings, than the path of suffering and sacrifice.[42] Others find the gratuitous and excessive amount of natural suffering to be intolerable as the direct intention of a creative God of love.[43] It cannot all be laid at the door of human 'fallenness', and so some Christian thinkers consider that there is a kind of fallenness in the whole of nature. I count myself among those who take this view, while insisting that it is not a one-point 'fall' at a specific moment, but a cumulative drifting away from the divine purpose for wholeness of being towards the state of 'non-being'; it is a 'slippage' from the good and a 'resistance' to the persuasive love of God dating from the very beginning of creation.[44] 'Loving the planet' will then mean *both* refraining from human acts of harm and seeking to work with the divine love to redeem what is broken.

---

[42] Christopher Southgate, 'Re-Reading Genesis, John and Job: A Christian's Response to Darwinism', *Zygon* 46 (2011): 387–88; Southgate, 'Divine Glory in a Darwinian World', *Zygon* 49 (2014): 804–5; Holmes Rolston III, 'Redeeming a Cruciform Nature', *Zygon* 53, no. 3 (2021): 743–5; Bethany Sollereder, *God, Evolution, and Animal Suffering. Theodicy Without a Fall* (London: Routledge, 2019), 105–10.

[43] See Fiddes, *The Creative Suffering of God* (Oxford: Clarendon Press, 1988), 225–9; Fiddes, *Participating in God* (London: DLT, 2000), 164–70; Michael Lloyd, 'Theodicy, Fall and Adam', in Stanley P. Rosenberg (ed.), *Finding Ourselves After Darwin* (Grand Rapids: Baker Academic, 2018), 248–55; Neil Messer, *Science in Theology. Encounters Between Science and the Christian Tradition* (London: T. & T. Clark, 2020), 84–98.

[44] Despite his espousal of the 'only way approach' (see n. 41), Southgate admits himself 'fascinated' by my proposal of 'resistance' within creation: see Christopher Southgate, *The Groaning of Creation: God, Evolution and the Problem of Evil* (Louisville: Westminster John Knox Press, 2008), 66–67.

It is this kind of picture that the Apostle Paul seems to have in mind when he considers the natural creation as being 'subject to futility' in hope that it will 'be set free from its bondage to decay'; he portrays it graphically as 'groaning' while it 'waits with eager longing for the unveiling of the children of God' (Rom 8:19–23). It would be easy to turn this vision into another version of the patronizing of nature by human beings, but it need not result in an anthropocentricity which has proved so destructive over the years. It can support a true reciprocity. Recognizing the need for redemption in *both* human and non-human life means that nature can be seen as God's agent of redemption for humanity as well as the other way round. But it does also mean that the use of human technology, whether in water-management on mountains, genetic modification of crops, or medicinal prevention and control of infection, is not necessarily an 'interference' in nature but can be an exercise of co-creativity and co-redemption with God.

I believe that there is another implication too of a reciprocity in love, not just between created beings, but between the creation and the Creator. If this is a true reciprocity, such as Buber envisages for inter-human relations, God must be in some way dependent upon the response of love that God receives, and will be frustrated by resistance to persuasive love. In short, God needs the world to be God, and the mystical poet Traherne does not hesitate to make this assertion, in a passage which Marcar does not quote:

> This is very strange that God should want, for in Him is the fulness of all blessedness ... He is from eternity full of want: or else He would not be full of treasure, infinite want is the very ground and cause of infinite treasure. It is incredible, yet very plain: want is the fountain of all his fulness. Want in God is a treasure to us. For had there been no need He would not have created the world, nor made us, nor manifested His wisdom, nor exercised His power, nor beautified eternity, nor prepared the

joys of heaven ... Infinite wants satisfied produce infinite joys. [45]

The word 'want' here means 'need', something required which is otherwise missing. Traherne is making the fundamental point that the joy of God springs from the meeting of needs and the satisfying of desires through a loving companionship with creation. Thus the love of God combines *agape* with *eros*, or the fulfilment of desires.

The question is how God can be 'in need' of response from creation, and still be the uncreated God, and here there are two main answers. First, it might be said that God's very essence is a love which desires relations with others, beyond the communion of God's own being. God is simply expressing the divine nature when creating a world that will fulfil God's desires.[46] Some, however, will feel—like Karl Barth—that there is a restriction upon a God who dynamically 'loves in freedom' in being necessarily bound by an 'essence', even God's own.[47] An alternative which I have proposed, and which has been adopted by others (including Ilia Delio),[48] is to say that God needs the world *because God freely chooses to be in need*, not because there is some intrinsic necessity of God's nature binding subsequent choices.[49] 'God needs our love, because he is the loving God that he has freely decided

---

[45] Traherne, *The First Century*, 42–3. Spelling modernized.

[46] Thomas Oord, *The Uncontrolling Love of God. An Open and Relational Account of Providence* (Downers Grove: IVP Academic, 2015), 146–9

[47] Barth, *Church Dogmatics*, II/1, 301–8.

[48] Delio, *Unbearable Wholeness of Being*, 77.

[49] I work this idea out fully in Paul S. Fiddes, *The Creative Suffering of God*, (Clarendon Press, Oxford, 1988), 63–71, under the heading 'The freedom of God to be in need'. There is some affinity with the proposal of John Zizioulas that in God 'person' is the cause of 'nature': see *Being as Communion* (Darton, Longman and Todd, London, 1985).

to be'.[50] As Karl Barth puts it, "God's being *is* .... his willed decision".[51] Building on Barth's thought, we might then regard creation as being part of God's self-definition, an integral factor in God's own self-determination, since God chooses to be completed through a created universe—or perhaps multiple universes.

This choice—which we should also describe as the *desire* of God—does not deny the *aseity* of God, if we distinguish self-existence from 'self-sufficiency'. Traditionally the two have been identified, and so for God to be the one reality which exists *a se* ('from himself') was thought to mean that God must be *totally* unconditioned by anything else. But there is no reason why a God who depends upon nothing else for *existence* should not choose to depend on others for some aspects of the *mode* of that existence. A God who is self-sufficient with regard to the very fact of existence is not thereby prohibited from electing not to be self-sufficient as far as the ongoing richness and value of divine life is concerned.[52] Moreover, such a decision does not detract from the perfection of God since perfection need not be a fixed total, and should be distinguished from completion. God can be perfect in relation to all the reality there is at one time, while there is still more reality to come through a project of co-creativity with the world. Thus, 'God's being is in becoming'.[53]

The idea of a God who has needs to be fulfilled will, of course, be contested not only by much traditional Christian theology, but perhaps even more strongly by traditional Judaism and Islam. I am not

---

[50] This is a quotation from Vincent Brümmer, *The Model of Love*, p. 237, in a passage where he is commending and adopting the approach that I had developed in Fiddes, *Creative Suffering of God*, 66–8.

[51] Barth, *Church Dogmatics*, II/1, 271–2.

[52] I develop this distinction in Fiddes, *Creative Suffering of God*, 65–7.

[53] The phrase is from Eberhard Jüngel, *The Doctrine of the Trinity*, trans. Horton Harris (Edinburgh: Scottish Academic Press, 1976), 61–64, although his exposition centres on God's becoming within God's triune self.

presuming for one moment to suggest that all essayists in this book will agree with me in drawing this implication from a scenario of reciprocity between God, human beings and the natural world. I do think that taking this view throws light on the question of whether loving the planet makes any difference to the situation of a ravaged and suffering earth, as my concluding section should make clear.

What difference does loving the planet make?

What difference might love actually make to the practical situations of environmental emergency with which we are faced—the over-heating of the planet by CO_2 emissions, the destruction of rain-forests which are the 'lungs' of the planet, the loss of bio-diversity with the potential extinction of millions of species (including humanity itself), and the polluting of earth's rivers and seas? In the face of such crises, already actualized in flood and famine, love may seem a sentimental luxury. But in the first place, love for the planet makes us more sensitive to its needs, and provides a motivation for welfare towards the earth. When governments and businesses pay only lip-service to 'zero' emission by 2050, exploiting more carbon fossil fuels in the meantime, love will provide more than an intellectual reason for taking action. This is the most pragmatic answer to the question, and it is not a weak one since it is often observed that governments could be much more effective if they only had the political 'will' to back up their policies. It is frustrating to see international agreements such as COP 26, embracing 197 nations that signed up to the United Nations Framework Convention on Climate Change, then failing to follow through on their promises. A mood of love could actually remove blockages to implementing good intentions. Love for neighbour and the 'stranger', including the planet, can also make a difference to the strategies of financial systems and encourage a green economy, as Tareq Moqbel maintains.

But second, the essays in this book have raised the intriguing idea that loving the planet can have more unseen results, if indeed there is a reciprocal relation of love between humanity and the natural world. If all living beings are bound in a 'meshwork', then an increase in love will have an impact on the life of the whole, in its interconnections, its interdependencies and even (in the way I have suggested) on its 'intersubjectivity' and 'consciousness'. Beneath the surface, there is an 'entanglement' to which the energy of love can make a difference, though it is hard (perhaps impossible) to spell out in scientific terms what this might be. An input of love from one part will have a transformative impact on the whole. It is the kind of vision that has some affinities with the image of the earth as 'Gaia' ('mother earth'), envisaging that the living organisms and inorganic material of the planet combine into one dynamic system that shapes the earth's biosphere and maintains the earth as a fit environment for life.[54] There is however a difference between the essays in this book and the 'Gaia hypothesis'. The essayists have a religious approach which derives from three major faith traditions: so they understand that the 'meshwork' of the natural world is sustained by the power and love of God working together with what God has created, and not by the earth alone.

This conviction brings us to a third answer to the question which may seem even more speculative than the second to a secular mind, but which people of faith will want to hold. When divine love is understood as 'energy' in the world, loving the earth will affect the flow, the fullness and the effects of that energy. DeMoor in her essay writes that hopeful love 'invokes and provokes love-energy into new possibilities, creating novel and distinctive lovescapes characterized by love, empathy, reciprocity and communion'. Here she echoes Ilia Delio, who writes that every action rooted in love 'affects God's own relational life', and that

---

[54] See James Lovelock, *Gaia: A New Look at Life on Earth* (Oxford: Oxford University Press, 2016).

every act of love is 'a personalization of God' on earth.[55] In relationships of love we co-create with God, so that our lives and God's life become ever more deeply entangled, releasing new energies of love. We may say that our love for the planet thus draws God deeper into the 'meshwork' of nature, fulfilling the desire and needs of God, and opening new possibilities for a symbiosis between the the created and the Creator which will redeem and transform a damaged world. In short, an eco-love-theology proposes that loving the planet has the potential to change human attitudes, the responsiveness of nature and the very life of God, and that each of these areas is so entangled with the others that they cannot be separated.

---

[55] Delio, *Primacy of Love*, 74, 82, 37.

Studies of Love in Religion 1
Love as Common Ground. Essays on Love in Religion

Edited by Paul S. Fiddes
Lexington Books, 2021

This book explores the way in which the study and practice of love creates a common ground for different faiths and different traditions within the same faith. For the contributors, 'common ground' in this context is not a minimal core of belief or a lowest common denominator of faith, but a space or area in which to live together, consider together the meaning of the love to which various faiths witness, and work together to enable human flourishing. Such a space, the contributors believe, is possible because it is the place of encounter with the divine. This book is the fruit of a Project for the Study of Love in Religion which aims to create this space in which different traditions of love converge, from Islam, Judaism, and the Christianity of both East and West. Tools employed by the contributors in exploring this space of love include exegesis of ancient texts, theology, accounts of mystical experience, philosophy, and evolutionary science of the human. Insights about human and divine love that emerge include its nature as a form of knowing, its sacrificial and erotic dimensions, its inclination towards beauty, its making of community and its importance for a just political and economic life

1. 'God is Love, but is Love God? Towards a Theology of Love as Knowledge', by Paul S. Fiddes.

Love in Islam

2. 'Love in the Holy Qur'an', by HRH Prince Ghazi bin Muhammad bin Talal of Jordan.
3. 'The Journey of Love and the Challenges of the "Self": Rūmī's View in Islamic Context', by Leyla Tajer.
4. 'Bridal Symbolism, Eroticization of Divine Love and Friendship Among Medieval Female Mystics in Islam and Christianity', by Minlib Dallh.

Love in Judaism

5. 'Judaism's Commandment to Love: "A Well-Tempered Banality" or the

Messianic Trumpet's Blast?', by Melissa Raphael.

6. 'Harmony of Mind and Body: Theories of Love in Rabbinic and Mystical Literature', by Naftali Rothenberg.

7. 'Tensions within the Study of Love in Religion: Reflections Arising from Conversation between Jewish and Christian Scholars', by Eleanor McLaughlin.

Love in Christianity

8. 'Transfiguring Love in Byzantine Theology: The System of St. Maximus the Confessor', by Smilen Markov.

9. '"Let him kiss me with the kiss of his mouth": Erotic Love in the Western Christian Mystical Tradition', by Louise Nelstrop.

10. 'Sacrifice and the Self: A Christian Mystery of Love', by Julia T. Meszaros.

Common Philosophical Traditions about Love

11. 'Love and the Limits of Platonic Desire', by Fiona Ellis.

12. 'The Universal and the Individual: Aristotle on Substance and Friendship-Love (Philia)', by Mircea Dumitru.

The Study of Love in Religion

13. 'Theological Reflections on "Christian" and "Human" Love', by Werner G. Jeanrond.

14. 'Love as Belonging: Towards an Interdisciplinary Understanding of the Human', by Oliver Davies.

15. 'The Potentialities of Love in Social, Political and Economic Contexts', by Paul Weller.

Index of Names

Printed in Great Britain
by Amazon

15692530R00139